Criminal Justice
Recent Scholarship

Edited by
Nicholas P. Lovrich

A Series from LFB Scholarly

Judicial Orientation
The Black Box of Drug Court

Kathleen M. Contrino

LFB Scholarly Publishing LLC
El Paso 2015

Library of Congress Cataloging-in-Publication Data

Library of Congress Cataloging-in-Publication Data

Contrino, Kathleen M., 1963- author.
  Judicial orientation : the black box of drug court / Kathleen M.
Contrino.
    pages cm -- (Criminal justice : recent scholarship)
  Includes bibliographical references and index.
  ISBN 978-1-59332-793-4 (hardcover : alk. paper)
1. Drug courts--United States--Case studies. 2. Drug courts--New
York
(State)--Case studies. I. Title.
  KF3890.C649 2015
  345.7302770269--dc23
                                      2015021093

ISBN 978-1-59332-793-4

Manufactured in the United States of America.

Table of Contents

Acknowledgments

I would like to thank the drug court judges and team members. who not only answered the phone when I called but also allowed me to sit in their sessions and shared their stories with me.

I would like to thank my research assistants, especially Suzanne O'Brien, Sarah Danna, Shraddha Prabhu, Tanya Carmosino, Patrick Zelno, Marese Dixon, Michael O'Neil, Melanie Dingeldey, Lettie Tellez, Sarah Tagliaferro, Yanell Brown, Ronald Winkelman and Shawn Hill, who helped me compile the data for this study and Frank Contrino for help with the analysis.

I would also like to thank Dr. Robert Granfield, Dr. Debora Street, Dr. Robert Adelman, as well as the rest of the faculty and staff of the University at Buffalo Sociology Department for providing everything else necessary to complete my research.

I would like to thank my husband, Ronald Winkelman, and his children, Jillian and Joel, who wiped my tears and hugged me when I needed it.

I would like to thank Dr. William Wieczorek for pushing me to complete my research.

Finally, I'd like to thank Dr. Thomas Nochajski who has been my mentor and advisor for the last 20 years.

Introduction

Sociology and the Development of Drug Court

Criminal justice is a policy-oriented discipline and drug courts fit squarely in the field of criminal justice. The focus of criminal justice research, generally, is to analyze what works in order to prevent crime. Reducing the cost of enforcing existing laws and lowering recidivism rates are critically important. Most research on drug courts has zeroed in on criminal justice concerns and has assessed the impact drug court has had on the individual client   (a micro level theory assessing recidivism and retention rates) .. Sociological inquiry, however, encompasses a broad range of macro (global) and micro (individual) theoretical foci, including the legal arena and addictions. As such, the discipline of sociology can help provide a critical analysis of drug court through the lens of social construction. One area for sociological scholars relevant to the study of drug courts is the social construction of the law, an area of sociology where the study of law and society includes a focus on culture and the relationship between culture and law. This area of study looks at the values and norms of society and how they shape law, or, alternately, how law shapes values and norms over time.

SOCIAL CONSTRUCTION OF THE LAW: THAT WHICH MADE DRUG COURT POSSIBLE

Social constructionists share the idea that law and culture are inter-related, that society has become more complex as it has evolved, and that, as society has evolved, individuality and diversity have influenced

1

the development and interpretation of law (Deflem, 2008). The belief that members of the legal community both construct and are constructed by the complex set of systems with which they interact is not a new concept. It has been a robust area of study for some time, and includes both macro and micro theoretical perspectives (Deflem, 2008). This area of sociology can help illuminate how the social institution of drug court developed.

THE GLOBAL PERSPECTIVE – DURKHEIM AND WEBER

The courts and the law are, in essence, arenas of dispute resolution (Boyum & Mather, 1983; Felstiner, Abel, & Sarat, 1980). Over time, scholars have looked at legal systems in different ways. One method of studying law from a sociological perspective is to focus on legal systems from a global view. Emile Durkheim reflected on the changing nature of society and its impact on the law. Durkheim proposed that law was not fixed in nature, but rather developed as a society evolved. Specifically, Durkheim argued that societies tend to move from mechanical states to organic states, and in a related way a society's legal framework moves from repressive law (mechanical) to restitutive law (organic) (Deflem, 2008).

Central to Durkheim's study of law was the concept of the "collective conscious," which was a reflection of that particular society's view of morality (the moral mind). This collective conscious creates the legal framework within which the society functions. While mechanical societies are more cohesive (solidarity), organic societies are more diverse. Thus, the legal framework has to evolve to adapt to the change from a simple mechanical society to a more complex organic society. Mechanical societies have legal systems that are relatively simplistic and focus primarily on excessive punishment to control individuals. In contrast, organic societies have more complex legal systems that incorporate restitution, alternative dispute resolution, mediation, and alternative paths to justice (Deflem, 2008).

Under repressive law (mechanical societies), rules are not explicitly stated as all members in the community are aware of them and infractions are immediately and severely punished as they threaten "the existence of the collectivity as a whole" (Deflem, 2008, p. 62). In organic societies, however, restitutive rules are codified and sanctions are used to restore the social relations between the individual and society (Deflem, 2008). Indeed, Durkheim proposed that the rise in civil law in organic societies reflected a society's move towards this concept of restitutive law (Deflem, 2008). Regardless of this evolution, criminal law would continue to serve a repressive function within a world of restitutive law.

Since Durkheim first proposed his theories on law and society, researchers have attempted to prove or disprove them. For example, Richard Schwartz and James Miller compared different societies regarding mediation, specialized legal counsel, and police systems in order to see if a society's evolution resulted in a more restitutive form of law (Schwartz & Miller, 1964). While Schwartz and Miller found partial support for Durkheim's theories, they found that alternatives to the traditional legal system are related to other characteristics arrayed along a rural to urban continuum (Schwartz & Miller, 1964).

One way Durkheim's theories are relevant to the rise of specialty courts, generally, and drug courts, specifically, is in the consensus model of criminal justice in which law is proposed to be a reflection of a society's moral mind. The consensus model proposes that crimes are determined through agreement of the community and there is no debate as to what should be illegal (Mays & Ruddell, 2008; Siegel, 2010). Durkheim demonstrates that legal systems are "alive" in the sense that they change over time and respond to external stimuli. Legal systems seem to change and grow in order to adapt to societal needs. According to Durkheim, the more diverse and complicated the society becomes, the more likely the legal system will evolve to a foundation of restitutive law to accommodate the diversity and rely upon alternative forms to the traditional court process in order to provide justice that is more tailored to the populace (Deflem, 2008).

Mediation is one such restitutive legal system that has arisen and allows parties to come together and agree to what would satisfy each other in order to resolve their dispute. In other words, what would be necessary to resolve the dispute and make each party "whole"? Another such restitutive legal system is juvenile court. Although juvenile justice reforms existed in New York and Massachusetts first, the first actual independent juvenile court was established in Chicago in 1899 (Ismaili, 2011; Platt, 1969). The idea of processing juvenile offenders separately from adult offenders sprang from the combination of a new perception of criminals and the growing acceptance of rehabilitation (Ismaili, 2011; Platt, 1969). In addition to reforming young criminals, the juvenile justice movement included abused and neglected children ("dependent children") in its benevolence. Within the new juvenile justice system, those parents who were deemed unfit to care for their children had them removed from their home and placed in a special school until the child reached an age to be released (Platt, 1969). This was a critical step in the development of the court system toward restitutive law and it allowed for the possibility for rehabilitation of a special population whose needs are unique.

Juvenile justice courts function on the concept of *parens partriae*; this is the idea that the state fills the role of parent for those children whose parents had failed to perform to the state's expectations for dutiful parenting (Neubauer, 2008; Platt, 1969). "The role model for juvenile court judges was doctor-counselors rather than lawyer" (Platt, 1969, p. 142). Thus, judges were reconstructed as therapists in American state legal systems by the end of the 19th century.

In its early days, juvenile court was diversionary in nature and judges were given great leeway in how they managed and implemented their courts. Due process rights were not granted to juveniles who appeared before juvenile court judges, but judges were expected to rule in the "best interests of the child" (Paik, 2011). Juvenile courts began carrying out a balancing act - namely the loss of due process rights for the possibility of redemption. It wasn't until court cases such as *In re Gault, 387 U.S. 1 (1967)*, and *Kent v. United States, 383 U.S. 541 (1966)* that juveniles were given some fundamental due process rights (i.e. right to counsel, right to notice of charges, right against self-incrimination). While some limited rights were ultimately adjudicated, American appellate courts were reluctant to place restrictions on a juvenile court's ability to work in the best interests of the child and fulfill its rehabilitative role (Platt, 1969).

As Durkheim foresaw, the evolution of courts to a more organic role took place in the U.S. The drug courts were the first step in the movement towards therapeutic diversionary courts for specialized offenders (veterans, gamblers, mentally ill), with the hope being in each case of reintegrating those individuals back into their respective communities. It is in the area of restitutive law that the concept of therapeutic jurisprudence also resides. Therapeutic jurisprudence incorporates idea that a civil court, governed by the core elements of contract law, can be the impetus for individual change with the goal of reintegrating a special population back into the community (Rosenthal,

2002; Wexler, 2008; Winick, 2013). In the case of drug court, it is the drug abuser who is reintegrated. While drug court can always return the client back to criminal court should the reintegration process fail, clients are given the opportunity to return to the community (drug court community and beyond) through a series of legal procedures, graduated sanctions and rewards for positive change.

The whole purpose of drug court is to make drug-addicted clients stop harming society through criminal conduct and become productive members of society through a less formal legal system. Thus, society is made whole as well as the drug offender. Durkheim's theories are supported in the evolution of the justice system from a purely punitive system to a system of justice that meets the varied needs of the population it serves. As Durkheim foresaw, the legal system in the United States has incorporated more and more non-criminal and quasi-legal systems to handle special populations within society. Juvenile Court, mediation, arbitration, and other problem-solving courts were created to allow members of a community to settle matters outside of the traditional adversarial legal system.

Max Weber also reflected on the evolving nature of the law in response to changes in society. He proposed that law was a primarily a reflection of the society from which it grew. Weber developed models of law (a system of rules and procedures) and dominion (political authority). Dominion, according to Weber, could be characterized as traditional, charismatic, or rational-legal. Traditional dominion was a system of authority that was maintained through long-established practices. Charismatic dominion was a system of authority established through a revered individual, while a rational-legal system was a system of authority enacted through rules and procedures reflecting logic and rational calculation (Deflem, 2008). Legal systems within dominions could be classified according to their relative formality and rationality. Thus, legal systems could be founded on logically formal rationality, formal irrationality, substantive rationality, or substantive irrationality (Deflem, 2008). Weber proposed that substantive law was decided on a case-by-case basis; each case was decided on its own fact situation (e.g., plea bargaining) without formalized or standard procedure, while formal law was codified law.

If a law was rational, the content of the law was based upon the general characteristics of the specific case, and if the law was irrational it was based upon religion or other systems of thought. Thus, substantive irrationality was more like mysticism, while logical formal rationality was considered a highly developed, properly enacted set of laws (Deflem, 2008). While rationality of law was important, over time it produced a process devoted to faithful obedience to mechanics which, ultimately, alienates people from the legal system. While Weber did not argue that the law evolved exactly (all four types could co-exist within a society) in this way, Weber's categories do imply a sense of progression (Boyum & Mather, 1983).

For Weber, individualism (self-interest and individualistic pursuits) was a social fact that must be addressed and underlies the fact that all societies tend to evolve into a more rational formal system which protects individual interests. Moreover, predictability in commerce and markets was the key to the rise of capitalism, and the evolution of legal systems followed suit. Liberal law, in the form of rational law, assumes the existence of community and rationality is efficiency-based and relies upon laws to provide for predictability and security of investments. If you have a rational formalistic legal system there is efficiency, but no particular meaning of justice being present - thus moving forward to Weber's concept of the "iron cage" phenomenon (Deflem, 2008).

Theorists over time have attempted to find evidence of Weber's theories in other aspects of our legal system. Boyum and Mather (1983) argue, for example, that the development of law in the United States has been generally toward a system which encompasses substantive rationality (Boyum & Mather, 1983). Duncan Kennedy (2004) presents a well-considered review of current perspectives on Weber's writings on law. Kennedy describes Weber in terms of three different schools of thought: classical legal thought ("Just the way we do things"), logically formal rationality, and the inquiry into the validity of legal systems. Kennedy was looking for threads of Weber in legal theory over the course of time, ending with critical legal systems where Kennedy found the strongest thread of Weberian thought. Further, Kennedy argues that where we find Weber in contemporary legal theory is not purely the original Weber, but a hybrid of Weber's theories and elements of contemporary intellectual thought (Kennedy, 2004).

Abel (1982) details the move from more formal legal systems to more informal legal systems, arguing that informal forms of justice did not really start in the 1980's as is broadly believed. Abel details the history of informal legal systems starting with the Knights of Labor Courts in the United States which arose in 1869 (Abel, 1982). Abel argues for a broader view of what constitutes informal justice, and analyzes the creation of Neighborhood Justice Centers in the 1970's and 1980's as well as the practices employed by the South Bronx Legal Services in his study (Abel, 1982). Finally, Abel proposes that Weber understood the danger of subordination inherent in formal law and informal law alike - namely the deliberate use of power to circumvent justice.

Abel argues in this regard that:

> ...[t]o the extent that law aspires to protect the weak against arbitrary authority, it must introduce formality, rational administration, rule-boundedness, and impersonal handling of cases. Yet when the law, is actually invoked to achieve social justice, that is, to compensate, protect, and guarantee the "economic and social life-opportunities of [the masses] in the face of the propertied classes," it typically represents an expression of informal, "ethical," concrete, and personalized varieties of "substantive justice" (Abel, 1982, p. 172).

It may be difficult to see Weber in the alternative systems of justice that have developed over the years such as: mediation, arbitration, and problem-solving courts. These systems of laws are more like the English problem presented herein. Alternatives to the traditional system are *outside* the formal codified laws. However, if predictability and guaranteed rights are key features of logically formal rational legal systems, then these alternatives still fit in a Weberian analysis. In alternatives to the traditional legal system, legal rights and responsibilities are detailed in the contract the parties sign before they are diverted out of the traditional system of justice. In this way, Weber's theories may still apply to legal systems such as mediation, arbitration, and problem-solving courts (drug court) as true types or hybrid social institutions.

Drug courts use multidisciplinary teams in their legal decisions in order to produce a swift response to client behavior. All of the client's treatment providers are given the opportunity to provide information on the client's current status. Moreover, any information related to the drug court coordinator by family members, other drug court clients, and/or health professionals is relayed to the drug court treatment team during its case conference. This includes information that may be criminally related, but more often than not is primarily socially related. Drug court teams consider whatever might have an impact on the client's ability to remain drug-free. Each case conference considers clients on a case-by-case basis with the goal of intervening in the client's life quickly and effectively to achieve sustained change in behavior. Graduated sanctions as well as rewards must be swiftly administered in order to be effective. Finally, there is no part of the client's life that is not subject to discussion if there is any possible connection between the information and relapse potential.

A detailed discussion of the client's life is what the case conference is for; it provides the opportunity for drug court team members. to discuss what is currently going on in the client's life, what effect (if any) issues in the client's life may have on the client in terms of relapse, and what response the team will have to those issues (regardless of whether relapse has occurred). Often, participation in drug court means the client must engage in activities that are not directly treatment-related. Drug court clients are often required to attend GED classes or participate in community service projects, as these are deemed "good for the client" (Paik, 2011; Team, 2006; Tiger, 2013). All of this information is presented and discussed in the case conference attended by the entire treatment team. If the team decides, for whatever reason, that the client is lying or non-compliant with the treatment program, sanctions are discussed and decided upon. Appropriate responses to client behavior are discussed beforehand in order to determine the most effective response. The team also makes decisions on whether the client can move to a certain location, move in with another person, pursue employment, go on vacation, spend time with a friend, or maintain an intimate relationship. All of these social factors can affect relapse and, as such, are fit aspects of a client's life subject to the control of the drug court treatment team. Weber becomes relevant in this realm where social factors become more important than legal rules.

ORGANIZATIONAL THEORY AND THE COURTROOM WORKGROUP – A
MICRO PERSPECTIVE:

Real courtroom practice usually revolves around routine procedures, plea bargaining, and quick justice (Blumberg, 1967). However, there are still many criminal matters where the tension that comes from two adversaries presenting their best case to a trier of fact (funneled through the rules of evidence) is still the best method of weeding out the irrelevant and producing a reasonable approximation of truth. In the end, the trial is still the defendant's last, best hope for an unbiased hearing of the government's case against him or her. Some cases must go to trial in order for a defendant to find justice. Many have tried to understand the exact nature of the courtroom drama, and to understand those actors who make up the play. Talcott Parsons, for example, through functionalist theory, looked at the legal profession in terms of the unique actors that are shaped by professionalism and bureaucracy (Deflem, 2008). Other theorists have also looked at the legal profession by analyzing how legal actors interact and function within an established courtroom setting.

Black (1989) presents the sociological concepts involved in the traditional court process (1989). Black argues that there is an informative analysis that comes from legal formalism which focuses on rules and the sociological perspective which focuses on the facts of the case. Black refers to the "sociology of the case" and discusses all of the factors which go into the social construction of the legal dispute. These sociological concepts include adversary effects, lawyer effects, and third party effects (Black, 1989). These effects are the "who" and "what" of the courtroom process and the difference they may make in the resolution of the disputes at hand.

Black also describes the sociological lawyer, the opposite of a lawyer who relies upon legal formalism. A sociological lawyer incorporates aspects of social justice in his or her practice of law. The sociological lawyer would include social factors in the decision to accept a case (i.e., preference could go to a socially superior client-that is, a client the jury would find sympathetic), structure his fee (hourly vs. flat fee), and design cases (choosing clients or opponents), as well as in making pre-trial decisions and managing trials (forum shopping and emphasizing sociological characteristics during trial for the jury's consumption) (Black, 1989). Like Weber, Black also proposes that the socialization of law occurs when more social characteristics are incorporated into the legal arena. Drug court incorporates a fair amount of the client's social characteristics in the evolution of the client's drug court case through therapeutic jurisprudence. In case status meetings, the drug court team acquires a great deal of information about the client's friends, family, and daily life (J. Miller & Johnson, 2009). Thus, the team is able to better direct the client away from "people, places, and things" which might trigger a relapse. None of these social factors are legally related; however, they may have an impact on whether the client can remain abstinent from drugs, thus affecting the client's legal position.

Also included in the social construction of the legal dispute are organizational theory and the courtroom workgroup. Organizational theory regarding legal disputes in court revolves around the actors involved and the courtroom drama that makes up the legal narrative (Black, 1989). The courtroom workgroup refers specifically to the actors who engage in the process of resolving disputes in the traditional court system (Eisenstein & Jacob, 1977). This typically has included judges, prosecutors, defense attorneys, and the jury (Hemmens, Brody, & Spohn, 2010; Jacob, Blankenburg, Kritzer, Provine, & Sanders, 1996). However, over time additional actors have been included in the courtroom workgroup by scholers. Bailiffs, law clerks, court clerks, and more recently, social workers have been included in the concept of the courtroom workgroup (Castellano, 2009; Hemmens et al., 2010). Social workers are often key members of the treatment team in that they are trained in the human component of drug addiction and provide useful information on treatment or treatment services for clients.

Nardulli (1978) discusses factors that influence the courtroom workgroup in his work. Nardulli proposes that the principal members of the courtroom workgroup, termed the "courtroom elites," have some common goals. The courtroom elite, (core group comprised of judges, prosecutors, and defense attorneys), share internal group considerations, environmental variables (external considerations), and court setting issues which affect how cases are normally resolved (Nardulli, 1978, pp. 69-77). Nardulli is unique in that he incorporates the criminal court setting and the idea of the courtroom elite in his organizational analysis (Nardulli, 1978).

There is no doubt, though, that judges, prosecutors, and defense attorneys are all from different branches of government and have very different mandates within the criminal justice system (Eisenstein & Jacob, 1977; Heinz & Manikas, 1992). While they all work within the framework of the criminal justice court system, their ethical obligations are quite different. Defense attorneys, for example, must zealously advocate for their clients. Advocacy for clients sometimes means that guilty people are found not guilty and are set free to commit future criminal acts. Prosecutors, on the other hand, zealously advocate for the state, which sometimes means that innocent people are convicted of crimes if a prosecutor withholds exculpatory information that is not requested under <u>Brady v. Maryland,</u> 373 U. S. 83 (1963). The judge, finally, has no alliance but to the legal truth that is being pursued during a trial. Organizational theory in the criminal court system promotes the idea that there are other considerations besides the ethical requirements of the rule of law at work in the courtroom.

The reality is that these actors work together day in and day out to dispose of the matters on their crowded shared calendar (Eisenstein & Jacob, 1977). According to the perspective of the courtroom workgroup, courtroom members work to efficiently dispose of cases through the use of formal and informal sanctions for courtroom actors who don't "play ball" (Eisenstein & Jacob, 1977; Jacob et al., 1996; Mays & Ruddell, 2008; Mileski, 1971; Spohn & Hemmens, 2009). This concept of how disputes are resolved is in direct contrast to the traditional beliefs of legal formalism (Black, 1989; Jacob et al., 1996).

Plea bargaining is an informal way to resolve disputes in which the prosecutor, judge, and defense attorney agree upon the disposition of a criminal matter in advance to court proceedings in order to extract a guilty plea from a defendant (Blumberg, 1967). In this way, plea bargaining is the major way the courtroom workgroup collaborates to dispose of criminal cases and it has a tremendous impact on the final adjudication of court cases (Blumberg, 1967). Most plea bargaining occurs in the prosecutor's office, between the prosecutor and defense attorney, or in the judge's chambers, with the prosecutor, defense attorney, and judge all in attendance (Maynard, 1984). There are few statutes which govern plea negotiations, nor is the plea bargaining process in any way a part of the formal record. Thus, through plea bargaining much of our legal narrative occurs in private, and it is in this private arena where cooperation reigns (Blumberg, 1967; Eisenstein & Jacob, 1977; Maynard, 1984; Nardulli, Flemming, & Eisenstein, 1985).

The courtroom workgroup, as this cooperative aspect of courtroom behavior is labeled, is more interested in the efficient handling of cases than in the pursuit of justice for individual defendants (Eisenstein & Jacob, 1977; Jacob et al., 1996; Mays & Ruddell, 2008). Incorporated in the concept of the courtroom workgroup is the idea of "the going rate," or the accepted punishment for a particular offense in a particular court of law. As long as the judge orders a sentence that falls within the unspoken agreed upon rate, neither the defense nor the prosecution will make an objection in court (Eisenstein & Jacob, 1977; Mays & Ruddell, 2008; Nardulli, 1979). These considerations suggest a set of expectations that are working within the system and that unexpected behaviors are problematic. The courtroom workgroup theory argues that the adversarial system is a great deal more fiction than fact. Proponents of the courtroom workgroup believe that trial court attorneys work cooperatively within a system that requires them to process cases as efficiently as possible (Spohn & Hemmens, 2009).

Drug court only exists as jurisprudence has evolved to allow for alternatives to the traditional court processes. Juvenile court, arbitration, mediation and the use of plea bargaining as alternatives to legal formalism gave breathing room to allow for a diversionary system that works completely outside of the traditional court process. Juvenile court, and the concept of rehabilitation, provided the opportunity to see the combination of legal processes and therapeutic processes to intervene in a person's life in a positive way.

Chapter 1

A look at Drug Court's Black Box: The Role of Judicial Orientation

WHAT IS DRUG COURT?

It is now commonplace for drug users with criminal charges to be referred to drug court. Drug courts are judicial innovations as a response to the steady increase in drug-related crime after criminal justice policy shifted from a more rehabilitative model (1960-1970's) to a more punitive model (1970-1980's) (Roper, 2007; W. Clinton Terry, 1999). During the late 1980's, more and more defendants poured into inner city courts and correction systems due to determinate sentencing policies (Inciardi, McBride, & Rivers, 1996). Judges found that after incarceration and release, defendants would very often return to court on new charges. After witnessing this revolving door of drug addiction, judges began experimenting with different variations of a treatment-related court (Nolan, 2001; Roper, 2007). The first of these therapeutic courts began in the 1980's, and while Dade County in Florida is generally believed to be the originator of treatment-based drug courts, New York City also began to experiment with creative ways to deal with drug offenders in the late 1980's (Fora & Stalcup, 2008; W. Clinton Terry, 1999). Other drug courts followed the Dade County experience. Orange County, Florida, Broward County, Florida, Maricopa County, Arizona and Portland, Oregon drug courts are also considered early drug courts which started in the late 1980's and early 1990's (W. Clinton Terry, 1999).

The Miami Drug Court utilized the team approach to encourage and supervise defendants in recovery, the Orange County Drug Court utilized an expedited calendar, and the Broward County Dedicated Drug Treatment Court was a diversionary court. These early courts pulled together a wide variety of local resources to treat the defendant's drug problem (Roper, 2007; W. Clinton Terry, 1999). Within these early models the different aspects of what would one day become the contemporary drug court were being created.

Drug courts are defined by several key elements: 1) integrating alcohol and other drug treatment services with justice system processing; 2) using a non-adversarial approach; 3) intervening early with front-loaded treatment services (before sentencing); 4) providing a continuum of treatment services; 5) monitoring abstinence from drugs and alcohol; 6) coordinating strategies for addressing non-compliance; 7) regular status appearances (judicial interaction); 8) monitoring and evaluating the court for the achievement of goals and program effectiveness; 9) continuing education for team members.; and 10) cultivating partnerships between treatment teams and community stakeholders (NADCP, 1997). Operating through the principle of therapeutic jurisprudence (the idea that law and legal processes can be used to accomplish desired behavior change through treatment), these courts employ judicial coercion to force drug users into compliance with treatment (Wexler, 2000; Winick, 2013). Indeed, therapeutic jurisprudence provides for a multidisciplinary information gathering process and allows for a wider range of options (both legal or social) to tailor a judicial response to compliant and non-compliant client behavior in order to end substance abuse (Bean, 2002; Winick, 2013).

Compliance with drug court rules typically involves weekly status meetings with the judge, regular attendance in drug treatment, use of self-help groups such as Alcoholics Anonymous (AA) or Narcotics Anonymous (NA), as well as any other requirement that the drug court judge or drug court team believes will be in the client's best interest (including, but not limited to pursing a GED, community service, parenting classes, job skills training, and/or in-patient treatment) (Tiger, 2011). Typically, drug courts utilize a series of rewards and graduated sanctions to enforce drug court and treatment compliance (Meyer, 2007). It is believed that treatment attendance and compliance, as well as length of time in treatment, will ultimately result in drug addicts who become successful in abstaining from drug use (Peters & Murrin, 2000; Rempel, 2006; Schmitt, 2006). Coercion in the form of jail time is the end point in a regime of graduated sanctions (Harrell, 1998; Meyer,

2007; Satel, 1999). Jail is the ultimate weapon in judicial coercion as participants who are deemed non-compliant with treatment can be sentenced on the spot to incarceration (Harrell, 1998; NADCP, 2005; Shannon Carey, Juliette Mackin, & Mike Finigan, 2008). Thus, the judge is the critical member on the team as the authority figure with the power to reward or sanction the client during drug court involvement.

One key aspect of drug courts is the focus on continuing education for team members. (NADCP, 1997). Drug court trainings emphasize teamwork, early identification and assessment, treatment interventions, accountability, and ongoing judicial supervision (NADCP, 2004, 2005). The National Drug Court Institute (NDCI) publishes a periodical entitled *Drug Court Review* which presents the latest research findings and process evaluations from across the country to drug courts. In addition, the NDCI holds national conferences yearly at various locations in order to bring together drug court professionals to share their practices and to learn from others. This national conference holds large seminars for all drug court professionals on current practices and controversies (e.g., medication-assisted drug treatment) and breakout sessions for team members (some team member specific – e.g., for judges only – or topic specific – e.g., stages of change research). New York State holds its own annual drug court meeting to provide training for their drug courts. These conferences help ensure that drug courts are dynamic and constantly evolving to become more efficacious in reforming and rehabilitating the drug-addicted clientele (NADCP, 2014).

DRUG COURT EFFICACY

Drug courts were developed in response to a perceived need within society and the criminal justice system. They offered a unique way to combat a rising crime problem by giving greater leeway to the judge to fulfill a rehabilitative role for individuals who needed help giving up drug use and becoming more productive members of the community (Bean, 2002; Fora & Stalcup, 2008; Rosenthal, 2002; Wiener & Georges, 2013).

Proponents of drug courts see therapeutic jurisprudence courts as the last and best effort to combat drug addiction. Looking for an alternative to the revolving door of drug addiction, crime, court, and prison, supporters of the drug court model see the marriage of rehabilitation and punishment, under judicial supervision, as a vehicle to help drug-addicted individuals and re-connect them to a more conventional lifestyle (McColl, 1996). Furthermore, the move from an adversarial system of justice towards a more benevolent and restorative court, with a focus on the defendant's needs, was seen as a positive step forward in our current system of laws (Wexler, 1999a, 1999b). Reform and rehabilitation is the goal all drug court teams struggle to achieve in their own unique way (Wexler, 2005, 2008).

While results from research studies have been varied, most studies have found that drug courts help reduce the negative impact (recidivism and jail time) drug addicted defendants have on the court system (Bavon, 2001; Belenko, 2001; C. West Huddleston, Douglas B. Marlowe, & Casebolt, 2008; GAO, 2005; Green & Rempel, 2010; Guydish, Tajima, Wolfe, & Woods, 2006; Rossman et al., 2011; Shaffer, Hartman, & Listwan, 2009; Turner et al., 2001). The conventional wisdom is that drug courts are successful in reducing drug addiction and drug-related criminal recidivism while being less expensive alternatives to traditional case processing. There have been a multitude of small and large research studies done on drug courts across the country, with a number of studies including multiple sites (Bavon, 2001; Belenko, 1999; Cissner & Rempel, 2005; Granfield, Eby, & Brewster, 1998; Green & Rempel, 2010; Joseph Guydish, Ellen Wolfe, Tajima, & William J. Woods, 2001; Rempel, 2006; Rossman et al., 2011; Shaffer et al., 2009; Turner et al., 2001).

Due to the ethical dilemmas presented in randomly assigning criminal offenders to different types of court interventions (no treatment, jail, traditional treatment, drug court), evaluation studies have either failed to include a control group or used weakly conceptualized control groups (unsuccessful drug court participants as compared to successful drug court participants) (David DeMatteo, Sarah Filone, & Casey LaDuke, 2011; Hoffman, 2002a, 2002b; Longshore et al., 2001; Popovic, 2000; Turner et al., 2001). Fortunately that is not the case for all evaluation studies on drug courts. Peters and Murrin (2000), for example, included comparison groups and examined recidivism at 12 months and 30 months (Peters & Murrin, 2000). At 12 and 30 months, graduates were less likely to be arrested than probationers and non-graduates. Peters and Murrin also found that being enrolled and retained in drug court related to better criminal justice outcomes (Peters & Murrin, 2000). Defendants in drug court did better if they remained in drug court at least a year regardless of whether they graduated. While these findings were based on two drug courts with a relatively small sample size, the published research and many evaluation studies conducted support the conventional wisdom. Retention and graduation are both related to a reduction in criminal justice contacts for drug court clients (Gifford, Eldred, McCutchan, & Sloan, 2014; Green & Rempel, 2010; Rossman et al., 2011; Somers, Rezansoff, & Moniruzzaman, 2014; Turner et al., 2001).

JUDICIAL ORIENTATION AND THE BLACK BOX

Over the years, some researchers have argued that there needs to be a more robust examination of drug courts as it tries to intervene therapeutically in drug-addicted clients' lives (Belenko, 1999, 2001; Goldkamp, White, & Robinson, 2001; Heck, 2006; Johnson & Wallace, 2004). Christopher Slobogin, for example, argues that the real problem in properly evaluating drug courts is in the difficulty of defining a complex legal system and assessing its benefits to society (Slobogin, 1995). Longshore and his colleagues echo this position and propose a theoretical framework encompassing five distinct dimensions - *leverage, population severity, program intensity, predictability*, and *rehabilitation emphasis* - as a more complete way to assess whether a particular drug court is employing an efficacious model (Longshore et al., 2001). Goldkamp, White, and Robinson have made a similar argument (Goldkamp et al., 2001). While Goldkamp et al. acknowledge the methodological problems inherent in drug court research, they propose the use of typologies using the structural components of individual drug courts in order to assess their impact (Goldkamp et al., 2001). The specific elements that make up individual drug courts has been referred to as a "black box" (Goldkamp et al., 2001).

Belenko (2001) emphasizes this point in his 2001 review of drug court evaluation studies, arguing that there is a relative lack of research related to the inner workings of drug courts despite their incredible diversity (Belenko, 2001). Drug courts, Belenko suggests, could benefit from more information on program services, courtroom dynamics, sanctions, and client supervision in order to understand the internal workings of drug court (the black box) and the impact that the black box has on client outcomes (Belenko, 2001). Qualitative studies,

ideally suited for collecting such information, should focus on the
unique characteristics of each drug court and staff perspectives, as well
as analyzing retention and graduation rates. Finally, Belenko suggests
that these qualitative studies should include individual interviews, focus
groups, and courtroom observations, because such methods allow
researchers to make sense of the unique characteristics found within
each drug court and assist in the interpretation of quantitative outcome
data (Belenko 2001).

Goldkamp et al. (2001) detail a variety of external and internal
forces related to drug court that can affect drug court client outcomes;
however, they specifically present the idea of the black box as the
"coordinated collection of functions, methods and activities that reflect
general and specific deterrent as well as rehabilitative aims"
(Goldkamp et al., 2001, p. 41). These functions, methods, and activities
are related to the drug court effect and are ultimately linked to the
courtroom experience through the judge. All things considered, it is
believed that this combination of courtroom activities and judicial
interaction has a greater therapeutic impact on the client than either the
traditional treatment process or incarceration (Goldkamp et al., 2001).
Thus, the black box is the unique courtroom experience that the client
encounters every time he or she attends drug court for a status
appearance. Goldkamp et al. have noted the challenge of detailing this
black box and measuring its exact impact on client outcomes
(Goldkamp et al., 2001; Longshore et al., 2001; Turner et al., 2001).

Burns and Peyrot (2003) have also attempted to understand the
inner workings of drug court and document its impact on clients (Burns
& Peyrot, 2003). Burns and Peyrot specifically looked at the
interactions between the judge and the client in order to measure client
behavior in the courtroom experience. Granfield et al. (1998) defined
the black box in a subtly different way (Granfield et al., 1998).
According to these researchers what was missing from the extant drug
court research was the "impact of the drug court on the general social
functioning of offenders, an examination of the network of associations
and partnerships established by the drug court, the impact of the drug
court on special populations such as immigrants and women, and an
examination of the subjective perceptions of offenders who participate
in the drug courts" (Granfield et al., 1998, p. 200).

Longshore et al., argued for a different type of examination of drug
courts (Longshore et al., 2001). According to Longshore et al., what

was missing from the research was an examination into the specific structural and process characteristics of drug courts and the impact those characteristics had on client outcomes (Longshore et al., 2001). Ultimately, Longshore et al. argued for grouping drug courts according to their adherence to specific structural and process characteristics (leverage, population severity, program intensity, predictability, and rehabilitation emphasis) and comparing the scores on those measures against client outcomes (Longshore et al., 2001).

Bouffard and Taxman (2004) focused on the black box as well, but narrowed their research to the delivery of treatment services. They examined the delivery of treatment services through a combination of direct observations, staff interviews and client surveys. They found that services were often eclectic in their approach thus potentially less effective for drug court clients in that clients were frequently given inconsistent messages. Bouffard and Taxman suggested that court-ordered treatment programs should not only provide a targeted approach to treatment, but also provide additional diagnostic services in order to address the multitude of needs that clients typically present (Bouffard & Taxman, 2004).

Deborah Shaffer examined the black box phenomenon through meta-analysis and surveys of drug court administrators, focusing on program elements which would be effective in treating clients (Shaffer, 2011). The focus of Shaffer's research was the impact of policies and procedures on effectiveness. Shaffer found that success in drug court depended on the clients which are targeted, leverage, additional support, establish clear expectations, and feature quality staff. Thus, she reported that well-trained staff ensures a good drug court program which promotes positive interactions and sets high expectations for clients.

Different researchers have attempted to define the black box as a way to measure the internal processes related to drug courts, but all agree that something more than outcome documentation is needed in order to understand drug court and its effect on client outcomes. The more nuanced the definition of the black box in the research, the better our ability to determine the exact ways in which drug courts impact client outcomes. Critical to any analysis must be the recognition that drug courts represent a hybrid entity within the criminal justice system. Drug court is multidisciplinary inasmuch as police, courts, and corrections come together to work cooperatively with treatment agencies and community resources to intervene with substance abusing clients (J. Miller & Johnson, 2009). Thus, any evaluation of drug court success needs to incorporate elements and models from various disciplines if it is to provide a more complete understanding of how drug court works.

Drug courts have allowed judges great leeway in how they construct and manage their courtroom, what rewards and punishments to use on clients to motivate them, what courtroom procedures will work in their drug court, and what is the best way to interact with clients to increase retention and compliance among drug court clients (NADCP, 2004). Judges construct who and what a drug addict is, how substance abusers gain the skills to abstain from drug use, and how clients see the judge for purposes of motivation. The construction of what the client needs inevitably affects how the judge constructs his or her role in the courtroom and influences his or her judicial response to client behavior (Meyer, 2007). Few drug court evaluations have looked at the impact the unique style of the judge has on client outcomes, even though the judge is considered the most important team member .in the room (Lloyd, Johnson, & Brook, 2014). Is the judge *a caring father figure* (a progressive or treatment perspective) or *a despotic authority* with the inclination to punish the client for minor violations (a traditional or sanction-based perspective)?

Chapter 2

Social Construction and Drug Court

Social construction of the law incorporates the idea that legal players construct the legal systems as they are constructed by it. In this vein, Sarat & Simon (2001) present a postmodern/deconstructive perspective that focuses on a constitutive theory of law and society by evaluating individual narratives in relation to their interactions with the legal system. These narratives may be related to specific cultures within the broader society (based upon race, gender, ethnicity, disability etc.), but as society has grown progressively more diverse, the law has had to adapt to these multiple individual narratives (Sarat & Simon, 2001).

Sarat & Felstiner (1988) focused on the social construction of lawyers and clients in their work. They reviewed attorney-client dialogs within the context of divorce law in order to demonstrate the fact that clients have different expectations from the relationship with their attorney. Lawyers, as they are taught to think like a lawyer, listen to client stories with an ear towards legal analysis, while clients are looking for empathy, sympathy, validation, etc. The different constructions of the attorney/client relationship affect the ability of the client and attorney to communicate with each other and, ultimately, affect client satisfaction with the final resolution of the case to a considerable extent (Sarat & Felstiner, 1988).

Alternatively, Hull (2003) analyzed a postmodern/deconstructive perspective in relation to privacy rights and the legal regulation of the availability of marriage. Hull found that even though same sex couples were unable to obtain a legal marriage, they would create the same or similar cultural norms as married couples. Hull argued that the desire to have legal marriages was not so much a desire for the same legal rights as married couples, but the desire to belong to that broader monogamous culture (acceptance as you will) (Hull, 2003).

Finally, Frohmann (2007) argued along the theoretical lines of Black's "sociological lawyer." Frohmann proposed that prosecutors review cases of sexual assault and make judgments based upon such social characteristics as whether the woman can be categorized as a "battered woman" or sympathetic victim (from a jurors point of view), and that category will determine whether the case is winnable (Frohmann, 1997). Thus, a prosecutor constructs a discourse in relation to the sexual assault by combining the facts of the case and the social factors related to the victim. Accordingly, Frohmann proposes that the use of discordant locales (discourse practice in a prosecutor's decision to pursue or dump a case) as a thinly veiled racism and misogyny (much like racial profiling) as the prosecutor's decision often relies upon whether the jury can favorably construct the victim from their own values and biases (Frohmann, 1997).

These examples illustrate the way that lawyers and clients construct the legal arena for their own purposes. These examples also suggest that, contrary to the idea of legal formalism, the socialization of the law is quite alive and well in the American legal system. Lawyers and clients come with expectations and understandings of how the law should work and how legal players should act.

Social construction theory in the traditional court system focuses in on key courtroom workgroup players (judge, prosecutor, defense attorney, client and jury), but drug court has less formalism and more ambiguity than normal courts. Drug court judges and their teams are given great latitude to create their own version of drug court. Through team building and education, drug court judges and teams do learn best practices, but they have the ability to choose how those best practices are implemented. Within best practices, ambiguity tends to reign and drug court judges and teams rely heavily upon their social constructions to guide them. These social constructions are critical to understanding the policies and procedures woven within the informal judicial system of diversionary treatment courts. *Judicial orientation in drug court combines the criminal justice models of corrections of deterrence and rehabilitation with the social construction of addictions to fill in the spaces left by ambiguity.*

The Social Construction of Addiction – Diseases of the Will

It is difficult to separate the idea of alcoholism and drug addiction. They are often joined together in the concept of addiction. It is no surprise that construction of alcoholism and drug addiction have the same roots in the temperance movement. Levine (1978) discussed the temperance movement and the social construction of addiction as a "disease of the will" (Levine, 1978). Drinking, or addiction, is a "disease of the will" through a loss of control, and abstinence is the cure. Levine also discussed the shift on the part of society from an assimilative reform (a sympathetic view of alcoholics) to prohibition (a punitive view of alcoholics) (Levine, 1978).

Gusfield (1986) examined social status as it related to the temperance ethic describing the interplay between temperance attitudes, the organized movement, and conflicts between subcultures (social status groups). Gusfield related that interplay in terms of the historical evolution of the temperance movement. The temperance ethic was religious, social in terms of status, and political and focused on moral reform while seeking to change the behavior of individuals. Drinking behavior (what is considered proper and improper) is typically controlled, defined, and enforced socially, just as abstaining is socially defined. As a reflection of the temperance and non-temperance ethics in America, drinking and drunkenness can give rise to a level of solidarity within groups (Gusfield, 1986). Thus, belonging to a group that is drinking and refusing to drink becomes a social *faux pas*. Behavior becomes a moral reflection of those who are drinking or not drinking.

Mariana Valverde (1988) also incorporated the concept "disease of the will" in her analysis of the construction of alcoholism. In discussing alcoholism as a "disease of the will," Valverde argues that alcoholism was medicalized (as a societal phenomenon) due to the belief that alcoholism is a loss of control and that alcohol consumption is considered a biological necessity for alcoholics (Valverde, 1998). Valverde argues that the disease model of addiction encompasses the idea that the alcoholic is seen as being ill. As the alcoholic does not choose to be sick, the logical conclusion is that the sick individual cannot be held responsible for any act committed while sick (Valverde 1998:192). Sick people must be treated and cured, so it follows that alcoholics must have treatment, practice self-help (Alcoholics

Anonymous), and demonstrate total abstinence from alcohol (remission) (Jellinek, 1952).

Notwithstanding the disease aspect of alcoholism, choice relates to "will" and the decision to drink (Valverde, 1998). A choice model of drug addiction is a very different construction (Valverde 1998). Under a choice model, there is nothing but responsibility for the act of substance abuse and every consequence related to that act of substance abuse. Addiction is a lifestyle choice or habit (Valverde 1998:23-42). Managing people who abuse controlled substances would include tolerance, harm reduction, and criminalization of socially offensive behavior.

Weinberg (2002) presented a critical survey of existing addiction research paradigms which detailed the considerable disagreement that exists regarding drug addiction (Weinberg, 2002). Weinberg discusses each principle paradigm of drug addiction - namely the neurological model, the social learning model and the symbolic interactionism perspective - and proposes that each has its own contribution long with serious limitations. The neurological model, according to Weinberg, suffers from the primary use of animal research which does not take sufficiently into account the social aspect of drug addiction (Weinberg, 2002). Social learning theories, with a focus on instrumental and classical conditioning, fail to account for the symbolic aspect of drug addiction, and symbolic interactionism for its part cannot explain relapse as a result of a compulsion to use despite a commitment to an abstinence lifestyle and identity (Weinberg, 2002). Weinberg proposes that drug addiction in practice is, in some respects, a hybrid of all of these theoretical contributions: "In opposition to such views, I would insist that people do literally *use* drugs in ways that are always personally meaningful to them. And this meaningful use of drugs is always embedded in, and at least to some extent, practically responsive to, socially structured contexts of action" (Weinberg, 2002, p. 16). Valverde also proposed that drug addiction, as viewed by professionals, is likewise a hybrid notion, fitting neither a pure disease model of addiction nor a pure choice model of addiction (Valverde, 1998).

In the United States the disease model is how alcoholism is generally understood in the law, but it is the choice model that became the vehicle for managing those who drink in excess as a preventive methodology (like a vaccine). If individuals pre-disposed to alcoholism are prevented from consuming alcohol, they can never contract the disease. In the alternative, if they have the disease, removing alcohol can help them manage the disease more effectively. Thus, a choice model, in the cloak of prohibition, becomes crucial in the fight to control the disease of alcohol addiction. Somewhere in the mix, controlled substances are pulled in and society must turn to the criminal justice system to enact and enforce this prohibition construction of the choice model in relation to substance abuse.

Within drug court, professionals have incorporated this social construction of the drug addict as both bad and sick (Tiger, 2013). The prevailing view is that most substance abusers must learn to control their disease through treatment and learn to abstain from the use of all controlled substances. In this way, drug-addicted clients are constructed as suffering from a disease and total abstinence is the goal. While the construction of the drug addict is a key piece to understanding how drug courts function, the construction of legal intervention is also important.

CRIMINAL JUSTICE AND MODELS OF CRIME CONTROL, DETERRENCE, DUE PROCESS AND REHABILITATION

Historically, judges have had only limited sentences for defendants who were found or plead guilty for a crime. The death penalty and public shaming were common sentences in colonial America (Knepper, 2001; Siegel, 2010). It wasn't until the 1800's that incarceration became common as an alternative to the death penalty in order to encourage repentance in convicts – thus the concept of the correctional facility or reformatory (Siegel & Worrall, 2013). Despite the belief that isolation from the community at large was rehabilitative, prison as a form of punishment is the traditional perspective of sentencing (Hoffman, 2002b; Mays & Ruddell, 2008). Traditionalist thinking in the criminal justice field is closely aligned with the crime control model and deterrence through swift, certain and harsh punishment (Mays & Ruddell, 2008).

The crime control model is concerned with the suppression of crime. Speed and efficiency are the focus of the crime control model, while actual guilt or innocence is a somewhat less critical concern. Accordingly, police and prosecutors are the most important actors and are relied upon to control crime in order to protect society from anarchy (Mays & Ruddell, 2008). Significant aspects of the crime control model include rational choice theory and the concept of deterrence. Rational choice theory relies upon the idea of consensus (there is a consensus in society of what is or should be right and wrong), and rational choice theorists believe that human behavior is governed in major part by rational hedonism so that criminal behavior can be controlled through a combination of specific and general deterrence (Siegel, 2010).

Deterrence is achieved through incarceration that is swiftly ordered, a certainty to occur, and is harsh in content and duration (Siegel, 2010). Sufficiently swift, certain and harsh, judicial sentences can prevent criminal behavior. Incarceration, whether in jail or prison, is the ultimate "time-out" for convicts where they can think about their actions and avoid committing proscribed acts in the future for fear of additional punishments. The traditional perspective incorporates policies such as determinate sentencing as well as consistent and public punishment through harsh sentences (Mays & Ruddell, 2008). It is through these public policies that the community at large sees that violating laws will result in predictable punishment. Thus, individuals will think twice before engaging in behaviors that violate the penal code. The traditional perspective is all about crime suppression.

It wasn't until the early 1900's that the American criminal justice system began to comprehensively incorporate treatment in the pursuit of rehabilitation (Knepper, 2001). This incorporation began in Cook County, Illinois through the Child Savers and the juvenile court system (Platt, 1969). Juvenile court, a diversionary system, devoted to the care and custody of abused and delinquent children was created in order to rehabilitate at risk children. Thus, individual case factors in the child's life were incorporated in the disposition of the case by the presiding judge. In other words, the beginnings of the socialization of the law were rooted in juvenile court (Platt, 1969). The individuals responsible for the advent of the juvenile justice system were considered progressives or reformists. Thus, the progressive perspective is focused on rehabilitation and the salvation of the individual (Cullen & Gendreau, 2000). The progressive perspective incorporates policies funneled through due process and focused on indeterminate sentencing, case-by-case tailored dispositions and individualized treatment to help people avoid violations of the penal code in the future. The due process model, on the other hand, presents a different view of the criminal justice system. Due process is fundamental fairness in the system of laws that prosecutes individuals for criminal acts. Critical facets of the due process model are substantive and procedural (Mays & Ruddell, 2008).

Substantive due process relates to fairness in the actual statutes that describe criminal acts. If the penal code for a particular crime is not fundamentally fair in its definition, it can be thrown out as a violation of due process (Neubauer, 2008).

Procedural due process focuses on fairness in the prosecution of individuals for criminal acts. Procedural due process includes the presumption of innocence and such rights as the right to remain silent, right to a speedy trial, right to be represented by an attorney and the right against cruel and inhuman treatment (Neubauer, 2008). It is by correctly identifying the guilty person and fixing their problem that will deter future criminality (Mays & Ruddell, 2008). The progressive perspective is all about the individual and fairness.

Drug Courts must incorporate both the crime control and the due process models in their therapeutic model. The crime control model relies upon the Judge's ability to swiftly punish non-compliant clients, but must consider basic constitutional rights that the defendant cannot waive in agreeing to participate in the diversionary court. Each court must decide for itself the extent to which these two models will be reflected in their court.

THE SOCIAL CONSTRUCTION OF JUDICIAL TEMPERAMENT:

Carol Gilligan (1982) presented the idea that men and women had very different ways of describing the experience of life, which she termed "voice" (Gilligan, 1982). Gilligan proposed that women experienced the world through an "ethic of care" and men through an "ethic of right." According to the ethic of care, women are more involved with activities of care and the relationship of connectedness On the other hand, according to the ethic of right men are more concerned with equality and separateness (Gilligan, 1982).

In Fox & Van Sickel's research, the ethic of care and ethic of right refer to different orientations to adjudicating clients. Fox & Van Sickel opined that the ethic of right orientation (the male "voice") was more authoritarian and focused on individual responsibility, while the ethic of care orientation (the female "voice") was more interested in the well-being of the individual and the connectedness of the defendant (Fox & Sickel, 2000). Fox & Van Sickel took Gilligan's ethic of right and ethic of care concepts and used them as a lens for observing judicial behavior on the bench (Fox & Sickel, 2000). They observed and coded both judicial instances (each judicial ruling) and judicial style (the overall style of the judge on the bench) in their study in order to see if male judges acted in conformity with the ethic of right and female judges acted in conformity with the ethic of care. After analyzing judicial instances and judicial style, Fox et al. determined that either voice could be observed in the behavior of individual judges (whether male and female) in the courtroom setting; however, legal factors held more weight in judicial decision making than did either the care or right perspective of the judges (Fox & Sickel, 2000). Fox & Van Sickel were creative in their attempt to examine the inner workings of the courtroom and how judges construct their role of judge in their interactions with defendants.

Fox and Van Sickel's study design and results can provide a framework for observing drug court judges in the field as they construct their role in the lives of drug court clients. Within the ambiguity of the drug court, judges create their *persona* based upon their construction of the drug-addicted client and belief on which model of corrections is most effective – traditional and the use of deterrence or progressive and the use of treatment. Should drug court clients be deterred from future drug use or should drug court clients be treated for their addiction, thus giving them the cure to their disease? Both constructions have the same goal, but the methods are very different.

PUTTING THE PIECES OF THE PUZZLE TOGETHER

It is in drug court that the elements of the sociology of law and social construction are found. Drug court contains Durkheim's understanding of the importance of consensus as well as the nuances of restitutive and repressive law and their respective roles in a diverse community. Weber's substantive law and the increased role of social factors in the law clearly came into play as do organizational theory and the courtroom workgroup, and even Gilligan's notions of voice can be seen in action. Theories related to sociology of law and social construction influence how the criminal justice concepts of crime control, punishment, due process, and treatment play out within the drug court setting.

Social construction theory in the traditional court system focuses on key courtroom workgroup players (judge, prosecutor, defense attorney, client, and jury), but drug court features for less formalism and a great deal more ambiguity. There are few requirements for drug court, other than having the key elements, thus drug court team members .have considerable discretion in their policies and procedures and how those policies and procedures are implemented. Given more ambiguity and a wide mandate, drug court judges and team members. must create and incorporate social constructions of the law in order to decide how drug court best practices will be implemented in their own court. The judge, the drug court team, constructions of law and addiction, as well as criminal justice crime control and due process models all come together in drug court planning meetings. Teams sift through the possibilities and incorporate elements of these ideas to create the drug court team they want to implement. Each drug court is made up of a set of sanctions, rewards, and unique policies which the drug court judge implements every day on the bench in his or her interactions with drug court clients. It is this set of policies and procedures, coupled with the judge's unique style of interaction, that makes each drug court unique.

It is through the courtroom workgroup that drug court teams are trained to create their version of drug court. Each team is put through a series of trainings (spanning three to five days) which incorporates long lectures on the principles of drug court broken only by periods of team planning meetings to design their individual drug court by applying the information learned in the lectures. Thus, drug court teams are encouraged to construct their own understanding of how to intervene therapeutically with drug addicts and how to work together to implement the basic tenets of the drug court model. Each drug court creates a unique entity and, like snowflakes, no two are exactly alike. Even those drug court teams that look to neighboring drug courts to help them design their own or to assist in drafting their manual make subtle changes in order to create something new.

Social constructions related to drug court, drug abuse and therapeutic intervention are created during the planning trainings, mentor courts and subsequent continuing education trainings. Field trips to mentor courts include transportation to the local court, adequate seating for all the drug court attendees, the opportunity to observe a "live" drug court session, and a Q&A with the drug court judge (moderated by the conference administrator). Attendees are encouraged to ask as many questions as they like, and each field trip emphasizes the unique aspects of the local court under observation. Each local court incorporates the key elements and focuses on treatment services in the area, including organized agencies and self-help support meetings (NA or AA). Thus, the drug court model is passed on within the court community through education, problem solving sessions, and purposeful modeling of best practices.

Drug courts capitalize on the idea of the courtroom workgroup, and it is a crucial aspect of therapeutic jurisprudence courts (Nolan, 2001). In drug court, some players are the same as in traditional court, however, there are additional extra-legal members in the courtroom (Nolan, 2001). Besides the attorneys who are prosecutors, defense attorneys, and judges, there may be probation officers, police officers, treatment providers, social service case workers, and drug court coordinators as well as other service providers (GED coordinators or client advocates) who are regularly included in the case management discussions and court hearings (Castellano, 2009). In terms o.f drug court, each drug court team member .has a traditional role (prosecutors win criminal cases, defense attorneys protect their client's rights, social workers and drug treatment counselors provide services to people in need, and judges make decisions) but each must set that role aside in order to work cooperatively to provide therapeutic services to clients. The diversionary nature of drug court translates into the transformation of traditional roles for key players in the courtroom. Transformation has ramifications that can be analyzed through social constructionism. Drug courts are created from the ground up through regular federally funded trainings in which drug court judges are encouraged to develop the *persona* that they will use to interact with each client. Initial drug court trainings are where drug court judges and drug court teams construct their understanding of how their particular drug court should function as a therapeutic intervention. This construction includes the team's collective vision of what a drug-addicted client is and, by necessity, what motivates an addict to abstain from drug use. Socialization of law takes hold as more social characteristics are incorporated into the legal arena. Where clients go, whom they interact with, how often the client attends treatment or not, the client's living conditions and family, and whether the client attends self-help are all factors discussed in the typical status meeting. It is here that drug court incorporates the client's social characteristics in order to carry out therapeutic jurisprudence and better direct the client away from unfavorable "people, places, and things" in order to avoid a relapse.

The social construction of judicial interaction is the black box phenomenon-that is, the interaction between the judge and the client and the unique set of practices (policies and procedures) that the judge (along with his treatment team) employs through his or her drug court to treat drug-addicted criminal offenders. A social construction perspective provides the tools to examine how the judge socially constructs himself or herself (which exhibits itself in the judicial orientation, using the unique set of practices created by him or her employed in drug court) in order to have a favorable affect on the drug court client. Given the literature reviewed, the theoretical perspectives reviewed would seem to suggest that judges may show wide variations in how they run their drug courts and how they interact with their clients. Indeed, it may be that judges will act in both progressively-oriented and traditionally-oriented ways or lean one way or the other in their interactions with client to best guide each individual to a sober lifestyle. Finally, empirical literature suggests that observation of the court and interviews with key members can provide rich information through which an analysis of these judicial interactions can be accomplished.

Chapter 3

A Qualitative look at Drug Court

The focus of this book is the day-to-day workings of each court, which includes the documentation of the unique policies and procedures each drug court has incorporated. Of course, the judge is a key component of drug court as the authority figure for the clients and the team members .who enforce the policies and procedures adopted by his or her drug court. Examining the way in which the judge interacts with the clients is critical in understanding the inner workings of any particular drug court (Marlowe, Festinger, & Lee, 2004).

The research described in this book investigates two questions.

- Can drug court judges be classified into the conceptual ideas of "traditional" and "progressive," thus providing key information regarding the black box of drug court?
- What impact do these particular approaches have on client retention in drug court and client graduation from drug court?

This research examines more closely the impact, if any, specific judicial orientations have on client success in drug court. These orientations will include the specific policies and procedures that each judge, along with the drug court team, has incorporated into the particular court and implemented through the judge's orders from the bench. Through the theoretical framework of social constructionism and data collection through court observation and staff interviews, this research provides a contextual understanding of how drug court affects client success. It is through research such as this that drug court professionals can come to understand the inner workings of the drug court in order to increase effectiveness regarding client outcomes reflected by retention and graduation rates (Goldkamp et al., 2001). The results of this study may provide information valuable to the development of judicial training materials, as well as provide content for training workshops for existing drug courts.

This is an observation-based study of judicial behavior, a fact which presents certain challenges. Case studies can measure how judges believe they will rule in certain cases, and surveys can measure what they say they think; in contrast court observations measure actual judicial behavior. Unfortunately, court observation as a research tool can feature reliability and validity problems because observations are subject to observer error and interpretational bias. This chapter will discuss these challenges, as well as the specific methods used to overcome these challenges and to collect unbiased information related to judicial interactions in drug court with clients.

PARTICIPANTS

The subjects in the study are drug court judges, and the study used court watching/team meeting forms in order to record and analyze judges' behavior in court. The study observed ten (10) judges within New York State from December 2011 to July 2012. Each judge was observed during both team meetings and drug court sessions. A pilot study (five observations of five courts) was also completed in the summer of 2011 to pre-test the reliability of the observation instruments. After the pilot study observations were complete, semi-structured interviews were conducted with four of the five judges in order to assess judicial behavior.

A total of 100 separate observations of drug court sessions and 81 team meetings were completed in this study (one court did not allow the research team into the team meeting, and one court did not hold team meetings for approximately half of the observation period), allowing the research team to code judicial style for 181 sessions. In addition, 2,612 instances of judicial interaction were coded during the court sessions for the study period. For each court, basic demographic information was collected, including location of court (urban, rural, and suburban) , how often the court meets, and the members of the team in attendance (judge, defense attorney, prosecuting attorney, project coordinator, treatment provider).

Site population demographics including total population of the community, where the court is located, and its racial makeup; are detailed in Table 1 and in the site descriptions below that.

Table 1: Site Population Demographics

2010 Census							
Courts	Total	White only	% of Total	Black Only	% of Total	Other	% of Total
A	122,3	102,55	84%	7,009	6%	12,79	10%
B	15,13	14,619	97%	138	1%	373	2%
C	15,46	13,831	89%	837	5%	797	5%
D	12,56	9,740	78%	770	6%	2,053	16%
E	261,3	131,75	50%	100,774	39%	28,78	11%
F	88,22	77,769	88%	7,069	8%	3,388	4%
G	18,14	15,215	84%	1,790	10%	1,136	6%
H	21,16	18,519	87%	1,526	7%	1,120	5%
I	50,19	35,394	71%	10,835	22%	3,964	8%
J	31,14	27,547	88%	1,273	4%	2,326	7%

*Other includes American Indian/Alaskan Native Alone, Asian

Table 1 presents the courts and is labeled according to their site descriptions. (Future tables and figures will alternate between their site description designation and demographic label in order to protect the privacy of each court and those who agreed to participate in this study.) All the courts recruited except one have adult drug courts that meet once a week. Many of the courts have more than one therapeutic court, but reserve one day to hear adult drug court status appearances.

Historically, drug court clients were misdemeanor-level individuals who were identified as good candidates for drug treatment through intake and assessment. If a potential drug court client appeared appropriate but was charged with a felony, the prosecutor could reduce the charge to misdemeanor so that the individual could be eligible to accept drug court. This was intended to ensure that drug court clients were "users" as opposed to "dealers."

In October 2009, Article 216 amended the Criminal Procedure Law allowing judges to offer drug court to non-violent drug-addicted felony offenders. These felony-level drug offenders are diverted to drug court after a plea of guilty to the felony charges. Drug court judges then monitor Art. 216 clients in the drug court program, and if they successfully complete the program to graduation these clients are entitled to have their conviction converted to a misdemeanor. Should the client fail, he or she is sentenced based upon the original guilty plea to the felony charges. Article 216 made it possible for more minorities to take advantage of drug court because minorities tend to have longer criminal histories while also being charged with higher offense level crimes (felonies) which in the past would make them ineligible for referral to drug court.

Site Descriptions:

The following details each site, providing information on each court, its observed sanctions, rewards, and unique policies as well as the judge's typical interaction and graduation ceremony.

Court A:
Court A is an adult drug court and is considered a large drug court serving a primarily white suburban population (2010 census). This drug court meets once a week and seeks to achieve the end of chemical dependency and criminal activity through counseling (substance abuse and mental health), community support (i.e., self-help groups), vocational/educational training, family involvement, and linkage to other services. Upon entry into the drug court, in lieu of providing a client manual clients are instructed to attend a mandatory orientation meeting where the client is provided with all of the necessary information related to policies, procedures, rewards, and sanctions. Once completing the treatment program and necessary court appearances, the client is required to complete a monitoring phase where he or she returns to court for mandatory drug screens before graduation from drug court. Clients are required to demonstrate a total cumulative clean time of six months before graduation, but one-year minimum participation is required before a client can become eligible for graduation.

Observed Sanctions, Rewards, and Unique Policies:
Sanctions: verbal warning, client instructed to figure out a plan for avoiding use in the future, 100% compliance, increased case

management contacts, subject to random urine screens for 60 days, community service hours, 90 meetings in 90 days, door-to-door, sanction pending, jail (long term).

Rewards: applause, handshakes, praise, small gift, green card.

Unique Policies: clients must be there at the start of the drug court session, but can leave after their case is heard, curfew, self-helps required, compliance court, monitoring status, transfer to different court.

Typical Interaction:

Drug court coordinator provides the client's status. The judge then looks at the client, giving him or her an opportunity to add anything to their status. After the client speaks, the judge then addresses compliance or non-compliance.

Graduation:

The judge delivers the history of the client's participation in drug court and presents the client as now graduating. The client receives a handshake, a book (*Metaphor For Success*), applause and congratulations. Finally, the client is given an opportunity to give a speech to the audience.

COURT A

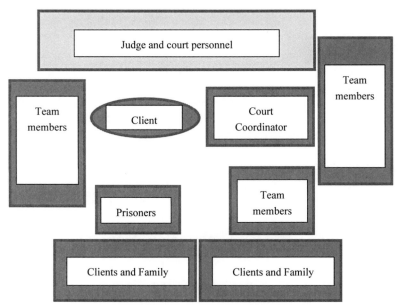

Court B:

Court B is a felony/misdemeanor/hub adult drug court and is considered a mid-sized to small city drug court serving a primarily white suburban population (2010 Census). As such, Court B accepts Art. 216 clients and, as a hub, clients referred from other town, city, or village courts. This drug court meets once a week and seeks to achieve the end of chemical dependency and criminal activity by emphasizing mandated treatment with judicial oversight, thus creating a long-term therapeutic environment. Upon entering the drug court, clients are provided with a handbook which details their responsibilities and gives them insight into the program they have entered. Clients are required to demonstrate a total cumulative clean time of six months before he or she can graduate.

Observed Sanctions, Rewards, and Unique Policies:

Sanctions: verbal warning, lecture, doo-to-door, higher level of care, sanction pending, jail (short term).

Rewards: handshake, small gift, praise, standing ovation, reduced status appearances, reduced treatment requirements.

Unique Policies: thought-provoking questions used to interact with clients, clients asked (by judge) to come up with own sanction.

Typical Interaction:

Judge calls the client to the bench. The judge then gives the client's status for the week, compliments client on compliance (or addresses non-compliance) and/or mentions something personal (kids, hobby).

Graduation:

The judge calls the client to the bench and provides the client's course of recovery. The judge then graduates the client, presenting a certificate and praising the client. Applause ensues and the judge offers the client an opportunity to speak to the audience. Finally, the judge finishes the client's criminal matter.

COURT B

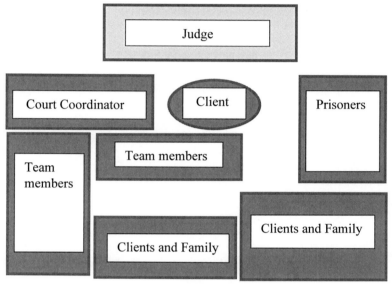

Court C:

Court C is also a felony/misdemeanor/hub adult drug court and is considered a mid-sized to small city drug court serving a primarily white suburban population (2010 Census). As such, Court C accepts Art. 216 clients as well as clients referred from other town, city, or village courts. This drug court uses intense supervision, treatment, and judicial monitoring to end the cycle of addiction by balancing therapeutic intervention and client accountability to the judge. Drug Court C meets once a week and clients move through four phases in order to successfully graduate. Upon entering the drug court, clients are provided with a handbook which details their responsibilities. Clients are required to demonstrate a cumulative clean time of one year before he or she can graduate.

Observed Sanctions, Rewards, and Unique Policies:

Sanctions: verbal warning, increased case management contacts, bed-to-bed, jail.

Rewards: small gift, verbal praise, every client receives applause at the end of their status appearance, group outing for clients.

Unique Policies: Clients must be there at the start of the drug court session, but can leave after their case is heard, an essay is required before phase advancement, community service requirement.

Typical Interaction:
The client is called up and the judge addresses the client: "How are you today?" The judge gives the client's status and asks relevant questions. Finally, the judge asks the courtroom to give the client a round of applause.

Graduation:
The judge gets off the bench to talk with the client, shakes his or her hand while standing next to the drug court coordinator. Client receives a certificate for graduation. They both congratulate the client on his or her progress and recovery. The client is given an opportunity to make a speech.

COURT C

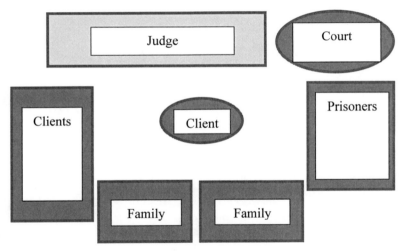

Court D:
Court D, a felony/misdemeanor/hub adult drug city court, serves a primarily white rural population (2010 Census). As such, Court D accepts Art. 216 clients as well as clients referred to them from other town, city, or village courts. This drug court uses timely and effective treatment in conjunction with supervision in order to protect the community from repeat substance abuse offenders. Court D seeks to

reduce costs to the criminal justice system and provide tools to clients in order for them to become abstinent community members. Drug court clients are provided with a handbook which details their responsibilities as well as the three phases the client must go through in order to complete the program. Clients are required to demonstrate a cumulative clean time of one year before he or she can graduate.

Observed Sanctions, Rewards, and Unique Policies:
Sanctions: verbal warning, small gift (compliance related), increased case management contacts, increased AA/NA meetings, 100% compliance, higher level of care, door-to-door, day reporting, community service, jail (short jail terms – weekends or three days).
Rewards: small gift, verbal praise, handshake, baked goods, lottery (reward for bringing in the calendar given to them by the court), group outing for clients (golf outing or picnic).
Unique Policies: GED is a requirement, client mentor is recruited to watch over the client within the community, clients get a weekly order (with a carbon copy for the court) of what they must do during the week in order to be compliant with drug court, clients are not allowed to leave until the drug court session is over, self-helps are verified in court, clients must complete drug court within two years or return to criminal court, termination hearing, community service is required of clients who don't have a job or are not enrolled in school, Must ask for permission to leave the county.
Typical Interaction:
Judge stands and shakes the client's hand when he or she approaches the table. "<client's name>, how are you?" Judge then provides the client's phase in treatment court and status. The judge then references the client's case worker, rewards or sanctions the client, and shakes the client's hand before the client leaves.
Graduation:
Two times yearly, a graduation ceremony is held in court for recent graduates. All clients are expected to attend and bring a guest. The ceremony opens with the Pledge of Allegiance, a moment of silence and recognition of veterans, opening speeches (mayor, minister, local judges, and drug court judge). During the opening speeches, metaphor is used to acknowledge the work done by the graduates in their journey to get clean and sober. The ceremony wraps up with closing comments, benediction, and a reception with food and drink. Those clients who

have made phase advancement are also recognized and applauded. Each graduating client is separately called to the podium, the client's course of recovery is detailed, congratulations, compliments, and handshakes ensue, and the audience applauds. Each client is given an opportunity to speak and given a small gift (i.e., a thriving flower that is described as a metaphor for recovery) . An additional award (Lighthouse award) is given to recognize a victim advocate/caseworker who is a "beacon of hope." The criminal matter is completed before the client leaves but after the reception.

COURT D

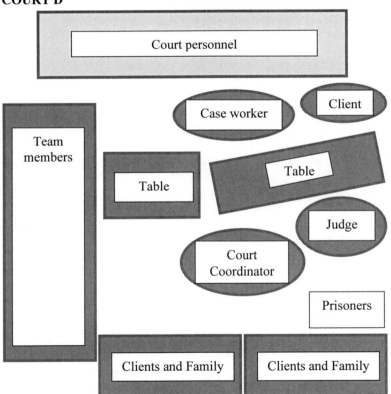

Court E:
Court E is a large adult city drug court serving a mixed race city (2101 Census). This drug court meets multiple times a week and accepts clients from other courts as transfers or as a hub Court. Art. 216 clients are also accepted in this court. Court E seeks to achieve the end of chemical dependency and criminal activity through counseling (substance abuse and mental health), community support (i.e., self-help groups), vocational/educational training, and linkage to other services. Upon entry into the drug court clients are provided with a participant handbook giving the client all of the necessary information related to policies, procedures, rewards, and sanctions for the court. Clients are required to move through four phases before they are eligible for their "day of recognition."

Observed Sanctions, Rewards and Unique Policies:
Sanctions: Judge enquires "What is going to be different?," community service, door-to-door, increased case management contacts, increased AA/NA meetings, Penalty Box, Higher level of care, Removal from program.
Rewards: Verbal praise, standing ovation from judge.
Unique Policies: The microphone is often turned off when discussing certain aspects of treatment, compliance, or criminal matters in order to protect the client's privacy. Clients are allowed to leave court when it their appearance is over. At the first appearance as a drug court client the judge gives a background of the drug court and instructs people on tips on how to stay out of trouble. The judge then breaks down what he expects of that person and gets to know the client. Clients must be there at the start of the drug court session but can leave after their case is heard.
Typical Interaction:
The judge addresses the client immediately: "Hello, how are you? You look…. Are you doing well?" Often the judge and client engage in some discussion about the client and his or her life. The judge then gives the drug court coordinator an opportunity to present additional information or speak to specific individuals about the matter before the court. The judge often instructs the client to "keep the focus" as a reminder to stay compliant until the next status appearance.
Graduation:
Graduation is called a "Day of Recognition." The judge gets off the bench and walks up to the client in order to give him or her the

certificate. Client is then given an opportunity to speak to the audience and then the judge gives a speech to encourage the rest of the clients by using the graduate as an example.

Once a year, a large banquet is held at a local hotel to recognize graduates, former graduates, case workers, and victim advocates. The banquet includes a silent auction as a fundraiser and speeches from former clients, judges, and special guests. Drug court judges who attend are also recognized during the banquet. The intention of this banquet is to celebrate every successful drug court client.

COURT E

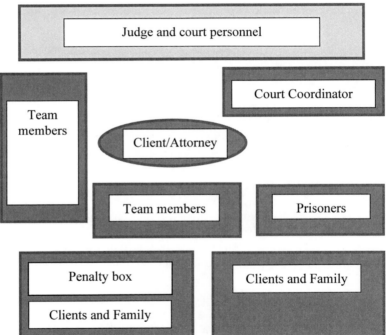

Court F:

Court F is an adult drug court and is considered a mid-sized town drug court serving a primarily white suburban population (2010 Census). This drug court meets once a week and seeks to achieve the end of chemical dependency and criminal activity through treatment, services, and judicial monitoring.

Observed Sanctions, Rewards, and Unique Policies:

Sanctions: verbal warning (i.e., diluted urine sample warning), essay or letter, attendance contract, increased case management contacts, 100% compliance, door-to-door, sanction pending, 90 meetings in 90 days, jail (short- or long-term).

Rewards: verbal praise, applause.

Unique Policies: compliant clients are sometimes let go without seeing the judge

Typical Interaction:

Judge addresses the client: "How are you? You look <some compliment> are you doing well?" The judge would usually ask about what brought the client into the program and their drug of choice. Finally, the judge would instruct the client to "stay on track."

Graduation:

The drug court coordinator tells the audience the course of the client's drug court program and announces that the client will be graduating. The judge congratulates the client, gives the client a small gift (i.e., pen/pencil set). The audience applauds and the client is afforded an opportunity to speak to the rest of the clients.

COURT F

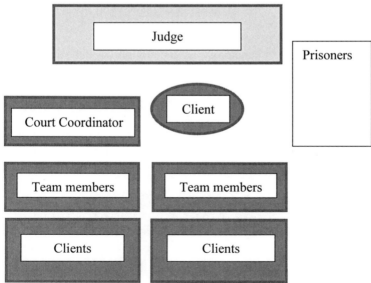

Court G:
Court G is an adult city drug court and is considered a large drug court serving a primarily white urban population (2010 Census). This court takes 216 cases and can provide a monitoring function for clients on probation. This drug court meets once a week and seeks to achieve the end of chemical dependency through substance abuse counseling, court supervision and engagement with additional services as needed. Additional program rules include mandatory employment or school enrollment unless a client has a documented disability. Clients are required to complete their treatment program and complete a minimum of twelve months of drug court participation and demonstrate a total cumulative clean time of six months prior to completion before he or she can graduate.

Observed Sanctions, Rewards, and Unique Policies:
Sanctions: verbal warning, essay, door-to-door, day reporting, sanction pending, jail (short or long term).
Rewards: verbal praise, applause, handshake, stage certificates, small gift.
Unique Policies: orientation for client, clients must be there at the start of the drug court session but can leave after their case is heard, transfer to different court, potential roommates or partners are examined for appropriateness, self-helps are verified in court, GED is required, some monitoring time between completion of drug court program requirements and graduation, twelve month clean time before graduation
Typical Interaction:
Court calls the docket # and the judge asks "How are you?" The judge then provides the client's status of compliance/non-compliance as the client approaches the bench. Then the judge asks if the client has any issues or concerns. At the end of the appearance, the drug court coordinator relates any additional concerns and the date for the next status appearance.
Graduation:
Judge tells the client's course of recovery and indicates that this is his or her graduation. The judge then congratulates the client, hands him or her the certificate, shakes the client's hand and the entire courtroom applauds. The client is then offered the opportunity to speak to the audience.

COURT G

	Judge	
Prisoners		Team
	Court Coordinator	
	Client	
	Team members	Prosecutor
	Clients and Family	Clients and Family

Court H:
Court H is a misdemeanor/hub adult drug court and is considered a mid-sized to small city drug court serving a primarily white suburban population (2010 Census). As such, Court H accepts clients referred from other town, city, or village courts. This drug court meets once a week. Court H uses mandated treatment with judicial oversight, creating a long-term therapeutic environment in order to stop clients from abusing substances and reducing criminal recidivism. Clients are expected to pursue appropriate educational and/or employment related opportunities.

<u>*Observed Sanctions, Rewards, and Unique Policies:*</u>
Sanctions: lecture, community service hours, service work, loss of clean time, higher level of care.

Rewards: progress in treatment and length of clean time is stated during client/judge interaction and praise and applause is given, reduced status appearances

Unique Policies: In-court GED program, treatment court support group.

Typical Interaction:

Judge addresses the client as he or she approaches the bench, "How are you doing?" If they ask about him, he says "Good, thanks for asking." After listening to drug coordinator on the client's status, the judge typically rewards the client (for good behavior) or sanctions the client if necessary. The judge will also discuss some positive aspect of the client's life with him or her during the court interaction.

Graduation:

Drug court coordinator states status of client and graduation status. Judge congratulates the client and the entire courtroom applauds. The client receives a stage certificate and is then offered the opportunity to give a speech.

COURT H

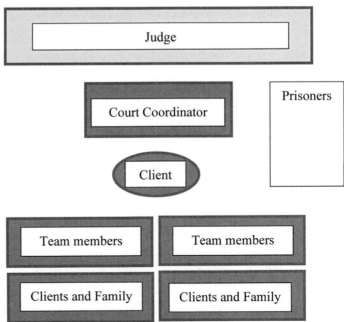

Court I:
Court I, a felony/misdemeanor/hub adult drug court is a mid-size to large city drug court serving a primarily white suburban population and accepts Art. 216 clients as well as clients referred from other town, city, or village courts (2010 Census). The community Court I serves is a relatively dense area, but Court I is the only drug court in the area, so the clientele is incrementally growing larger with the increase in categories of clients this court accepts. This drug court uses intense supervision, treatment, and judicial monitoring to end the cycle of addiction by balancing therapeutic intervention and teaching clients to be responsible for their actions. Drug Court I meets once a week and clients move through four phases in order to successfully graduate. Upon entering the drug court, clients are provided with a manual which details their responsibilities and they must attend an alumni group session which serves as an orientation to the court.

Observed Sanctions, Rewards, and Unique Policies:
Sanctions: lecture, essay, community service hours, additional self-helps, higher level of care, door-to-door, sanction pending, jail (Long-term).

Rewards: praise, handshake, applause, stage certificates, holiday cookies, small gifts, reduced status appearances, special treats: i.e., holiday: clients allowed to leave after status appearance, head of the class

Unique Policies: GED addressed, curfew, life works, roll call, detailed in-court intake procedure, head of Class, six month goal sheet, self-helps are verified in court, community service project, all clients remain until court is over (unless using a head of the class), alumni group, twelve months clean time before graduation.

Typical Interaction:
The judge addresses the client as he or she approaches the bench. "Good morning, how are you this morning? What do you want to talk about today?" Often the judge asks about what the client learned in treatment (after completion) or any struggles or triggers the client may have. In the alternative, the judge will ask about what the client is working on in treatment. Finally, the judge will ask about the client's family, living situation, or hobbies the client has.

Graduation:
The client approaches the bench and the drug court coordinator congratulates the client on graduating and the judge comes off the bench in order to shake hands with the client. The client receives a stage certificate, praise, applause, as well as a small gift. The gift is a key chain, which holds "a whistle to know how to call for help when they need to, a thermometer [is] on there, [so] they know when a situation gets too hard, a magnifying glass to help them see things clearly, and a compass to help point them in the right direction." The client is then given an opportunity to make a speech to the rest of the clients.

COURT I

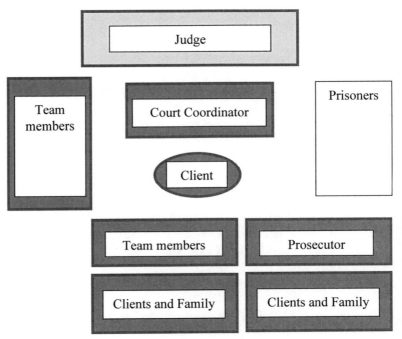

Court J:

Court J, a felony/misdemeanor/hub adult drug court, serves a primarily white rural population. As such, Court J accepts Art. 216 clients as well as clients referred from other town, city, or village courts (2010 Census). This drug court offers an expedited case processing method providing treatment and supervision in a timely and effective manner. Court J focuses on problem resolution, team collaboration, and comprehensive service delivery to clients in order to reduce costs to the criminal justice system and to prevent recidivism. Drug court clients are provided with a handbook which details their responsibilities and the three phases the client must work through in the treatment program. Clients are required to demonstrate a cumulative clean time of one year before he or she can graduate.

Observed Sanctions, Rewards, and Unique Policies:

Sanctions: verbal warning, small gift (compliance related), letter of apology, increased case management contacts, community service hours, higher level of care, door-to-door, jail (short-term).

Rewards: applause, praise, speech, stage certificates, reduced treatment requirements

Unique Policies: clients must be there at the start of the drug court session but can leave after their case is heard, curfew, judge asks for how many self-helps the client completed during the week and instructs the client on the number of self-helps he or she must complete during the week at the end of the interaction, self-helps are verified in court, clients must enroll in school or get a job.

Typical Interaction:

The drug court coordinator calls the client. The judge asks for a status from the coordinator: "What does <client name> have for us today?" At this point the coordinator reports the amount of self-helps the client attended while the judge checks to make sure the client attended his or her required set of self-helps. The judge compliments compliance or extra self-helps. In the alternative, the judge addresses the client for failure to complete the week's self-helps. The judge then addresses any other status issues before the client is let go for the day.

Graduation:

Drug court coordinator gets the certificate from the judge in order to give it to the client. The client is given the opportunity to say a few words to the other clients. The judge praises the client's success in finishing the drug court program and takes care of any final criminal matters immediately.

COURT J

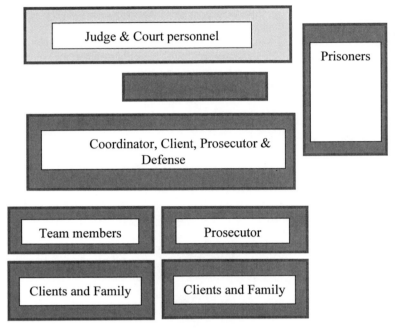

These site diagrams portray the physical atmosphere the clients are in during drug court. Each set-up can mean the difference between a harsh environment in which the clients are expected to stand in front of the judge, looking up at him or her and experiencing the full force of judicial admonishment or other sanction (as well as the "atta boy" or other reward) or having an attorney by the client's side to mitigate and advocate for him. Altering the courtroom can transform the courtroom from a more traditional environment into a more therapeutic environment in the same way that the creation of drug court has transformed traditional criminal justice players into therapeutic agents. This transformation and its reflection on judicial orientation is elaborated on later in the discussion.

TEAM MEMBERS.

Team members typically include those professionals who work with the drug court clients at the judge's request. Potential team members are found in the community and include the Department of Social Services, caseworkers and/or employees of the treatment agencies, employees of other service agencies (e.g., GED providers), court personnel, prosecutor or representatives from the district attorney's office, defense attorneys, police officers, social workers, drug court coordinator(s), probation officers, judges, and anyone else the client sees during the course of the drug treatment program.

Team members for each court differed in quantity (from 2 to 13 members in attendance), and composition (some teams had probation officers and/or police officers). Some courts were limited to only one or two treatment providers in attendance. Not all team members would attend the team meeting or stay for the actual court session. Prosecutors, for example, may come for the team meeting in order to voice their opinion, but may attend to other duties during the drug court session. Along that same vein, a defense attorney would attend the drug court session in order to represent the client but, not attend the team meeting. The team members who participate in drug court are determined by judicial recruitment, the community and its resources, and budgetary concerns. Each team member interviewed for this study attended the team meeting and the drug court session, so each had the opportunity to observe the judge and his interactions with the clients. Each judge was interviewed at least once during the course of the study, and a total of 12 interviews of team members were completed (5 drug court coordinators, 1 prosecutor, 3 defense attorneys, 3 treatment providers). Semi-structured interviews total 26 for the whole study; 22 were collected for the full study, and 4 were collected for the pilot study.

The study participants included one African American judge and nine White judges; all were men with a mean age of 59.4 years and mean judicial experience of 19.62 years. Of the team members interviewed, all were White college graduates with a mean age of 46.5 years for defense attorneys, 42 years for drug court coordinators, and 43.33 year for treatment providers. Finally, one prosecutor was interviewed, - a White man, age 53. Demographic information related to judges and team members. is detailed in Tables 2 and 3. The original study design required that three individuals representing each key team member would be interviewed for the study. Table 3 details those team members interviewed for the study.

Table 2: Demographic information-Judges

Years attorney	Years judge	Education	Race	Sex	Age
18	12	Juris Doctor	White	Male	44
24	0.25	Juris Doctor	White	Male	58
24	19	Juris Doctor	White	Male	57
26	36	Juris Doctor	White	Male	61
31	26	Bachelor's	White	Male	61
33	21	Juris Doctor	African American	Male	57
34	28	Juris Doctor	White	Male	62
37	20	Juris Doctor	White	Male	63
39	18	Juris Doctor	White	Male	64
40	16	Juris Doctor	White	Male	67
Mean 30.6	19.625				59.4

Table 3: Demographic Information-Team Members.

Defense	Race	Sex	Age
1	White	Female	34
2	White	Male	59
3	White	Male	Unknown
		Mean Age	46.5
Drug court coordinators	Race	Sex	Age
1	White	Female	31
2	White	Male	50
3	White	Male	57
3	White	Female	48
4	White	Female	44
5	White	Male	36
5	White	Female	28
		Mean Age	42.00
Treatment providers	Race	Sex	Age
1	White	Female	59
2	White	Male	26
3	White	Male	45
		Mean Age	43.33
Prosecutors	Race	Sex	Age
1	White	Male	53

It was during the study observations that it was discovered that prosecutors were not found to be very regular or active team members. in **both** the team meeting and the court session, so finding three prosecutors was impossible. It was important to include team members who had the ability to observe the judge in the team meeting and the court session in that it increased their ability to speak about their judge specifically as well as the role of the judge generally. Of the ten courts in the study, only one prosecutor met that criteria and he agreed to be interviewed for the study. To supplement for the missing interview subjects, two more drug court coordinators were selected to interview in order to provide additional insight into the role of the judge in drug court.

Privacy of the courts and their clients was protected by assigning a random number to each court and printing pre-marked forms for court watchers to use in the courtroom. No identifying information was collected on any form or interview other than gender and race of team members .and clients. The code sheet noting the random number assigned to each individual court was accessible only to the principal investigator.

Measures

The independent variables related to this research revolve around judicial behavior in relation to team members and drug court clients.

Independent Variables

Judicial orientation refers to which side of the therapeutic jurisprudence spectrum a particular judge is on - that is the *therapeutic* side of judicial orientation (**progressive**) or the *jurisprudence* side of judicial orientation (**traditional**) .

Traditional vs. Progressive Orientation

By starting out with the basic models within the criminal justice system, as well as the traditional perspective of punishment and the progressive perspective of treatment, in combination with the theoretical constructs of "voice" as developed by Fox and Van Sickel, it is possible to see the development of traditional and progressive judicial orientations. Fox and Van Sickel's ethic of care and ethic of right refer to different orientations when adjudicating clients. Fox and

Van Sickel opined that the ethic of right orientation (the male "voice") was more authoritarian and focused on individual responsibility, while the ethic of care orientation (the female "voice") was more directed to the well-being of the individual and the connectedness of the defendant (Fox & Sickel, 2000). Thus, the ethic of right would be more aligned with a traditional perspective while the ethic of care would be more aligned with the progressive perspective. Through direct observation of drug court judges, it was possible to see that different judges were able to express their "voice" (male-aligned with a traditional perspective and female-aligned with the progressive perspective) when given great leeway to develop a relationship with the client. Thus, a drug court judge is able to express his (and his team's) construction of how to best motivate a client through his orientation.

Judges who employ a progressive orientation focus on the contextual aspect of the drug court client's life and the community support the client uses in his or her struggle to stay clean. The use of positive reinforcement, or a system of rewards, is the primary tool the judge uses to encourage clients to refrain from using drugs. In addition, the progressively oriented judge is often concerned with fairness in the drug court process and will incorporate some elements of due process:drug court in the drug court environment even though diversionary systems have no such requirement. Due process is fundamental fairness in the system of laws that prosecutes individuals for criminal acts. Critical facets of the due process model are substantive and procedural (Mays & Ruddell, 2008). Thus, the independent variable of a progressive judicial orientation is related to the progressive model, derived from Fox & Van Sickel's research, and the criminal justice model of due process. The progressive judicial orientation is examined through measures related to the concepts of context, community, and due process (Fox & Sickel, 2000; Mays & Ruddell, 2008).

Judges who employ a traditional orientation focus more on the individual's choice and responsibility in drug addiction and the rule of law. The use of negative reinforcement, or graduated sanctions, is believed to be the best way to ensure compliance with treatment requirements and, through treatment compliance, the end to addiction. Judges who employ a traditional approach are as much concerned with the impact of this approach on all of the drug court clients in the courtroom. Thus, traditional judges need to ensure that everyone receives the same sanction in regards to non-compliance, and non-compliance must be dealt with harshly in order to increase its deterrence value on others. Through both general and specific deterrence, individuals can be dissuaded from future criminal behavior if the punishment is swiftly given, certain in its delivery, and harsh enough that the rational mind weighs in on the side of "too great a cost to bear" and decides against committing a particular crime (Knepper, 2001). Thus, the independent variable of a traditional orientation is examined through the specific measures related to the concepts of individualism, rule orientation, and crime control.

The context, community, rule orientation, and individualism measures were adopted from Fox and Van Sickel's study, while the due process and crime control measures were adopted from criminal justice models. Each measure was adapted to the drug court setting and modified through a pilot period of observations in courtrooms (Fox & Sickel, 2000; Mays & Ruddell, 2008). In the end each orientation – progressive and traditional - were examined by three measures a piece. Whichever orientation the judge uses relates to how they socially construct their role of "judge" in drug court and the guides them in choosing between policies, graduated sanctions and rewards. Thus, judicial orientation is examined as the independent variable to what, if any, impact that orientation has on the dependent variables of client retention and graduation.

Judicial Orientation: Judicial Instances and Judicial Style
My research examined judicial orientation by coding judicial instances and judicial style during drug court sessions and drug court team meeting sessions on the pre-printed observation sheets. Judicial style was coded using the court watcher's overall impression of the judge during the drug court session (i.e., Does the judge focus on bringing other team members. into the discussion with the client during the court session? or does he conduct himself as the only person in the room whose opinion matters?).

The court watching instrument (see appendix) records judicial instances (interaction with a client) according to the category of progressive or traditional. Progressive measures include judicial behaviors that convey context (reward given, considered context of any violation, asked for context or additional information related to a positive or negative event) and community (encouraged client to use community support and/or required the client engage in restoration activity) in their interaction with that client. Context and community are concepts that come from Fox and Van Sickel's development of "voice," adapted for the legal arena of drug court (Fox & Sickel, 2000). The traditional measures include judicial behaviors that convey rule orientation (focused on complete compliance, considers only the black and white and/or sanction given) and individualism (focused on individual responsibility for any violation and/or incapacitation for any violation) in his interaction with that client. Rule orientation and individualism are also concepts that come from Fox and Van Sickel's development of "voice," adapted for the legal arena of drug court (Fox & Sickel, 2000).

Each client was considered one instance, and all behaviors for that particular instance (client) were marked on the court watching instrument (see appendix). The judge could exhibit multiple behaviors for each client (i.e., the judge may sanction – marked on the form in the section for traditional – but ask the client for the context surrounding the violation, like "what were the facts and circumstances that led to the violation of the drug court rules?" which would be marked in the progressive section, under context. Thus, for each client, a multitude of marks may be coded on the form for different sections (measures) related to either progressive or traditional. It is possible that, for some clients, only one or two of the behaviors will be coded on the court watching form. In the end, up to nine clients could be coded as instances on the form. The court watcher had additional forms to use in case the judge saw more than nine clients during that session.

Context and community (as measures of the progressive) and rule orientation and individualism (as measures of the traditional) were coded and totaled for a final score for the ten sessions for a particular judge. Thus, for each judge, there would be a score for judicial instances of context, community, rule orientation, and individualism. The court observers were able to note any specific impressions of the court, race and sex of each client in the judicial instance, rewards/sanctions given, and any reaction (if they were in a position to observe it) from the client to those rewards/sanctions. This provided valuable contextual information related to each individual drug court and the judge who presided.

The judicial style section of the observation instruments (team meeting and court session--see appendix) were related to the overall impression of the judge's behavior. Thus, during each session, the court watcher coded the judicial style (see pg. 2 of the court watching instrument) the judge exhibited that day (marking yes or no or not applicable on the court watching form).

The tendencies that the judge could display in court that would fall under the progressive category included: 1) sought middle ground or solution most of the team was happy with (consensus); 2) elicited input from treatment team members.--beyond the drug court coordinator (inclusion); 3) discussed client's employment, family relationships, childhood; 4) discussed extenuating circumstances; 5) emphasized treatment/rewards; 6) agreed with treatment recommendations (in court or team meeting); 7) relied on input from others beyond the drug court coordinator; 8) considered the context of any offense – if any; and, 9) focused on attitude and demeanor of client in courtroom. Consensus and inclusion are measures developed by Fox and Van Sickel and adapted to the particular characteristics of drug court (Fox & Sickel, 2000).

In contrast, due process judicial behaviors included: 1) discussed client rights; 2) discussed whether client could be innocent; 3) discussed client need to talk with attorney; 4) relied upon the defense attorneys; 5) relied upon the drug court coordinator; 6) considered each client on a case-by-case basis; and, 7) allowed for the contesting of evidence. Due process behaviors are based upon the due process model and adapted for the possibilities that can occur during drug court (Mays & Ruddell, 2008).

The tendencies that the judge could display in court that would fall under the traditional category included: 1) made unilateral decisions (authoritarian); 2) quick processing of case based upon rules (not specific facts); 3) discussed need to be compliant with treatment/law abiding lifestyle (circle which applies); 4) discussed past non-compliance with drug court rules; 5) discussed acts of lying; 6) discussed offense only: seriousness/prior history; 7) emphasized rules; and, 8) emphasized sanctions. Authoritarian and procedural are measures developed by Fox and Van Sickel and were adapted to the particular characteristics of drug court (Fox & Sickel, 2000).

Crime control behaviors include: 1) focused on punishment; 2) quick to sanction; 3) assumed guilt; 4) sanctions based upon team member assertions.; 5) speed in disposal of issue at hand; 6) uniformity in case disposition; and, 7) routine handling of cases. Crime control behaviors are based upon the due process model and adapted for the possibilities that can occur during drug court (Mays & Ruddell, 2008).

For judicial style, progressive and due process are separate measures that are related to each other, but different, and as such will be totaled separately (the same for traditional and crime control). These four measures were coded and totaled for a final score for the 10 sessions for a particular judge (see appendix). Thus, for each judge, there will be a score for judicial style of progressive, due process, traditional, and crime control.

Dependent Variables – Client Behavior: Client Retention and Graduation

Two conventional measures of success for drug courts are client retention and client graduation (Johnson & Wallace, 2004). Client retention relates to the overall average number of months and days that clients stay in any particular drug court, and client graduation rate is the percentage of clients who successfully complete the drug court program (Bavon, 2001; Goldkamp et al., 2001; Granfield et al., 1998; Joseph Guydish et al., 2001). Client retention is critical because it has been shown that length of time in drug court translates into length of time in treatment, which is associated with better client outcomes (Belenko, 1999; Gifford et al., 2014; Somers et al., 2014). Graduation rates are also important as drug court clients who graduate have lower rates of recidivism than do drug court dropouts (Belenko, 1999; Green & Rempel, 2010; Rossman et al., 2011).

This study looks at client retention rates and client graduation rates for each court. Client retention will be determined through official court records kept by the drug court coordinator of each court, and are expressed as an average for all drug court clients. Client graduation will also be measured as the average for those clients who are successfully discharged from each court. Data on client retention and client graduation was gathered for specific judges during the time period of the study, and no identifying information related to specific clients is included in either the data collection or analysis.

Research Procedures: Drug Court Reports

Before data collection began, each court was observed three times from the beginning of the drug court session until the end of the drug court session. These general observations provided valuable information about each individual drug court in terms of the unique characteristics of each court (i.e., unique procedures, sanctions, and rewards) as well as insight into the judge's personality and style (*persona*) in the court room. These observations were critical as they were done before data collection began and were used to create training materials.

Training is essential in order to be able to code more complicated judicial behaviors correctly. When a judge says "keep focused," for example, the comment can be coded differently depending on whether the judge is rewarding a particular client for doing a good job or as a reminder to focus on compliance and emphasizing individual responsibility. In addition, a judge may elicit information from clients by a look or stare upon the client's approach to the bench. This subtle behavior would be missed during the early data collection if court watchers were not forewarned to be aware of such behavior.

The scouting reports gave a first look at critical judicial behavior that might otherwise have been missed during the early stages of data collection. Thus, the drug court reports provided initial information regarding general courtroom behavior the judge may engage in on a regular basis and assisted in coding this behavior properly. Observations were written up in a report detailing the observations of each court and any impressions that the observer came away with after the three observations were complete.

Court Watching

Court watchers, in research teams of two, attended each court watching session from the start of the session until the end of the session. Court watchers were trained for field experience through three training sessions (Session 1: drug court and how it functions, Session 2: drug court judges and their interactions, Session 3: field work with experienced observer). Newly trained court watchers were paired with a more experienced court watcher in the early stages of their field work in order to supervise them and continue the training in proper completion of drug court watching forms. Training manuals were provided to court watchers during Session 1, and were later referred to throughout the training experience.

During the drug court session court watchers coded each judicial instance as one client before the judge. Thus, if there were nine clients before the judge that day, there would be nine judicial instances. (For

Fox and Van Sickel, the researchers counted each judicial instance as a legal decision that was before the judge during a court session. Drug court clients generally comprise one legal decision for the judge during one drug court session). Every behavior-related judicial action was scored on the court watching form for each category the judge exhibited for that instance. Court watchers also noted the sex and race (if possible to identify) of each instance before the judge. No other identifying information related to team members. or instances were noted on the form. Judicial style was scored on the court watching form from the overall impression the judge presented during the drug court session (see Appendix).

Court watchers completed the date, time (start and end) of session and sex/race of each team member (judge, prosecutor, defense, drug court coordinator, treatment provider) .. Finally, each form included a notes section so the court watchers could write down additional information on the session, the courtroom, as well as any noteworthy events and impressions which were reviewed later for valuable insights.

At the end of the drug court session, court watchers discussed the observations and form coding in order to come up with a completed observation form through an interactive process to establish inter-observer reliability for the session, data which were used for analysis. Individual code sheets were used for notes.

Drug Court Team Meetings

For the drug court team meeting the research team entered the team meeting conference room before all the team meeting members were there. Team meeting watchers attended each team meeting session from start to finish. During the team meeting session, only judicial style was scored on the team meeting watching form from the overall impression of the judge during the team meeting session (see appendix).

Team meeting watchers completed the date, time (start and end) of the session and the sex/race of each team member . (judge, prosecutor, defense, drug court coordinator, treatment provider). No identifying information related to drug court clients or any member of the team, other than race and sex, and only information related to the impression given from judicial behaviors was noted on the form. Finally, each form included a notes section so that the court watchers could write down additional information on the session, the courtroom, as well as any noteworthy events and impressions that were reviewed later for valuable insights.

Once the meeting was called to order and the team began its deliberations about the upcoming session, the team meeting watchers observed the proceedings. The watchers then coded the elements of the judge's judicial style during the team meeting based upon the behavior of the judge on that day. Thus, the team meeting watchers determined if the judge displayed any of the listed tendencies and marked yes, no, or n/a on the team meeting watching form accordingly. The tendencies that the judge could display in the team meeting for progressive, due process, traditional, and crime control measures are the same as the measures on the court watching instrument. However, it is possible that the style the judge displays in the privacy of the team meeting with drug court professionals will be different from the judicial style in the courtroom with drug court clients. Thus, there was a need to measure both contexts.

As with the court watching instrument, judicial style of progressive and due process are separate measures that are related, but different, and as such were totaled separately (the same for traditional and crime control). These four measures were coded and totaled for a final score for the ten team meetings with a particular judge. Thus, for each judge, there is a score for judicial style of progressive, due process, traditional, and crime control.

At the end of the team meeting, court watchers discussed the observations and form coding in order to complete an observation form for the session through consensus; the consensus-derived coding was used for analysis. Individual code sheets were used for notes.

Semi-structured Interviews

At the end of the observations, each judge was contacted for a semi-structured interview during which the judge's ideas, attitudes, and beliefs regarding drug court were explored. In addition, semi-structured interviews were conducted with representatives of each key drug court team member. – namely, drug court coordinator, prosecutor, defense attorney, and treatment provider.

Judges: All ten judges involved in this study were recruited for the semi-structured judicial interview during the data collection period. Judges were contacted to schedule an interview for a date and time of their choosing. Semi-structured interviews were held in the privacy of their offices and recorded for later transcribing. These interviews covered demographic information (sex, race, education level) as well as information regarding the policies and practices in his courtroom.

Examples of questions for the judges included the following: What kinds of performance-related procedures has your team come up with that are unique to your court? What is the most important behavior, intervention or procedure you utilize in your court in your role to impact drug court clients? What do you like best about drug court? What are your opinions, thoughts, and feelings about your drug court team? Examples of probes include the following: What have you learned? What do you do differently than the training recommended? Can you tell me a story about that? Can you give me a for instance? (See appendix)

Team members: . Team member semi-structured interviews were conducted for each role of the key team members. This study conducted six drug court coordinator interviews (four individual drug court coordinators and two male/female team drug court coordinators), one prosecutor, three defense attorneys, and three treatment providers for a total of twelve semi-structured interviews. These semi-structured interviews were held in the privacy of each of their offices, and all interviews were recorded for later transcribing.

These interviews covered demographic information (sex, race, education level) as well as information related to the policies and practices in the courtroom. Examples of questions for team members include the following: Which sanction used by your court has the greatest impact on clients? Are rewards used regularly? Are they effective in motivating clients? What are your thoughts about the role of the judge in drug court? What impact that you have been able to observe does the judge have on clients? Is there any way that the judge interacts with the clients that has had the greatest impact on them? Examples of probes include the following: Can you tell me a story about that? Can you give me a for instance? Could you tell me more about that? Can you give me an example? (See appendix)

Informed Consent Process: Waiver of signed consent is applicable to the Drug Court Reports and the Drug Court Session

Drug Court Reports and Drug Court Sessions: This was an observation-based study of drug court judges. The drug court itself is a public forum and what is observed is activity that subjects and non-participants performed in their everyday life. Notifying court patrons (anyone who attended that court session on that day, whether they were a client or not) that they were being observed could cause changes in the choice of courtroom activities by any of the court patrons. Additionally, it would be an interruption of the court's activities in order to obtain permission.

Informed Consent was obtained for the team meetings
Team meeting session: The drug court coordinator was contacted and provided with an information sheet on the study (see appendix). It is standard procedure for the drug court coordinator to discuss any matter related to the drug court with the team members.. A team meeting session was scheduled for the research team to be present, and at the beginning of the team meeting, the Ph.D. candidate (hence forth PI) presented the information sheets to the drug court team, and written informed consent was obtained at that time by the PI (see appendix). All questions were addressed immediately before the session was watched.

Semi-structured interviews Judges: The judges were contacted separately to discuss the drug court and team meeting observations. Each drug court judge was provided with an informed consent for the court/team meeting observations as well as for the semi-structured interviews. All questions were addressed during this interview. (See appendix)

Team members: During the data collection period, individual team members were identified and contacted to see if they were interested in participating in the semi-structured interview. Once the team member agreed to be interviewed, an informed consent for the semi-structured interview was obtained before the interview began. (See appendix)

Recruitment/Initial Contact (where applicable) Drug court session: Initial Contact-- The PI made the initial contact by phone in order to set up a meeting with the drug court coordinator and/or the drug court judge. At this meeting, the PI provided the "Information Sheet" (See appendix) to the drug court coordinator and/or the drug court judge to inform them about the project. This initial contact was to notify the judge that the research team was going to be in the courtroom and to discuss the team meeting observations.

Team Meetings: For the team meetings, the PI contacted drug court judges and teams through the drug court coordinator. The PI would request that the research team be allowed to sit in on the meetings and observe the judge's behavior during the team meeting session. This contact was done prior to any team meeting observation.

Semi-structured interviews: Judges and team members were contacted in order to see if they would participate in the semi-structured interview. Interviews were conducted in the team members' office or attorney conference rooms.

Maintaining Consent (where applicable):
Observations began in November 2011 and continued through the summer of 2012. Consent for the team meeting observations was established through signed informed consent documents signed by each team member, and regular contact with the drug court coordinator occurred to schedule team meeting observation. Consent for the semi-structured interviews was obtained right before the interview began.

Privacy:
Privacy of the courts and clients was protected by assigning a random number to each court, as well as by using pre-printed, pre-marked observation forms. No identifying information was collected on either the court watching form, the team meeting watching form, or in the semi-structured interviews, other than gender and race of team members and instances for purposes of statistical analysis. Some individual courts had a confidentiality agreement that everyone in the courtroom must sign before the session began; this provided an extra layer of confidentiality.

Assessing Rigor: Pilot study
During the summer of 2011, a pilot study was conducted to test the validity of the observation forms to be used in this research. A two-person research team was sent out to observe five courts in New York State. Court proceedings were observed five times for each of the five courts and team meetings were observed for three of the courts approximately five times for each of those three courts (two of the courts declined to allow us to observe the team meeting).

The forms were initially developed by adapting the observation variables in the Fox and Van Sickle study, including the concepts of due process and crime control models. Once the observations were concluded, four of the five judges were interviewed in order to identify the judge's intent in his court behavior. The pilot study was used to test whether two people could code the judge's behavior on the observation form the same way while observing the same court/team meeting session to ensure that the form correctly captures the judge's behavior during the court session/team meeting.

A number of things were learned during the pilot study that resulted in changes in the form and helped in developing the training and procedure manuals for this study. After each observation, the research team engaged in a conversation about what they saw and how they interpreted and scored what they saw. Rate of agreement was measured by looking at the total number of codes for each coder and taking the number of agreements and dividing it by the total number on each form. After analyzing the rate of agreement between the two observers for the court sessions, the overall reliability rate for each of the forms are as follows: judicial style (team meeting) original pilot form was 88%; judicial style (court watching session) original pilot form was 78%; court watching (instances) original pilot form was 85%. Some measures were more reliable than others. For example, the progressive measure, which details the positive reinforcement or treatment oriented, was more reliable than the due process measure, and the traditional measure was more reliable than the crime control measure.

Midway through the pilot study, the forms were revised to reflect the changes that were deemed necessary after the observers' discussions. For example, "consider context for any violation" was moved down to below "sanction given" on the court watching form. While they are related to different measures, the two responses were easier to code if violation-related questions were grouped together. For the judicial style forms, the due process and crime control measures were more clearly defined: "Focused on substantive and procedural due process," for example, was changed to "discussed client rights" to more clearly reflect the judicial behavior being sought. Other changes included shading and color in order to better aid the observer in quickly being able to fill out the form and in knowing which forms belonged to which court, as well as which type of proceeding the observer would be watching.

After revising the forms, the reliability rate increased to judicial style (team meeting) new form registering 93%; judicial style (court watching session) new form coming it at 83%; Court watching (instances) new form attaining 93%. The most significant change that came from the pilot test was the continuation of use of two-person research teams in the final study. It became clear that court watching was a difficult task; the length of time court is in session, the multitude of events that occur, and the fatigue that sets in from sitting in one spot for a long time all culminate in court observer inattention at critical moments when noteworthy information can be missed or lost.

The pilot test demonstrated that two people watching the same event can both increase the amount of information that can be coded and increase the quality of the observations for each session. Thus, two-person research teams were used during the full study in order to help ensure the reliability of the data collected during the observations. Teams would agree on one version of the observation instrument for that team meeting and drug court session while the other version was retained for later textual analysis of the comments the research assistant noted on the form.

Data collected with the observation instruments for the full study were subjected to double data entry for the purpose of ensuring the reliability of the data entered. After all of the observation forms were entered twice, the resulting data was compared with the original observation instruments and any errors found were corrected. A final, corrected set of spreadsheets was used to analyze the information recorded on the team meeting and court watching instruments.

The drug court session observation instrument recorded and coded information on 2,612 clients which whom the judges interacted (each interaction could have multiple interactions coded on any of the four measures – ethic of care, due process, ethic of right, and crime control). During the observation period judges were observed at times to have lengthy conversations with clients that contained statements spanning measures. In addition, interactions that could not be coded were collected during the observations. Thus, the information collected and coded on the observation instruments provided a rich set of data for analysis.

More than 30 hours of interviews were recorded and transcribed for the final study (an additional 10 hours were taped and transcribed for the pilot study). The 30 or so hours of transcribed interviews were analyzed in Dedoose (an online text analysis software specifically designed for research that involves mixed methods) in order to identify common themes regarding a judge's construction of himself as a therapeutic agent and the unique policies and procedures used in each drug court to achieve effective therapeutic intervention. Results found in the data and interviews are combined in order to elaborate on those judicial constructions and unique aspects found for each court. While no identifying information was collected on clients during the court sessions, observers did collect information on gender and race as they could observe in order to better understand the gender and racial makeup of the drug court clients in the study.

Chapter 4

Judicial Orientation in Court

Each court differed in the gender and racial make-up of the clients, although there were some unexpected results in this regard. Figure 1 displays the gender breakdown in the observed drug courts categorized by size of court calendar and urban, suburban, or rural setting characteristics (see Table 4).

As demonstrated by Figure 1, drug courts differed markedly in the percentage of women clients involved. The range, between Suburban Ct 8, where women were observed to make up only 16% of the drug court population, and Suburban Ct 1, where women make up almost 38% of the drug court was unexpected. While women outnumber men in American society, they are underrepresented in the criminal justice statistics in terms of arrest, conviction, and incarceration (Siegel, 2010). In drug court, women clients often appear in family treatment court, a non-criminal alternative court.

After the breakdown of individual observed courts according to the size of their court calendar, it was found that larger courts tend to have more men clients enrolled than smaller courts (with the exception of Urban Ct 7). Additional research would be needed to uncover the reasons why large courts and small courts have this kind of gender disparity in drug court. One possible explanation is that the characteristics of the community itself could have an impact on the number of women arrested for drug-related crimes. If the community is a small, rural community, where women are more tightly controlled, formally or informally, there may be fewer female arrests, while a large community with a significant college or university student population may have more female drug-related arrests. Another possible explanation relates to systemic chivalry in the criminal justice system, which could result in the diversion of female suspects to family court while males are arrested (Siegel, 2010). In any event, the gender disparity in the gender composition of the clients is significant.

Figure 1: Gender in Drug Court

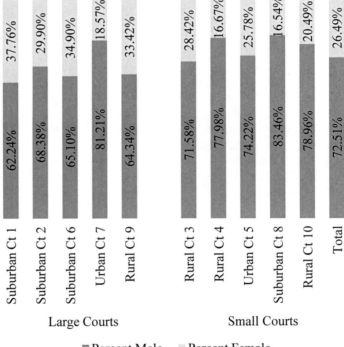

In terms of the racial makeup of the drug court clients, Figure 2 presents the drug court clients observed in each court as well as the 2010 census figures for those courts broken down according to individual court characteristics (see Table 4).

The census categories include African American only and Hispanic only. As this was an observation-based study, it was not always possible to make those distinctions. To the best of the observer's ability, clients were categorized as White, African American and Other, but listed here as White and Other so as to compare what was observed to what is known to exist in the community. The racial makeup of individual drug courts resembled, to some extent, the racial makeup of the community, while a few communities were observed to have significant differences in their minority makeup in drug court (i.e., Rural Ct 3, Rural Ct 9 and Rural Ct 10).

Figure 2: Race in Drug Court compared to 2010 Census

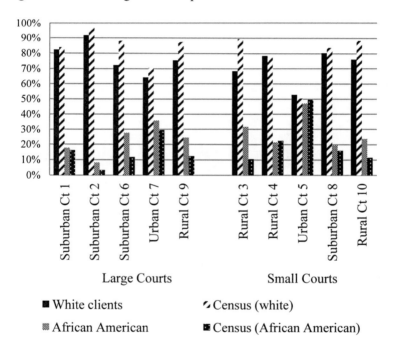

Figure 3 presents the collapsed mean percentages for large and small drug courts to see if there is any trend once individual court characteristics were removed.

Figure 3 demonstrates that drug court clients generally represent the racial make-up of the greater community, with a slight increase in minorities in drug court over the greater community found in the 2010 census. Drug courts with a larger clientele or court session calendar have greater numbers of white clients than appear in the community, while smaller courts have higher numbers of minorities than appear in the community. Regardless of the community, drug court appears to be largely a white male phenomenon. Larger percentages of minorities in both larger and small courts were expected, given that minorities are over-represented in official statistics for drug arrests (Provine, 2007; Walker, 2011). However, minorities may well be excluded from drug courts due to eligibility requirements and the offender's current crime and criminal history. Drug courts were intended to be reserved to rehabilitate drug-addicted criminal offenders, not drug dealers or suppliers. Future research in the area of race in drug court could provide valuable insights into the reasons why minorities are underrepresented in drug court.

Figure 3: Race in Drug Court: Large Courts versus Small Courts

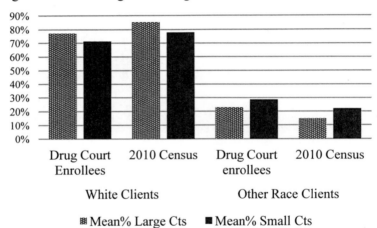

Moving inside the drug courts themselves and to the judges who preside there, one of the most noticeable differences in judicial orientation came down to the size of the community in which the drug court sits, and the size of the drug court calendar.

THE IMPACT OF COURT SIZE

Irwin (2002) examined drug courts in urban and rural areas, proposing that drug courts in rural areas are somewhat better able to implement the drug court model of therapeutic intervention (Irwin, 2002). While small towns may have more limited treatment options, drug courts are better able to reach out to the community and engage the stakeholders in the drug court model. Moreover, Irwin believed that the size of the community (small towns and mid-sized city drug courts) would allow for greater "collective control," thus providing for better drug court outcomes. Finally, Irwin concluded that drug courts will be valued by members of the community if they are seen to be "changing lives for the better" (Irwin, 2002).

Irwin's model is rooted in Weisheit and Wells (1996) research examining social organization of rural areas in terms of crime and justice (Irwin, 2002; Weisheit & Wells, 1996). Weisheit and Wells proposed that while urban communities allow for greater opportunities for research in crime and justice in terms of survey and official data research, rural communities can provide more information in terms of "social context, local community and interpersonal networks" (Weisheit & Wells, 1996). In other words, rural communities have been overlooked due to their limited population numbers even though their careful study can help inform criminal justice research by providing more breadth and depth of information about the community in which crime and justice system response exist (Weisheit & Wells, 1996).

Observations for this study included drug courts in both rural and urban areas. While only two of the drug courts existed in communities considered urban, these drug courts can be categorized as small or large in terms of their court calendar. Table 4 details each court in terms of the community characteristics and mean court calendar across ten observations.

Table 4 was used to create the descriptive identifiers used in the figures and tables, as courts were categorized in terms of their court calendar and community characteristics. As Table 4 demonstrates, judges managing large court calendars could see as many as 40 or 50 clients over three or four hours, while judges with small court calendars would see as few as 10 to 20 clients in a drug court session. The size of the court calendar could have a significant impact on judicial behavior on the bench, especially at the higher numbers, given time restraints for any given judicial session. Judges with large court calendars were observed to balance the need to address non-compliant behaviors with the importance of rewarding compliant clients as the court session wore on. Often, the necessity of addressing those non-compliant clients won out so the judge could set a public example.

Table 4: Court Characteristics (using site description designations)

Courts	Urban	Suburban	Rural	Small Court	Large Court	Average Daily Calendar *	
C				X	x	9.5	
H		x			x	13.3	
D				X	x	16.8	
E	x				x	22.5	***
J				X	x	36.6	****
B		x				x	29.1	
A		x				x	29.4	**
F		x				x	19.2	**
I				X	x	40.1	
G	x				x	44.7	

* Average calendar is number clients seen during an observation

**Average is for clients seen (many are let go per green card policy)

***Large Court but multiple days hearing drug court cases

****Large calendar/rural court.

    While all the judges in this study understood the importance of rewards in motivating clients, not all the judges were able to emphasize rewards or even see each court client in attendance. One large court in the study was observed to have created the concept of a "green card." This green card was given to clients who were determined by team members. to be in full compliance. The judge would release these clients midway through the drug court session without meeting with them. This procedure was created by the judge and his team as a reward for compliance. While a creative practice, this "reward" had the consequence of reducing the opportunity for judicial praise for compliant clients. However, this was the only way for the judge to get through the court calendar on any given day. Without the green card, this court would not be able to function given the number of clients enrolled in its drug court.

    The green card was one way a particular court allowed compliant clients the opportunity to leave without ever seeing the judge. It was also observed in other courts where time constraints put pressure on large courts to allow compliant clients to leave without positive reinforcement. Positive reinforcement for compliant behavior is one of the most important rewards that a drug court judge can provide to a client (e.g., "good job" or "well done" for attending all treatment meetings) and can help the client get through a difficult week, knowing that "atta boy" would be forthcoming should the client show up in court at the next court appearance.

In smaller courts the judges have more time to speak to individual clients and to provide rewards to each client in the drug court session. In speaking with a team member .about one of the judges with a smaller court calendar, the team member indicated that "He's always positive. First, recognition of the accomplishment and then words of encouragement. He always does that." In this particular court, the client's accomplishments (any new events in the client's life, his or her status in treatment and cumulative clean time) are stated as the client approaches the bench, thus giving the judge the opportunity to reward the client and emphasizing the positive accomplishments to the audience (other clients). Given the time constraints in courts with a large calendar, even judges who believe in a more reward-oriented progressive model drug court would struggle. They simply run out of time before the end of the morning or afternoon sessions.

Positive reinforcement is only meaningful to the client if he or she cares about the judge's opinion of him or her. In other words, positive reinforcement has an impact only if the client is able to establish a relationship with the judge to the point where judicial feedback is valuable to the client.

RELATIONSHIPS BETWEEN THE JUDGE AND THE CLIENT

One key element in fostering a relationship link between the judge and client was observed during court. Personal attention to the client and/or the client's family was found to be a valuable tool for judges when creating a personal relationship with the client and encouraging positive, reward-oriented interactions. During interviews, judges and team members. alike discussed the importance of the judge establishing a relationship with the client. One interviewee said in the regard: "It [motivation] is like the dog. Rule by love, the dog will want to make

you happy. I'm trying to get those people to want to make me happy."
One judge also observed that

> No one has ever cared about them [clients] before. They
> finally found one person that believes they can succeed.
> There's something that can be transforming in that. For some
> of these people, getting that certificate - it may be the only
> thing they have ever done that has been successful. They
> might be able to go forward and build on that success. I think
> that is a big basis for drug court. Small successes, small
> rewards, phase advancement, small successes build towards
> big successes. Some of them don't remember being clean. It
> is a whole new experience for them.

One judge was observed to start the drug court session with a thought-provoking question and to engage in an extended conversation with the audience (clients). The judge clarified this practice:

> I say drug court is a court of love. Then I did a little session
> out there. What does that mean? It is the court of love because
> you love your family, you love your mother, you love your
> kids, you get back together again, you talk all kinds of love
> and then one kid says "Judge, it is about loving yourself. I
> never loved myself, now I am starting to love myself."... Great
> answer, right on target.

Other thought-provoking questions were used in this courtroom in order to invoke insight and stimulate reflection in clients. Observing sessions in this court was very compelling. The clients were observed to raise their hands and fully participate in the conversation with the judge. These clients would offer their opinions, fully expecting the judge to listen and respect what they related. The judge was observed to acknowledge their participation and verbally reward their attempts. Thus, the session began on a very positive note and overshadowed the rest of the session, even if individual clients were judicially admonished or otherwise sanctioned.

Throughout the team member .interviews, judges were discussed in terms of their role as a "parental figure" in the relationship, and their being central to a client's successful completion of drug court.

DRUG COURT AS FAMILY

Tiger (2011) researched drug courts by analyzing organizational documents and interviewing client advocates (team members) about drug courts. During his interviews advocates discussed the importance of the drug court judge and sanctions by presenting the judge as a "parental figure." One advocate elaborated on that parental relationship, claiming that the clients didn't want to disappoint the judge by their behavior, suggesting that a kind of parental transference occurred for the client (Tiger, 2011, 2013).

This idea of the judge as a "parent" and the relationship between the client and judge as quasi-parental in nature was repeatedly reaffirmed in many of the team member interviews. Judges as well as team members discussed clients who had established a relationship with the judge. These clients wanted the judge to be proud of them and didn't want to disappoint him (above and beyond the mere threat of a sanction). If the client does make that "parental" connection with the judge, it can be a powerful motivator; the judge presiding in the drug court is often mentioned in graduation speeches. One judge laid it out particularly well:

> I wholeheartedly believe that it's like a well-drawn family structure where the Judge sits as the father figure or the parent figure with giving rewards and incentives for behaviors. That's how we all grow up I think, you know if you do well and succeed you get praise from your parents and most of us like praise and do well under those circumstances, and if we step out of line then there are consequences. It's like your parent might ground you or take away certain benefits or things. We try and play within those circumstances, understanding wholeheartedly that addiction fights against those parameters of punishment and reward.

The judge noted that this relationship is a reciprocal one: "You do become affected because of the family approach that we're trying to take; you do become invested in what they're doing." More than one judge discussed the fact that clients often form this parental connection. One judge put it simply: "when I give them a fatherly phrase I think they will remember it. I try to make them not want to disappoint me."

Put another way, "So to be honest, sometimes breaking bread with people is like social. They haven't had really nurturing families or anything, so if you bake a bunch of funfetti cookies, what does it take? ... Families eat together." Put a little differently, "We're the protection. We are the family accountability, the family reliability source that they don't have – that they never had. If we put them back into the community without this therapeutic intervention, they would revert back."

Another judge noted how in-depth that connection often is:

> We know all our participants. We know their family background, we know their education backgrounds, we know their medical backgrounds, their employment backgrounds, we just immerse ourselves to try and know each individual. I'm sure, in a lot of respects that [has] come to allow us to be more compassionate because we now understand what the picture is like. On the other hand you can get very close to people and then you may not be operating in their best interest because you have that affection for them and compassion. You got to really balance it.

Judges are not the only people in the room to notice that relationship-building between the judge and client. Team members. are in a unique position to observe this relationship between the judge and the client. One drug court session demonstrated just how strong that relationship can be. A client, who was having a particularly difficult time as he was recently homeless and estranged from his family, had been late for an appointment or two. Initially, the judge was inclined to sanction the client, but as a team member intervened and addressed the court with the underlying circumstances this particular judge was moved to come off the bench and hug the client in an effort to give comfort and reassurance. While this is uncommon behavior in a traditional court, it is not uncommon in this drug court.. A team member indicated that "Yeah, once in a while he does stuff like that. First of all he grew up there. The [community] is small. It is like a big family. You know everyone in [the community]. If he does not know the person there, he knows their parents or something like that."

Another team member noted that "when [the client] is facing that judge, that father, we all feel that same intimidation, that same I think 'I gotta tell the truth' and 'Oh my God if I'm in trouble can I get away with it.' I mean it's all those feelings that we feel when we see a father figure come out. And, part of me, I have to wonder if sometimes these people are reenacting that whole family conflict that they had, you know, and trying to redo that."

That relationship between the client and judge becomes more apparent over time. One vivid example related to a female client with a long-standing substance abuse addiction that resulted in the termination of her parental rights with her biological children. When the woman entered drug court she looked strung out and run down from her addiction, but after some time in drug court she began to dye her hair, dress in her best clothes, and wear make-up. Even when given the opportunity to reduce her status appearances, this woman would come week after week and seemed to enjoy the time she spent talking with the judge, laughing and joking. And the client thrived for quite a long period of time. This woman wanted the judge to be proud of her accomplishments and, as a result, began to take pride in herself. Prior to this connection, giving up her addiction was a hurdle that she could not overcome, either for herself or for her children, but it was doable once she was able to connect to someone she cared deeply to please.

Finally, team members .cautioned on the dangers of a judge who was not invested in the process: "Then what happens to that drug court when you really don't have someone who's open to the idea? We were talking the judge being the most important person to have contact with the client. If that judge has no interest in the clients, you see what happens in a family when there's a father who has no interest in their kids."

Each judge presented himself differently, some saw themselves as a "dad," some as merely an authority figure, and one categorized himself as a "benevolent despot." Whether a judge constructs himself as a dad or a despot showed some real insight into whether a judge believed himself to be more progressively or traditionally-oriented. Judges who presented themselves as a dad were well-versed in the area of rewards as a powerful motivator for clients and would employ rewards often in their courtroom. Virtually all of the judges had been through extensive drug court training and were well-trained in the drug court model. Thus, individualized attention and rewards were well understood, but when it came down to employing the more reward-progressively-oriented, model, whether or not the judge accepted himself as a parental figure was important in understanding his official actions on the bench.

Even dads can be quite harsh and punitive, so merely seeing oneself as a parental figure did not ensure a progressive orientation. How a judge perceives his role in drug court provides insight into how he constructs himself as a therapeutic agent for drug court clients – a judge who creates and maintains a relationship with his clients rather than interacting with them in a more distant, formalistic way. At that point, whether the judge is more progressive or traditional may boil down to his personal vision of parenting.

It should not be a surprise that the relationship between the judge and client is so crucial to drug court outcomes, given that the client is also a component of the courtroom workgroup. Increased contacts and length of time with individual clients would argue for clients' greater role in the courtroom workgroup than one might find in traditional court. The client is also essential to the smooth functioning of the court session or to the disruptive functioning of the court session, depending on the events of the day.

During the interviews, some team members. discussed how that the family concept associated with a drug court went far beyond the relationship between the judge and client.

FAMILY AND THE COURTROOM WORKGROUP

Legal formalism, the traditional way of looking at legal disputes, proposes that these cases should be disposed of through rules, evidence, and argument (Deflem, 2008; Nardulli, 1978). Weber, however, discussed substantive law and the frequent use of non-legal factors in the legal arena. Organizational theory in the criminal court system also promotes the idea that there are other considerations besides the ethical requirements of the rule of law at work in the courtroom. This is no less true in drug court where cooperation and "playing ball" is arguably even more important.

Whether a team works cooperatively or combatively is, in part, dependent on how the judge constructs, manages and relies upon his team. The other team members. have some role to play in this for sure, but primarily it is the judge who sets the tone and encourages or discourages a cooperative atmosphere or a non-cooperative atmosphere.

Interviews with other team members extended that parental figure narrative to include the marriage between the judge and the drug court coordinator, presenting "her" as a maternal figure for the clients. Judges and drug court coordinators were observed calling the other a "work wife" or a "work husband." Judges were also observed to rely upon their respective coordinators in different ways. Some judges relied upon the coordinator to provide the information to him in open court, while other judges were briefed only in the team meeting, thus running the drug court on their own with minimal support during the drug court session. Some judges would ask for additional information from the team during the court session, while one or two judges required more active involvement from team members during the court session.

Whether the judge relied on the team during the court session seemed, at least in part, on the role the judge saw the team playing in terms of the clients. In other words, how does the judge construct the team? One judge, for example, saw the team members as a way to mitigate his power as judge:

> I welcome and relish their experience and knowledge.... They're a vital component to my team in filling out the knowledge and experience, number one. Number two, they bring a particular character to my bench. And when I find an individual that needs that type of character that's why so many times, "<team member>, step up here, talk to this little girl about something."; "<team member >, you come up and talk to this kid and his son." So they bring their personality to the bench, and then I pick and choose that personality to share it with my clients. So that's important. The other thing is, again, just the knowledge in a profession. There's so many issues, insurance and different things in this business that I can call on people to "go make a phone call right now, I want an answer quickly," etc., etc. So you're tapping - you're fully tapping the resource...The other thing is that we play good cop, bad cop... I'll bring someone in and sit them down and I'll say, "Look, I'm going to beat him up a little bit, and then I want you to come to his rescue a little bit. And then I'll make a decision and you're going to be the hero." Sometimes it's

vice versa. But I believe in that. I believe in that because you strengthen the bond between the client and the treatment team.

Other interviewees expanded on the idea of family to include the entire team as aunts and uncles, and suggested that clients fared better in drug courts where teams were on the same page. One advocate suggested that drug court and the family unit therein allowed clients to successfully renegotiate dysfunctional family relationships in ways that would allow them to remain compliant in drug court and ultimately graduate.

As one team member suggested, "just building that relationship and them <the clients> feeling a part of this team as a family member, versus a court system that's adversarial" is an important advantage of drug court. Another team member elaborated on how team members are involved with clients: "I always say it's almost like treating our addicts just like you would treat a child… it's a very symbiotic relationship."

Finally, one judge incorporates other clients in that concept of family. In this drug court, the team assigns a client mentor (a veteran drug court client) to mentor a newly-admitted client. This judge sees drug treatment and drug court as a kind of holistic healing of the individual and focuses on the whole client. The judge related, "Well, I think it's helpful because with our numbers, we have between, at the most, 40 to 50 people and not everyone's here every week, but it's still a small enough group that they get to recognize who is here. Who they see …, maybe, in the waiting rooms at treatment. Who'll they see at self-help….they're learning from each other…That they're not unique with their problems. Other people have the same problems."

Just like any family or social group, not everyone plays nicely all of the time. When individuals fail to work together, courtroom workgroup theory argues that formal and informal consequences are imposed. Judges, as the key team member of the courtroom workgroup, are in a unique position to encourage the team to work together to maximize client outcomes. Alternatively, clients viewed as part of the courtroom workgroup can work against team members to serve their own interests, which may not include achieving and sustaining sobriety.

TEAM COHESIVENESS AND JUDICIAL ORIENTATION

Ongoing success of any drug court rests on the ability of team members. to come together and share a vision of therapeutic intervention (J. Miller & Johnson, 2009). Teams can be made up of any number of professionals, including treatment providers, police agencies, probation officers, and client advocates in addition to the judge and drug court coordinator. Defense attorneys and prosecutors were not observed to be participating members in drug court, nor did they participate in both the drug court session and the team meeting. The mix of team members and their ability to work together is crucial to having a solidly functioning drug court.

Of course, as the interviewees suggested, problems often start when the drug court has team members who do not get along. This circumstance was likened to the problems that come from dysfunctional families:

> Everyone is sort of dysfunctional in every family, like I always say there's no such thing as the perfect family...I always say you always pick up that rooftop and you look in there, you're going to find something in that there's going to be a problem and just remember when you were growing up and if you had a sibling, or even if you didn't have a sibling, and your mother would say "Why can't you be like Jane?," "Why can't you be like your brother?" "I didn't have problems with your brother like I have problems with you." So, is there such a thing as a functional court and a dysfunctional court? I think there's probably no such thing as a functional court.

Interviewees repeatedly related stories illustrating the dangers of drug court teams that were "not on the same page." One judge related a particularly rough period for his team:

> [W]e had no direction, no wind in our sail and our rudder was broken... the participants could tell. Because we were not on our game. They could get away with things that they would never try now. Only because they were so entrenched in their personal lives, we can tell when somebody comes now

whether they're on their game or they are not. It they're not
firing on all eight cylinders we're going to know that. Or if
they're not we'll figure out based on what we know that
individual where the problems might be, we stand a better
chance of diagnosing a problem, identifying a problem and
then try to resolve that problem.

One way conflict can seep into a team is when an individual agenda
overwhelms the team concept. One judge, for example, discussed
treatment providers and their agenda thusly: "they would be here for no
other reason other than they would be looking for clients. So that
interfered with what we were doing here as far as I was concerned.
And I didn't adopt the model where the individual treatment providers
provided the counselors for the individual participants to report to me
in court...I didn't do that at all." The judge was recognizing the fact
that in drug court clients are a commodity to treatment providers. The
more they treat, the more money the treatment facility makes, and the
longer clients stay sick the more money they are worth to the treatment
facility. In fact, each team member .on the treatment team has an
obligation to some other organization in addition to the drug court.
    Judges are not oblivious to these competing agendas

> You know I have said this before, but you are always going to
> have differences of philosophy. As much as we can say that
> we can put this team together, and everyone is going to be
> pulling in the same direction, you got a prosecutor, you have
> certain obligations to the defense attorney, you have the
> people in treatment who have... a certain way that they
> approach things and I have always said it is like taking the
> head of a horse and a tail of a cow and the legs of a dog and a
> cat and trying to put those together so they walk-and
> sometimes surprisingly it does.

Judges quickly learn that they need to balance giving team
members the opportunity to voice their differences and the need for
team peace. One said, "the defense attorney may feel that for some
reason that his client or her client is not getting a fair shake and then it
can very quickly become litigative in nature, and learning from the past

I think it is probably better just to be the decision maker rather than to, you know, throw some gas on the fire."

One treatment team struggled with whether to incorporate jail into its drug court. This was one of the family court treatment teams in the pilot study, and the team's struggle illustrates the issue quite well. As a general rule, family courts cannot sentence parents to jail for the abuse and neglect of their child. However, some family treatment courts include jail as a sanction in the contracts that parents sign and have used it as a form of punishment for non-compliance. Jail, of course, is the ultimate weapon in judicial coercion as participants who are deemed non-compliant with treatment or are lying to the court can be sentenced on the spot to go to jail for any length of time the presiding judge chooses (Harrell, 1998; NADCP, 2005; Shannon Carey et al., 2008).

Family treatment courts have more opportunity to struggle with the concept of jail than do adult drug courts, which are criminal in nature and are well-accustomed to having jail at their disposal. This particular treatment team was split in its opinions on jail in family treatment court and the judge was undecided. The judge said that during this time period

We made a conscious decision not to use jail as a sanction for fear that it is actually a violation of a participant's due process in a civil proceeding... especially since we have, what, about eight lawyers on our team. Due process is very fundamental. We had many discussions on our team about the appropriate procedures, and I remember when we were in our training we even included the words due process... in our mission statement or in at least some of our training. So we wanted to ensure that our people were treated with due process, and we weren't going to let them voluntarily give up their due process rights, which we didn't think they should give up.

For the judge, the crux of the issue boiled down to "whether or not a participant in a civil proceeding could voluntarily agree to be incarcerated... we grappled with that...It is almost like agreeing to be flogged ...The team and the judge hold a certain amount of power over these people and they may not be [giving up] their rights freely and voluntarily if we were to ask them to do that, so we chose not to do that." The judge in this treatment court allowed the team members .to weigh in on the issues and he made the ultimate decision to not include jail in the procedures of his treatment court. Team members. were strongly committed to their position on this matter as jail can be an important motivator to convince clients to be and remain compliant in drug court. Judges walk a tightrope with team members and clients alike. As Peter Parker's Uncle Ben said in the Spider Man movie (2002), "With great power comes great responsibility." For drug court judges, however, continuing conflict between his team members can affect the ability of that court to deliver services to clients in that their clients, like children, know if the team members can be exploited for purposes that serve the client's addiction. One team member put it thusly,

> You know because this is one of the few times that they <clients> get into a situation that is fairly similar to the family situation and … they look at it from that perspective … "how can I do this?" and "how can I do that?"… "who can I lie to?… who can I scam?,… "man, who will stick up for me?"… "who's gonna cover for me?"… and I've seen that <teams broken by the conflict> done…in a number of ways, you know, when… you have the team meeting and you come to a conclusion…about what's going to happen and…because they know the connection of the judge as the ally, whatever trump card they have or whatever they know works with the judge… out it comes and then all the sudden then everything that was discussed is gone.

Clearly, team cohesiveness is crucial in drug courts to ensure that clients focus on their recovery. How that cohesiveness is achieved relates to judicial orientation and judicial temperament. All the judges in this study expressed appreciation for their drug court team and its value in giving the judge tools to interact effectively with drug court clients.

Team cohesiveness, however, also relates to organizational theory and the courtroom workgroup. When a client achieves the loyalty of one team member .that team member may go out on a limb for that client and advocate for lenient treatment. As courtroom workgroup theory proposes, one client may be sacrificed for the benefit of another.

Failure to "play ball" can bring informal consequences to force the appearance of team cohesiveness. Defense attorneys spoke of clearly understanding their vulnerable position in drug court in having to advocate for clients against strong opposition. This position meant, at times, being excluded from some team meeting discussions because of their role as defense attorney and needing to pick and choose when to advocate and prioritizing what to advocate for in order to avoid informal sanctions.

One potential danger for judges who preside over small courts which may interfere with their ability to remain a reward-oriented, progressive, court is expanding court calendars in many jurisdictions.

EXPANDING COURT CALENDARS

As mentioned above, one consideration in whether a court is classified as small or large is the size of the court's calendar. One of the larger urban courts, for example, could be classified as a small court given its small court calendar. The judge in Urban Ct 5 has a large number of clients enrolled in his court; however, he maintains a relatively small court calendar due to the judge's ability to see clients throughout the week. This court runs multiple therapeutic courts (i.e., veteran's court, drug court, mental health court), but each exists as a dedicated therapeutic court set on different days and thus each has the ability to distribute client status appearances throughout the week. The other courts in this study have to manage a criminal calendar as well as their drug court (and often multiple therapeutic courts). While this relatively large drug court had the opportunity to keep its daily calendar small, most drug court judges don't have that ability.

City drug courts, for example, can also be designated as hub courts. This means that other courts in the neighboring communities can send over eligible clients to the hub court in order to allow defendants to participate in drug court who would otherwise be barred due to a lack of drug court in their own community. Of course, drug courts can transfer cases from within (from drug court to mental health court) and without (from one jurisdiction's drug court to the client's community of residence or from one jurisdiction's drug court to another jurisdiction's veteran's court). Being able to use a neighboring hub court is a valuable tool for a poor county to expand the benefits of drug court to eligible clients without having to spend the funds to start a whole new drug court. Further expanding drug court calendars are the previously discussed Article 216 clients. Figure 4 details the observed drug courts and their 216 clients.

Figure 4: Art. 216 clients (sorted by highest percent of calendar)

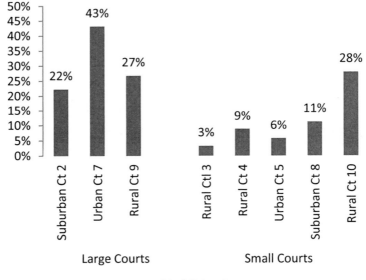

The addition of Art. 216 clients is both a blessing and a curse in some jurisdictions. It allows drug addicts previously excluded from drug court to receive services that assist them in becoming productive members of the community; however, it also adds clients who have a longer history of drug use, crime, and addictive behaviors to the drug court rolls. One judge put it simply: "[t]hese [Art.] 216 clients... like the one yesterday he was coming off sanction. He is really -- he is a sophisticated guy. He knows what he is doing. It has to be hard because he is more manipulative than that young girl. She has not been in the system enough. She is not hardened enough."

Judges also discussed the benefits of including Art. 216 clients in their calendar: "I think the [Art.] 216s fit in well," one judge related, "I think it was appropriate to have them sent to the drug treatment courts for supervision. I think it would have been a mistake to have the county court judges ... try to supervise them in a drug and alcohol setting – outpatient or try to monitor the in-patient state. I think the drug courts are perfectly suited for them to come in and be monitored." Another judge indicated he would welcome more Art. 216 clients: "[D]iversions have been coming in slowly you know. Probably at one point in time with diversions and felonies, I probably had about eight to ten. You know I would like to see those numbers up to 25." The addition of Art. 216 clients can transform a small rural drug court calendar to the size of a large city court calendar.

Size, in terms of drug court, is a complicated matter. As observed in this study, it is possible that a small rural community can have a very large drug court calendar, while a large urban community can have a small drug court calendar. Does court calendar have an impact on judicial orientation?

OBSERVED - PROGRESSIVE VERSUS TRADITIONAL

Judicial behavior coded during court observations on the court watching instrument support the possibility that small courts provide a judge with a better arena for a progressive orientation. Figure 5 presents the percent of progressive behaviors, calculated from the court-watching observation instrument, per judge, over ten observations.

Figure 5 demonstrates that virtually all the individual judges scored high on asking for context during the court session for those clients with whom the judges actually interacted. This reflects the fact that each of the judges in this study, generally speaking, asked the client or team member for additional information about the client's situation. This could be as simple as a judge asking the client how he or she was that day, or as complicated as asking the client for the surrounding circumstances of a relapse or police contact.

Judges from Rural Ct 10, Rural Ct 4, and Rural Ct 9, for example, regularly asked about the client's community connections (including family members and self-help attendance). The judge in Rural Ct 9 runs a very large court calendar in a rural community and would regularly discuss the client's life, interests, and hobbies. Rural Ct 9 is presided over by a judge whose knowledge of the client's life stems from a very thorough in-court intake procedure which includes questions related to

Figure 5: Progressive measures ethic of care court watching instrument

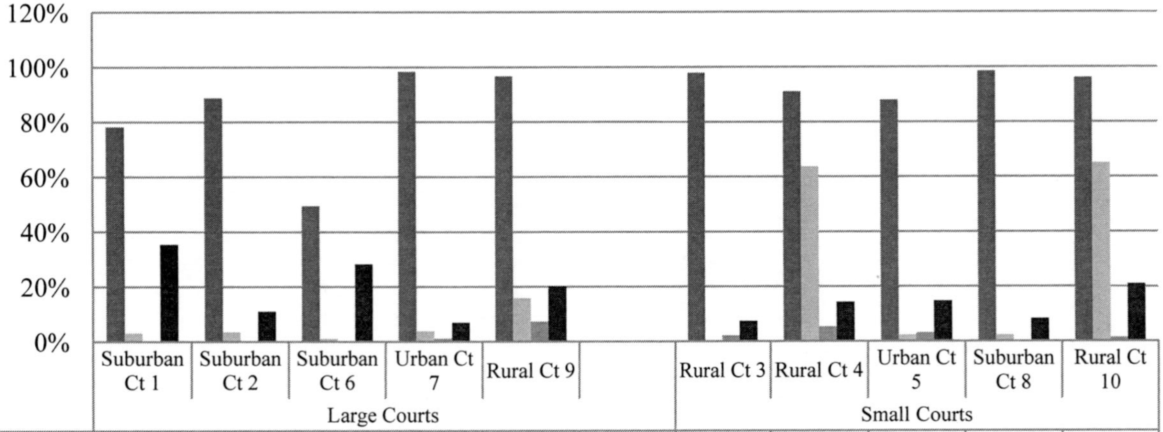

	Large Courts					Small Courts				
	Suburban Ct 1	Suburban Ct 2	Suburban Ct 6	Urban Ct 7	Rural Ct 9	Rural Ct 3	Rural Ct 4	Urban Ct 5	Suburban Ct 8	Rural Ct 10
Asked for Context	78.23%	88.66%	49.48%	98.43%	96.76%	97.89%	91.07%	88.00%	98.50%	96.17%
Community	3.06%	3.44%	1.04%	3.80%	15.96%	0.00%	63.69%	2.22%	2.26%	65.03%
Restorative	0.34%	0.00%	0.00%	1.12%	7.23%	2.11%	5.36%	3.11%	0.00%	1.37%
Considered Context	35.37%	11.00%	28.13%	6.94%	20.20%	7.37%	14.29%	14.67%	8.27%	21.04%

the client's social history as well as the client's drug and criminal history. The judge in Rural Ct 9 was observed to take notes during that intake procedure and refer to that material in subsequent conversations with the client in court.

This attention to detail comes at a cost of time, however, and the busier that court gets the harder it is for the judge in Rural Ct 9 to get through the calendar before the morning session is over. Balancing the benefit that comes with strengthening the judge's relationship with the client and supporting the lessons learned in sobriety and the cost of time is a delicate dance the judge in Rural Ct 9 manages every week when he holds court.

The large courts scored higher on considered context as well, but those courts were more often observed to sanction clients. Considered context was coded, typically, when a client was being sanctioned and the judge was taking into account some mitigating circumstance when sanctioning the client. Suburban Ct 8, for example, scores very low (8.27%) on considered context, but that was largely due to the low number of times the judge was observed to sanction a client. Most of the courts scored low on the restorative index, except for Rural Ct 9 and Rural Ct 4.

High percentages for Rural Ct 4 and Rural Ct 10 for community are related to those courts' incorporation of community service hours for every client who is unemployed (a restorative action with a relationship to the ethic of care). Finally, the due process measure was found to be a mixed indicator of a progressive orientation.

Given the considerable variations inside individual courts, small and large court categories were collapsed into mean scores in order to determine if, in fact, there were any variations based upon size of court. Figure 6 presents those collapsed mean percentages for each of the ethic of care variables. As demonstrated by the results in Figure 6, once individual differences in courts are collapsed into small and large court categories, courts in rural communities and/or courts with small court calendars tended to score high in the measures designated progressive (except for considered context which is likely due to the fewer observed sanctions meted out in those courts).

In terms of the traditional measures, Figure 7 details the judges observed during their drug court session and where they scored in terms of the ethic of right measures (considered violation only, focused on compliance, individual responsibility, and jail).

Figure 6: Progressive Orientation in Court – Large versus Small Courts

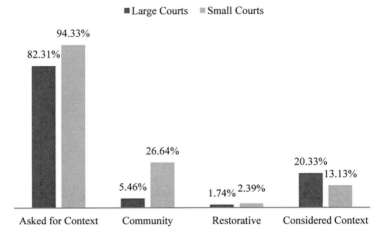

As demonstrated by the results set forth in Figure 7, larger courts generally score higher on traditional measures. Suburban Ct 6, Rural Ct 9, Suburban Ct 1, and Urban Ct 7 are all courts with a large court calendar. Rural Ct 4 scored high in terms of focusing on compliance and individual responsibility in large part because the judge would draft a weekly order for each client before they would leave the court. This was a procedure used to remind each client of their obligations in the community and to stay compliant during the week. The judge would keep a carbon copy of the weekly order in the client's file for reference at the next status appearance. That level of detail in the client's life is a measure of Rural Ct 4 being a smaller court in a rural community that had the time and ability to add structure to the client's life. That ability diminishes when the judge has 50 to 100 clients to get through in a morning or afternoon calendar. Notably, the judges in courts Suburban Ct 2 and Urban Ct 7 scored lower in focused on compliance and individual responsibility even though those courts have a large court calendar.

Once again, small and large court categories were collapsed into a mean score in order to determine if, in fact, there were any variations based upon size of court. Figure 8 presents those collapsed mean percentages for each of the ethic of right variables.

Figure 7: Traditional measures Ethic of Right court watching instrument

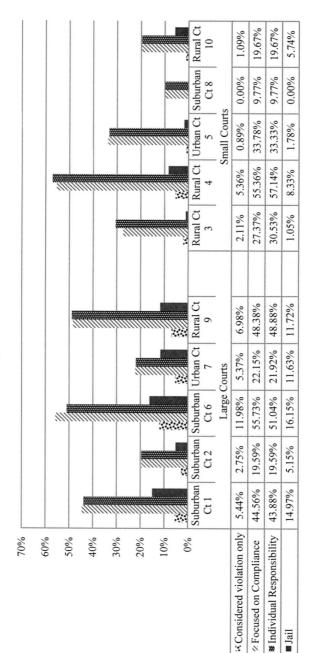

| | Large Courts | | | | Small Courts | | | | | |
	Suburban Ct 1	Suburban Ct 2	Suburban Ct 6	Urban Ct 7	Rural Ct 9	Rural Ct 3	Rural Ct 4	Urban Ct 5	Suburban Ct 8	Rural Ct 10
∴ Considered violation only	5.44%	2.75%	11.98%	5.37%	6.98%	2.11%	5.36%	0.89%	0.00%	1.09%
⁒ Focused on Compliance	44.56%	19.59%	55.73%	22.15%	48.38%	27.37%	55.36%	33.78%	9.77%	19.67%
ℬ Individual Responsibility	43.88%	19.59%	51.04%	21.92%	48.88%	30.53%	57.14%	33.33%	9.77%	19.67%
■ Jail	14.97%	5.15%	16.15%	11.63%	11.72%	1.05%	8.33%	1.78%	0.00%	5.74%

Figure 8: Traditional Orientation in Court: Large versus Small Courts

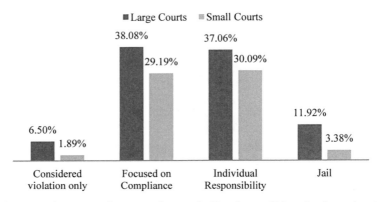

Here consistent results were observed. For the traditional orientation in court, the collapsed mean percentages for large courts scored higher on all of the traditional orientation variables.

In terms of the judicial style measures in court, judges from rural communities and smaller courts show up in the progressive measures when examining the overall impression of the judge while on the bench. Figure 9 details the progressive measures for the judicial style instrument.

As Figure 8 illustrates, some of the larger individual courts score quite high on both the ethic of care and due process measures. One aspect of the judicial style instrument is that observers would code "yes" if a judge asked for context of an event or required community service in the ethic of care measure and "yes" for relying on the defense attorney or protecting the client's rights in drug court. However, more progressive judges were not faced with as many non-compliant clients (due to their smaller court calendar) and/or did give as many sanctions to clients (for similar reasons), and thus were not faced with an issue related to due process (which was coded as N/A on the instrument). So, those judges from rural communities and/or with small court calendars scored lower on the progressive measures than the other judges. In terms of comparing the collapsed mean percentages of small and large courts for progressive measures according to judicial style observed in court here, too, larger courts score higher than smaller courts, as demonstrated in Figure 10.

Figure 9: Judicial style in court progressive measures

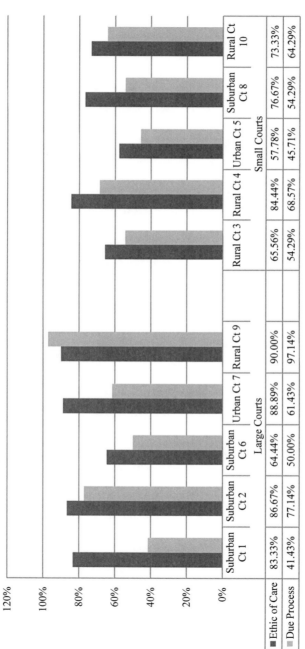

	Suburban Ct 1	Suburban Ct 2	Suburban Ct 6	Urban Ct 7	Rural Ct 9		Rural Ct 3	Rural Ct 4	Urban Ct 5	Suburban Ct 8	Rural Ct 10
			Large Courts						Small Courts		
Ethic of Care	83.33%	86.67%	64.44%	88.89%	90.00%		65.56%	84.44%	57.78%	76.67%	73.33%
Due Process	41.43%	77.14%	50.00%	61.43%	97.14%		54.29%	68.57%	45.71%	54.29%	64.29%

Percent = number of times observed to act in accordance – limited to one time per visit/total number of times observed - 10

Figure 10: Progressive Measures Judicial Style in Court: Large versus Small Courts

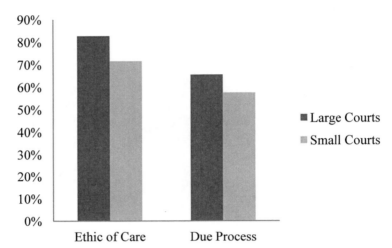

Figure 10 presents findings suggesting that larger courts demonstrate a slightly higher collapsed mean score in the progressive measures of the ethic of care and due process. This may well reflect the greater occurrence of non-compliant acts in the larger courts, thus increasing their need to address context and due process issues.

As Figure 11 demonstrates, Court Suburban Ct 1, in a large suburban community with one of the largest drug court calendars, scores quite high on both the ethic of right and crime control measures, while many of the courts in the rural communities with smaller court calendars are clustered lower on these measures.

Figure 12 presents the collapsed mean percentages for the traditional orientation measures coded on judicial style in court observation instrument.

Figure 11 and 12 reflect clear differences observed on the traditional orientation measures in larger courts versus the smaller courts. Regardless of some of the variations observed in individual courtrooms, when grouped together, larger courts demonstrate a higher percentage of traditional orientation measures than smaller courts do.

Figure 11: Traditional Measures Judicial Style in Court.

Traditional Measures
Judicial Style in Court

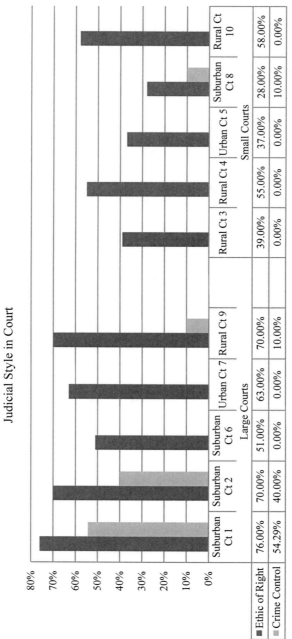

	Suburban Ct 1	Suburban Ct 2	Suburban Ct 6	Urban Ct 7	Rural Ct 9	Rural Ct 3	Rural Ct 4	Urban Ct 5	Suburban Ct 8	Rural Ct 10
			Large Courts				Small Courts			
■ Ethic of Right	76.00%	70.00%	51.00%	63.00%	70.00%	39.00%	55.00%	37.00%	28.00%	58.00%
▨ Crime Control	54.29%	40.00%	0.00%	0.00%	10.00%	0.00%	0.00%	0.00%	10.00%	0.00%

Percent = number of times observed to act in accordance – limited to one time per visit/total number of times observed - 10

Figure 12: Traditional Measures Judicial Style in Court: Large versus Small Courts

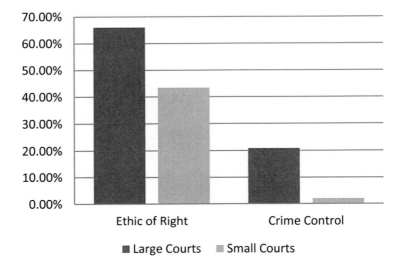

To some extent, a judge's style in court does not completely reflect his attitudes towards community, context, authoritarian manner, or focus on crime control measures in that judges in court must worry how he is viewed by the members of the audience (other drug court clients) as well as the client before him. Thus, some of the behavior in court is a function of what the judge wants to project to the audience for purposes of general deterrence.

A more complete understanding of each judge and his focus in terms of client compliance and judicial responses comes from examining his style in the team meeting, and how he interacts with his drug court team members.. Figures 13, 14, 15, and 16 detail the judicial style of each judge in the team meeting.

Figure 13 shows that the judges from smaller and larger courts ask similar questions regarding the ethic of care when in the team meeting and clients are not around, while small courts appear to be scoring visibly higher on the due process measure. This pattern is also found in Figure 14 which presents the collapsed mean percentages for the progressive measures derived from the observations of the team meeting.

Figure 13: Judicial style in team meeting Progressive measures

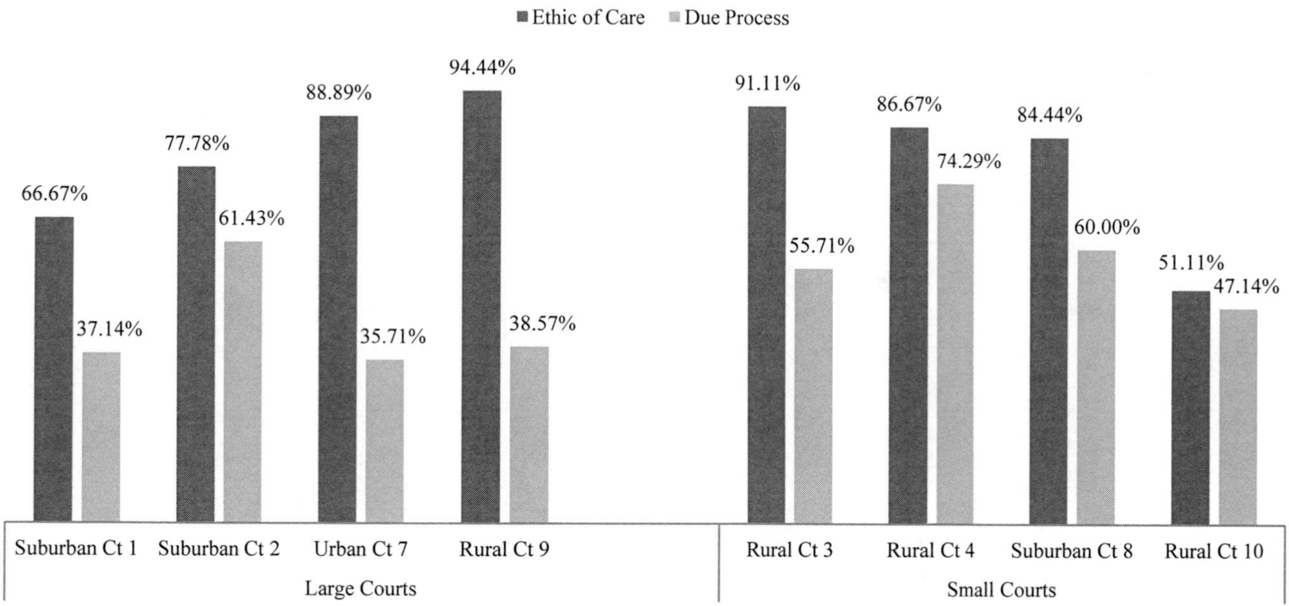

Percent = number of times observed to act in accordance – limited to one time per visit/total number of times observed – 10. Two courts are missing as the team meeting was not observed in those courts.

Figure 14: Progressive Measures Team Meeting: Large versus Small Courts

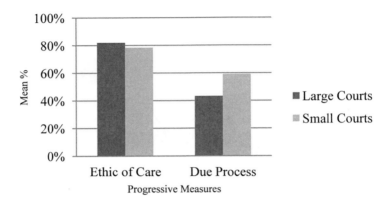

The collapsed mean percentages for the ethic of care measures shown in figure 13 are closely matched across courts of all sizes, demonstrating that judges express many of the same questions and concerns when speaking to the team members. under unobserved conditions, perhaps reflecting the progressive nature of therapeutic courts. This "ethic of care" for context and community the judges discuss in the team meeting may reflect the judge's desire to obtain the best possible information from the team in order to be fully prepared to interact with the client during the drug court session as possible.

Conversely, the larger courts scored higher on the traditional orientation measures outlined in Figures 15 and 16.

Figure 15 displays findings which demonstrate that the large courts, without exception, scored higher on the ethic of right measures than small courts, with Rural Ct 3 scoring as high as the larger courts in terms of the crime control measures, thus indicating a clear pattern in terms of the traditional measures for large and small courts. Figure 16 also presents evidence of these considerable differences between large and small courts in terms of their collapsed mean percentages.

Figure 16 reflects the significant differences found between large and small courts across courts found for individual courts in Figure 15. These collapsed mean percentages regarding the traditional measures in the team meeting demonstrate the most consistent differences observed between the small and large courts.

Figure 15: Judicial style in team meeting traditional measures

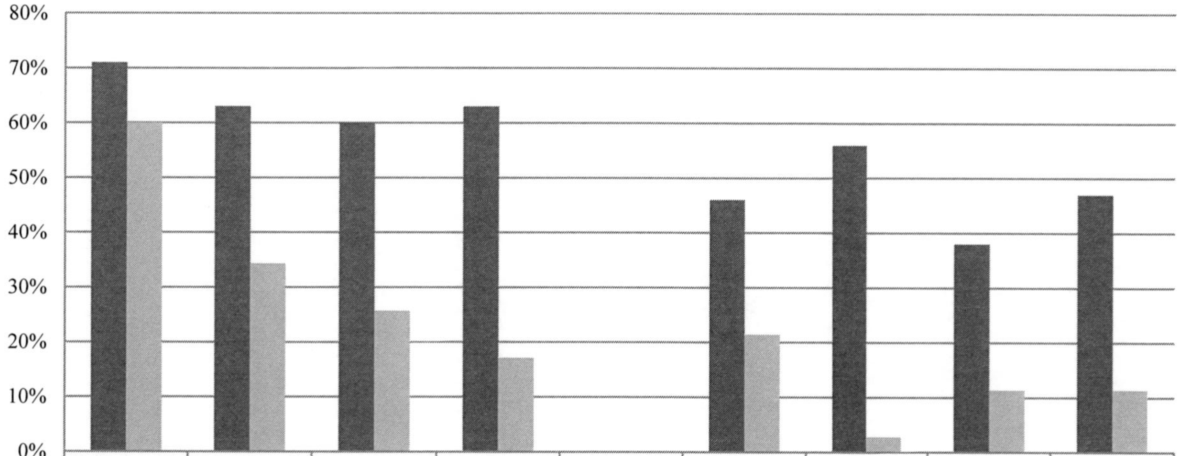

| | Large Courts | | | | Small Courts | | | | |
	Suburban Ct 1	Suburban Ct 2	Urban Ct 7	Rural Ct 9	Rural Ct 3	Rural Ct 4	Suburban Ct 8	Rural Ct 10
Ethic of Right	71.00%	63.00%	60.00%	63.00%	46.00%	56.00%	38.00%	47.00%
Crime Control	60.00%	34.29%	25.71%	17.14%	21.43%	2.86%	11.43%	11.43%

Percent = number of times observed to act in accordance – limited to one time per visit/total number of times observed - 10

Figure 16: Traditional measures team meeting – Large versus Small Courts

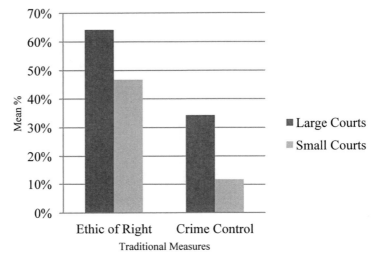

In the end, the above analyses demonstrate that larger courts reflect a more traditional orientation than smaller courts do. In other words, the smaller courts engage in positive reinforcement and the therapeutic side of therapeutic jurisprudence, while larger courts fall on the side of the jurisprudence end, using more negative reinforcement.

DOES COURT SIZE MATTER?

The conclusion drawn from the observations made of drug court team meetings and courtroom sessions is that the size of the court seems to have a major impact on the judicial orientation of the judge who presides, a finding which supports Irwin's proposal that small drug courts in mid-sized cities and rural communities have better capacities to implement the drug court model in terms of therapeutic intervention than large courts which seem to practice the traditional role of punishment. More importantly, the conclusions drawn from this study suggest that large drug courts can implement the therapeutic jurisprudence model with the same progressive orientation as the smaller drug courts do if the court calendar is managed to keep it small and/or the judge is strongly dedicated to the therapeutic model.

It is here that Durkheim can also provide some insights in terms of understanding how these drug courts differ. Durkheim proposed that in organic societies punitive systems would still serve a function in terms of social control. Thus, should restitution and reintegration fail, the penal system would still serve to punish individuals who could not be reintegrated back into society. Drug courts, as civil courts operating within an organic society, provide that opportunity to restore individuals to the community at large, and should the opportunity fail the criminal justice system would still be available as a punitive system.

Spitzer (1974) suggested that under a Durkheimian analysis the "relationship between punitive intensity and social development is actually curvilinear – in the sense that sanctions are lenient in simple egalitarian (reciprocal) societies, severe in non-market (redistributive) complex societies, and lenient in established market societies (Spitzer, 1974). Thus, according to Durkheim, it would be natural to find a punitive system in an organic society if it served a purpose. Here, smaller communities would fall into the simple, egalitarian or cohesive community category and large communities fall into larger, more complex community category.

When examining individual courts, a clear pattern between small and large courts emerges regarding the traditional orientation, but the pattern is more ambiguous regarding the progressive orientation. One explanation for the clear pattern of a traditional orientation in large courts may be related to other issues inherent to big courts (e.g., crime control or wide diversity in client population). This is an aspect of drug courts that would be explained by further investigation.

Another piece of the drug court model involves the pattern of use of rewards and sanctions. The rewards and sanctions a judge uses during his drug court session are central to the understanding of whether a judge's orientation is more progressive or more traditional.

REWARDS AND SANCTIONS: THE BREAD AND BUTTER OF DRUG COURT

Rewards and sanctions are the primary motivators in drug court. Judges and team members. in interviews all elaborated on the importance of the use of rewards over sanctions. One defense attorney put it plainly when he said,

Of course, [clients] have [their] stumbles along the way
because addiction is addiction. But I think that motivation is
not recognized enough. The approach too often is "I will
provide the motivation for you. Here's the motivation. If you
don't do this, we'll inflict more pain on you." That's effective
with a great number of people to some degree, which is a bad
thing because then people become convinced that that's the
way to do it, and this is the way to motivate people. You can
beat a horse, and they'll move, but that is not evidence that
that's the best way to get a horse to move."

THE PURPOSE OF REWARDS – MOTIVATION:

Judges learn the importance of rewards one way or the other: "If we
disregard all these little goals," commented one judge, "even though
the big goal hasn't been reached, I think we do much more harm than
good. I can tell you now – if you're never giving any credit for those
13 little goals, this party will never complete the program and probably
will come out as screwed up or worse than when they came in because
they couldn't even get an 'atta-boy' out of you."

Rewards generally consisted of praise, applause, and handshakes
for clients who attended treatment session, followed team requests, and
had drug-free toxicology tests. Tables 5 and 6 present the most
observed client compliant behaviors and the most common rewards
used in court. (Complete list of observed behaviors, sanctions, rewards,
procedures as well as descriptions are listed in the appendix)

Some judges recognized each client's progress during the week in
the drug court session: The judge or drug court coordinator would
relate the client's total number of days clean, treatment sessions
attended, and/or the receipt of good reports from the treatment
providers for that particular client, while other judges were observed to
only hear or relate a client's major accomplishments (i.e., the
completion of a treatment program, phase advancement, or graduation).
The most commonly used rewards included judicial praise, applause,
and handshakes. Table 6 relates the more frequently observed rewards.

Table 5: Top compliant behaviors (Table uses Site Description designations)

| Compliant behavior | Courts | | | | | | | | | | |
	A	B	C	D	E	F	G	H	I	J	Total
Attended treatment sessions	8	79	37	24	40	17	196	41	31	208	681
Followed team requests	3	44	23	12	20	6	206	12	5	190	521
Drug free urines	4	18	21	11	13	5	165	37	1	58	333
Phase advancement	41	12	7	8	8	22	7	3	7	23	138
Obtained employment, a GED, or graduated high school	1	2	2	8	8	0	2	8	2	12	45
New to program	0	0	0	0	0	0	0	0	6	15	21
Positive attitude	1	4	2	0	1	0	0	4	4	2	18
Doing well/good reports/doing better	0	0	0	1	3	1	0	1	7	5	18
Rescheduled appointment	1	2	0	0	4	0	0	2	2	7	18

The complete list of observed behaviors, sanctions, rewards, procedures as well as descriptions are listed in the appendix

Table 6: Top rewards (Table uses Site Description designations)

Rewards	Courts										
	A	B	C	D	E	F	G	H	I	J	Total
Praise	19	61	67	18	32	31	18	81	52	159	538
Applause	35	14	83	8	9	20	7	32	2	21	231
Handshake	20	2	1	168	2	0	0	0	0	0	193
Stage certificates	21	7	4	0	4	8	7	2	8	10	71
Small gift	46	1	3	1	1	7	7	0	1	2	69
Speech upon graduation	27	1	1	0	0	10	7	1	0	5	52
Reduced status appearances	0	16	4	2	0	4	0	3	6	6	41
Encouragement	0	0	3	1	1	2	0	0	10	0	17
Reduced requirements	0	0	1	2	1	1	1	0	3	6	15

The complete list of observed behaviors, sanctions, rewards, procedures as well as descriptions are listed in the appendix

Graduations are the ultimate reward for continued compliant behavior, but even here judges differed in their approach. They all included a description of the client's progress in drug court, official recognition of graduation, judicial praise, certificate, and the opportunity to give the remaining clients an encouraging speech. However, one judge does not label that final success a graduation, and he schedules what he calls a "Day of Recognition" where clients receive the usual applause, graduation certificate, and judicial praise. When asked about this procedure, the judge replied as follows;

> Early on when we starting treatment court we would always use the term "graduation," but graduation sometimes connotes a completion or finishing and so we like to call it "a day of recognition," recognizing where a person stands today in their recovery and their sobriety or stability in their life, and at the same time, it affords us an opportunity to further emphasize that it does not end today, but it's a continuation in the things that they need to do in order to keep the disease of addiction in remission.

This judge also hosts a banquet each year to celebrate and recognize clients who are successful in their sobriety. Other drug court judges are invited to this celebration so that everyone involved is able to partake in the success of the graduates.

DRUG COURTS AND THE USE OF METAPHORS:

Drug courts use metaphor extensively. This is often observed during graduation ceremonies. Some graduation ceremonies can be quite elaborate. One of the smaller communities manages a really "grand ceremony" twice a year. Stakeholders in the surrounding communities are invited to share in the ceremony for recent graduates. Current clients must attend, and they are encouraged to bring a family member or significant other as a guest. The drug court judge explained, "One of the things we try to do with the graduations is honor the person by giving them flowers. Since I like gardening, I always bring in a corny story about flowers. So if its sunflowers and how they progress... follow the sun. From the morning till the evening. And how that's what you should be doing in recovery, you focus on following the sun, the light. The goal of recovery and sobriety."

Other drug court judges gave gifts which often represented a metaphor for recovery. One court gives each graduate a book upon graduation. As one judge put it, the "idea behind *The Little Engine That Could* is a tradition. We give them the engraved medallion when they go on to monitoring status, we give them the certificate and the book when they finish, and we allow them the opportunity to speak to the rest of the people, to share what was important to them that made their success possible, the book I think is something that I think the participants eagerly work to get."

Another drug court judge relates the meaning behind his court's gift this way: "...anyone that graduates currently receives the key chain, which is a whistle to know how to call for help when they need to, a thermometer is on there, they know when a situation gets too hard, a magnifying glass to help them see things clearly, and a compass to help point them in the right direction; it's just a survival key chain...which is kind of a kitschy souvenir to remind them of the programs." One judge has given pens for graduation, while another used to give flashlights. Graduation is that goal toward which every client strives, and the more other clients see that it is possible to graduate the more they believe that they themselves can reach it.

For one reward-oriented judge, even sanctions issued should be therapeutic: "See sanctions should be constructive, should be progressive, not regressive. If they're regressive, you've got the wrong sanction." This sentiment was echoed by other judges who believe that in drug court, a therapeutic court, sanctions should not be used as punishment. It is a concept echoed in juvenile court where the best interests of the child are the sole consideration for the judge. There, placement (sometimes in a juvenile facility – the same concept as jail or prison) is not punishment, but is ordered to keep the juvenile safe or to help rehabilitate the juvenile. This particular judge uses jail sentences of a few days instead of a week or more, which is common in drug court for relatively minor acts of non-compliance:

> Short-term incarceration is absolutely vital and necessary in our system.... because somebody has to understand a consequence is in order and they have to live it, smell it, taste it, and then don't want it any longer. And that is very, very

important. So I'll do short terms. And sometimes when they come back, what I'll do is I'll ask them to draft me a letter as to why they want to remain in drug court, draft me a letter as to what their problem is, why they relapse, because you have to understand that.

THE PURPOSE OF SANCTIONS - DETERRENCE:

In the same way that progressive judges focus on rewards, the more traditional judges focus more heavily on non-compliance and sanctions in their typical interactions with clients. The questioning regarding compliance is more the norm when the client approaches a traditional judge rather than a discussion regarding a client's successes. In one of the larger courts, the judge characterizes his role as that of a benevolent despot, and he described it thusly: "There has to be somebody that requires accountability and responsibility. There has to be somebody that makes the final decision. There has to be somebody that they will obey and accept guidance from whether they like it or not. My role on the bench can vary from patient, gentle listener to on occasion extraverted and somewhat controlled arrogance for consistency... that compliance with drug court rules will lead to sobriety." The judges who followed a more traditional orientation all expressed a desire for consistency, both for the individual client who is in front of the judge as well as those clients present in the audience.

Even in more reward-oriented courts, judges are very aware of the role that general deterrence (as opposed to specific deterrence) plays in drug court. As one judge noted, "There are 63 other people listening...Sanctions are very good – very good, a strong part of these programs." Another judge put it slightly differently "...consistency in response patterns. If they don't self-report, there's a problem. Consistency in rewards and sanctions...Fairness and understanding legal ramifications is important, but I have to be consistent so I meet expectations." Failure to be consistent would open up the possibility of accusations that the judge was being unfair or arbitrary. One judge made it clear that "if you don't believe this, go to a court where somebody's taken on the assignment because their supervisor sent them to the assignment without training and without any background. And watch how punitive it is. You'll get a perfect idea as to what we're talking about as to how not to set this model up."

A team member put it bluntly: "[a sanction] should be immediate and it should be severe whether it's good or bad. It's got to be to the point where the individual gets the message the first time. It is unfair to that child. It's unfair to that participant in drug court to let them get a different message and let them face more punishment further down the road just because you didn't get it across to them the first time." The same team member presented the concept of graduated sanctions, and describe how they can be effectively used thusly:

> Graduated sanctions are a wonderful concept. Graduated sanctions should not be graduated as how they're doled out to an individual. They should be graduated based on the offense that is causing the difficulties. So graduated means "Yes, we go from A-Z." You can put in new ones if you want, but my point is it doesn't mean that client A gets to go to sanction one first and then sanction two next and then finally when they get to sanction five, which is the worst, being thrown out of the drug court, they still haven't learned because nobody taught them anything. Sometimes a punishment needs to be more severe.

In some respects the courts with larger calendars have little choice but to focus on those clients who are not in compliance. There are only so many hours in a morning or afternoon session and, for some courts, the clients who are non-compliant get most of the attention in order to figure out why they are non-compliant and what to do to motivate them. Larger courts often had a probation officer as a key team member who was able to report on client compliance. Small communities that lack the resources to include a probation officer as a team member are missing a key factor in compliance. Other resources that assist a court in monitoring compliance are SCRAM bracelets (ankle bracelets that monitor alcohol level in a client's blood stream), 80-hour alcohol tests (measuring a personal alcohol level over 80 hours), and home curfew checks. Even something as small as monitored toxicology samples can help in determining compliance. Clients have many ways to circumvent drug court rules, and even when caught, many provide elaborate explanations or excuses for being called on their non-compliant behavior.

One court has handled clients who refuse to admit their non-compliance by putting in place a procedure that allows them to contest a positive instant toxicology test or any other allegation of non-compliant behavior. Should the test later come back positive from the lab or there is any evidence that the client did in fact engage in non-compliant behavior, the sanction is doubled. This procedure can lead to clients serving more than one long jail sentence during their participation in drug court.

Of course, here Weber's substantive law comes into the picture. Drug court judges decide what do to with each client on a case-by-case basis, with the increased role of social factors in each decision. Those social factors, or non-legal factors, play a larger role in rewards and sanctions rather than whether or not a client has relapsed and used some illegal substance. That is the whole idea between sanctioning proximal behaviors more harshly than actual relapse: "[A]bstinence is a distal goal for the addict because treatment support is often necessary before change will occur for that target behavior. Thus, for the addict, treatment is a proximal behavior and a high magnitude sanction is warranted for treatment non-compliance. Although abstinence may be a distal goal for the addict, there is always a consequence for use" (Meyer, 2007, p. 4).

Thus, failure to attend a treatment appointment or multiple treatment appointments without any reasonable emergency may lead to a week in jail, while substance use admitted by the client before detection by a positive toxicology result may in contrast warrant only an essay on the client's struggles with his or her addiction. The theory is that drug court needs to discourage the behaviors that will lead to a relapse, especially if there is a failure to call in or admit to this behavior in order to avoid a relapse. Indeed, if you handle the proximal causes of a relapse, you will ultimately avert a relapse altogether. Finally, any social factors that are the proximal cause of a relapse - failure to attend treatment, lies to the court, relationships with known drug users, people, places, things - will gain greater attention (and sanction) than the distal behavior of relapse (criminal offense).

Tables 7 and 8 list the top non-compliant acts and sanctions used to enforce compliance. The most serious non-compliant behaviors are drug use, failure to attend treatment appointments, and failure to follow team requests. An interesting pattern in the judicial responses to non-compliance was that if a client admitted to the drug use or re-scheduled the treatment appointment, he or she was rarely sanctioned by the court. If they lie, however, about their drug use or fail to re-schedule their treatment appointment, they are sure to receive some kind of sanction. For many clients who relapsed, there could be multiple sanctions for one incident (e.g., loss of clean time, essay in jail, and removal from the program). A full list of non-compliant behaviors and sanctions observed, as well as their descriptions, are found in the appendix.

Table 8 details the most frequently used sanctions observed during the study. Jail tops the list and "no sanction" is second as many clients do self-report their non-compliance. While they may lose their cumulative clean time, they will not usually be sanctioned to jail time for their relapse if they self-report, as the drug court model recognizes that relapse is an expected and inevitable part of recovery. Other forms of sanctions include increased case management contacts, higher level of care (often referred to as "bed-to-bed" or "door-to-door" which includes jail time as a sanction or to reduce the possibility of another relapse before going into in-patient).

Other sanctions include warnings, deferred sanctions, and 100% compliance which attempts to let the client know they are dangerously close to going to jail or being removed from the program if there is any further deviation from judicial expectations. Community service hours and essays can be used as program requirements or sanctions depending on how they are incorporated. Court D and Court J require clients to perform community service if they aren't working, while Court I uses community service as a sanction for non-compliance. Court I, however, requires every client to complete a community improvement project before they can become eligible for graduation. Thus, community service is reinforced as clients move forward in their recovery in the hopes of reintegrating them back into the community. Another sanction requires the client to make an appointment, sign up for social service benefits, or provide a doctor's prescription for a newly discovered set of pills, depending on what the basis was for their non-compliance. Finally, essays can be used as a requirement either for phase advancement or as a sanction for non-compliance. The purpose, however, is the same; essays are used to promote reflection and insight to help clients come to grips with their addiction.

Table 7: Top Non-compliant behaviors (table uses site description designations)

Non-compliant behavior	Courts										Total
	A	B	C	D	E	F	G	H	I	J	
Drugs found in toxicology test	54	22	5	9	14	32	36	5	30	19	226
Failed to go to treatment appointments	26	20	8	13	16	34	34	7	15	21	194
Failed to follow team requests	13	3	2	6	0	9	31	1	12	7	84
New criminal charges	7	5	0	4	13	9	10	2	5	9	64
Unknown/other	11	6	1	2	1	8	3	1	6	12	51
Lied about non-compliance	10	1	1	3	0	2	14	0	17	1	49
Failed to go to court	5	2	0	0	5	11	4	1	4	2	34
No sample provided or diluted sample	6	1	1	0	2	7	4	0	3	2	26
Curfew violation/failed to call in	6	1	0	3	0	0	0	0	9	6	25
Fled treatment/violation of program rules/kicked out of program	4	0	0	1	1	6	3	0	6	2	23
Associated with drug addicted friends	0	1	0	0	0	0	1	0	5	11	18
Self -report use	10	0	0	0	1	2	1	1	2	0	17
Late for court/treatment appointments	5	4	0	3	0	0	2	0	1	0	15
Failed to pay fines/treatment	1	1	2	0	0	0	5	0	1	2	12
Suspected drug use or inappropriate behavior	7	0	1	0	0	1	0	0	2	1	12
Police contact	0	0	0	0	0	0	0	1	7	1	9

The complete list of observed behaviors, sanctions, rewards, procedures as well as descriptions are listed in the appendix

Table 8: Top Sanctions (table uses site description designations)

Sanctions	Courts										Total
	A	B	C	D	E	F	G	H	I	J	
Jail	45	17	1	13	4	31	55	0	47	18	231
No sanction *	9	10	5	5	3	8	23	8	25	14	110
Increased case management contacts	2	0	1	0	9	6	2	0	1	13	34
Higher level care/detoxification program	4	4	0	5	4	3	5	2	2	2	31
Warning	2	5	0	5	0	6	1	1	3	6	29
Sanction pending	2	1	2	0	0	16	0	0	0	1	22
Additional requirement **	4	1	2	3	1	6	2	0	0	1	20
Unknown/other	3	1	1	2	7	2	1	0	0	3	20
Community service hours	2	0	0	0	6	5	0	0	4	2	19
Returned to criminal court	12	3	0	1	1	0	0	0	0	2	19
Increased self-helps	1	1	0	1	3	4	0	0	7	0	17
Essay/letter	0	0	0	0	0	3	3	0	6	0	12
100% compliance	2	0	0	0	6	0	0	0	0	0	8
Loss of clean time	0	0	0	0	5	0	0	1	0	0	6

*Clients typically will not receive a sanction if they self-report a substance use before a positive toxicology test

**Obtain a doctor's note/make a plan in order to become compliant/make a doctor's appointment

In the final analysis, the use of any one reward or sanction did not signify whether a particular court was more traditional or progressive, but rather whether the judge's use of rewards or sanctions were incorporated in the judge's daily practice. In other words, did the judge focus more on compliant behavior and rewards during the drug court session? Or, alternatively, did the judge focus more on non-compliant behavior and sanctions?

REWARDS OR SANCTIONS WEAVED THROUGHOUT THE COURT SESSION:

Some of the judges in this study would consistently reward clients with judicial praise and encouragement, and these rewards were incorporated into the unique dialogue the judge has with the client. The judge in Court H, for example, was observed to directly address compliant clients and praise them for their accomplishments, while the judge in Court D would shake each client's hand when he or she reached the bench and praise any accomplishment the client achieved. In addition, the judge of Court J never failed to praise a client for reaching or exceeding the assigned number of self-helps as well as any other positive events in the client's life (e.g., completed treatment or obtained employment), and the judge in Court C was observed to applaud every client who came before him in the status appearance (with the possible exception of clients who are sanctioned to jail). The praise is incorporated into the ritual the judge uses to interact with the client.

One judge discussed his decision to use rewards in his typical interaction with clients by relating a story in which he was encouraged by one of this team members. to reserve his applause for special occasions. The judge told the team member the following.:

> I have done it because I just thought that it was important that we recognize people, but you know let's give this a chance. Okay? What we will do is we won't do the clapping after every person. We will wait until we get something significant. So the first day back we had our mental health court and I got down and I said start calling "next case" and I hear [clapping] in the background. Loud -- it was loud. Whether or not they were trained -- I don't think so…. I think it was something that

they wanted to do because they wanted to support and be supported. So I am going to keep doing it.

Another judge spoke about his decision to shake every client's hand this way: "you shake their hands and you treat them like a human being that you would want to be treated in that situation, so you call them up, obviously, by the first name, shake their hand, have them sit down. Even if they're in shackles…." Another judge put it this way: "[S]ometimes, and we don't do it often enough, I'll come out without my robe and sit outside the table. Sit across from me. You know, what do you want to talk about? One-on-one just so they know I care. And you know what happens, it becomes they care. And they ask how you doing? Well I'm doing ok, but it's not about me, it's about you. Well ok, well thanks for asking."

Finally, one judge defined his role in terms of rewards: "My role is more so to encourage them, to compliment them and praise them if they're doing positive things in their life. It's also to ask them what happened. How did you get here? What's going wrong? There are so many different things that are going on in people's lives."

Some judges presided over courts where sanctions permeate their daily court calendar in typical interactions used to motivate clients. It may be that the distinction between a progressively-oriented judge and traditionally-oriented judge boils down to how the judge looks at sanctions. One reward-oriented judge put it this way: "while that person is in drug court…I think everything has to be therapeutic, you know. Whether it is a positive thing…It's some praise or one point where we are trying to support somebody, help somebody, a good thing some person has done, that's -- we have to do it in a therapeutic manner and I think also with the sanctions. Sanctions aren't there to punish people. They are there to push a person toward a certain modification in their life." However, for judges in larger courts, the court calendars force them to focus more on non-compliant clients, which automatically permeates the court calendar with sanctions. Judges in rural communities with a small court calendar (or a larger court with a small court calendar) have the luxury of spending more time with individual clients and give rewards to all the compliant clients. For those judges, the time spent with rewards softens the overall impression of the court, regardless of the time spent sanctioning non-compliant clients.

Rewards and sanctions do not operate in a vacuum. They are largely supported and administered through the unique policies and procedures developed by each judge and their respective drug court teams.

POLICIES AND PROCEDURES: THAT WHICH MAKES EACH DRUG COURT UNIQUE

Drug courts are like snowflakes; even given their commonalities, no two are alike. To a great extent that uniqueness comes from the procedures the team creates and/or implements to motivate clients. Newly created drug courts turn to model drug courts to inform them on best practices, and many existing courts look to their neighboring drug courts for ideas to improve their drug court. This borrowing of procedures rarely results in carbon copies, however each drug court looks within to its resources, stakeholders, team members, and community of likely clients and assesses the best way to incorporate any particular procedure. Once adopted, the judge, with his or her unique style, implements and enforces procedures. Finally, after months, or even years, a procedure may be examined to see if it is effective or should be adjusted, and the procedure may be either discontinued or continued in a different form.

This study cataloged a significant number of unique policies and procedures. Some, like the green card, have been discussed in previous sections. A complete list of unique procedures observed and the drug court they were observed in is found in the appendix (Tables 16, 18, and 19). Complete descriptions of each procedure are listed in the appendix as well (Tables 12, 13, and 14).

Notably, both progressively- and traditionally-oriented judges have used some unique and creative policies. The penalty box is among the most unique policies observed. It was surprising to see clients enter the courtroom and voluntarily sit in the penalty box, thereby proclaiming to everyone else in the room (clients and judge alike) that they were non-compliant. It is one of the better examples of reintegrative shaming in the court system. In most of the criminal justice system, shaming is used to label individuals as offenders and thus exclude them from legitimate opportunities. However, reintegrative shaming occurs when the offender is embraced after the punishment is served (Ray, Dollar, & Thames, 2011). The penalty box provides a vehicle by which clients can admit their non-compliance to the group, receive their punishment for the inappropriate behavior (whatever that may be), and be re-accepted into the group.

There are many creative policies with rewards and sanctions designed to motivate clients. The judge of Court I used the "head of the class" reward for many client behaviors that he wanted to encourage. A client earns this reward by doing something appropriate (e.g., attending a Life Works meeting, the alumni group for this court). The reward can then be used at any time the client wishes to be called before other clients and allowed to leave immediately. In Court I, clients are expected to be sitting in drug court before the session starts and to remain until they are dismissed. An earned head of the class reward can mean the difference between getting to a doctor's appointment or missing it, so it is highly prized. At one point, head of the class rewards were being given for sending letters to service men and women who were in the hospital overseas. This provided the troops with an encouraging letter and motivated the client to perform community service activity.

The judge of Court I also required clients to involve themselves in some community improvement project before they were eligible for graduation. Again, this judge is motivating the clients to engage in community service. It is no surprise that this judge scores high in the progressive measures of ethic of care, as he focuses on community and restorative items. While this judge presides in a rural city court, he has a large calendar as his court is designated a hub court and accepts Art. 216 clients. Since his is only one of a few drug courts in a large geographic area, his court is heavily relied upon. This may explain this judge's focus on community service not often observed in the urban courts. The judge in Court I also scores high on due process in that he relies extensively on his assigned defense attorney by suggesting that clients consult with the attorney after any sanction he may issue.

The judge in Court A instituted a monitoring status for clients who had completed their treatment and drug court requirements, but were not yet eligible for graduation. It is a time period for which clients did not need to return to court for status appearances, but they did have to be tested for substance use and must lead a law abiding life. If the client is able to remain compliant while on monitoring status for the required period of time, the client would become eligible for graduation. This judge also created a compliance court for those defendants who came into his court for a substance abuse-related offense, but did not have a dependency diagnosis. The clients in his compliance court needed to maintain compliance with the rules of the drug court, but would not need to make status appearances unless found to be non-compliant (i.e., positive toxicology test or new criminal charges).

Another unique procedure, previously discussed, was the thought-provoking question delivered in lecture hall fashion in order to encourage reflective thinking. One such question, "Why is a drug court a court of love?" was intended to help clients understand that being sober is more about the love of self rather than the love of others. Clients need to learn to become clean for themselves first and foremost. Another question, "Why are your friends not always your friends?" addresses the concept of people, places, and things, which is important in understanding the danger in falling back into the drug addict lifestyle.

Another unique aspect of Court B's judge is his use of team members to work with clients during the court session to discuss issues of non-compliance that came up during the week and having the clients come up with their own sanction. This judge is one of the few drug court judges interviewed and observed who actively uses the team members. in his court to work positively with the clients who are struggling. Asking clients to come up with their own sanction typically occurs in discussion with team members who talk to the client about their non-compliance and possible sanctions. It is during these interventions that the judge is able to understand the situation better without coercing the client in open court. This was observed to encourage reflective thinking on the part of the client and to help mitigate sanctions for the client when the situation called for it.

Judges in this study use different techniques to encourage clients to engage in reflective thinking. While one judge used a thought-provoking question and team member intervention, other judges used an essay for minor acts of non-compliance or stage advancement, and the judge in Court I required the composition of a six-month goal sheet. The six-month goal sheet is required within the first few status appearances and the clients must hand it to the judge in a sealed envelope. The judge returns this goal sheet to the clients in six months (unread) for clients to review and reflect on where they were in the early stages of recovery as well as where they are six months in. Essays can be used before phase advancement, as in Court C, or after a non-compliant act. If an essay is used regularly for phase advancement, its purpose is to encourage the client to reflect on the consequences of his or her addiction and the positives of sobriety. However, if the essay is used as a sanction, it is assigned to get the clients to think about what they are doing wrong, the harm they are causing, their ongoing commitment to the program, and/or a plan for how they can start to become compliant with the program. This was observed in the pilot study courts as well as in the full study courts.

Judges sometimes would discover things about the client that would lead to a change in the treatment plan. The judge in Court G had assigned an essay for a woman sanctioned to jail who was really struggling to comply with drug court rules. The essay revealed significant abuse history which made her a better candidate for mental health court, and she was accordingly transferred. Mental health court, another therapeutic diversionary court, would allow the team to focus specifically on her mental health issues resulting from the trauma experienced as well as the substance abuse. This judge presides over a large urban court as well as a criminal calendar and a mental health court. This judge tries to balance the needs of his clients and the demands of presiding over a large drug court calendar by listening to his staff as well as to the clients. Finally, most of the drug courts studied tried to provide special treats to the clients. Small gifts, food, and group outings are common, and then treats are used as an extra reward for the clients who are working on their treatment phases and to foster a feeling of community.

One simple procedure used in some courts involves the judge or the drug court coordinator stating the level to which the client has been compliant. In Court H, for example, as the client approached the bench, the coordinator would state that the client went to his treatment appointments, obtained employment, was testing negative on all substance use tests, and any good things that were happening in the client's life. Then, after the judge was done speaking to the client the coordinator would announce the client's cumulative clean time and everyone would applaud. This simple procedure gave the overall impression of a very positive court emphasizing client progress. While many other courts have also adopted this procedure, in whole or in part, the articulation of the client's cumulative clean time before the client left the courtroom gave everyone the opportunity to give this client a pat on the back for his or her accomplishments for the week.

Weber's substantive law really encompasses the entire concept of therapeutic jurisprudence by focusing on the individual social factors of each client. Rewards, sanctions, and unique procedures all rely upon individual clients and a cases-by-case analysis of the individual improvements each client has made when they walk into court. This is far from the idea of legal formalism and actions detected by the facts of the case. Drug court focuses on the time and attention each judge can spend on individuals in order to coax, encourage, and coerce them into becoming conforming members of the community. Policies and procedures can be used in conjunction with sanctions and rewards by progressively oriented judges or traditionally oriented judges. Another aspect of a progressive or traditional orientation can be the arrangement of the courtroom itself.

DESIGN: REWARDS AND SANCTIONS - THE ARCHITECTURE OF THERAPEUTIC INTERVENTION

Mulcahy, (2007) presents the idea that the current physical design of the courtroom is used to marginalize the spectator in order to remove the "public" from the public trial (Mulcahy, 2007). Mulcahy opined that current courtroom designs are the result of territorial struggles in which the litigants and members of the public are increasingly pushed out, crowded, and humiliated (Mulcahy, 2007). Arguing that current courtroom design is deliberately planned for an intended effect on the public or litigants may be controversial, but direct observation of the courtroom does give impressions, even to a novice, as to the legal system. Traditional courtroom design provides for two parties, standing parallel and equal to each other, facing a central figure who looks down upon them in judgment. The architecture of the adversary system reveals itself. The jury is often on the side of the courtroom: up higher than the litigators and at the middle of the activity to provide the best view of the action. Thus, hierarchy and function is used for the trial to take place in the most efficient manner.

The notion that courtrooms can be used for more than the mere mechanics of routine justice has not escaped drug court judges. The use of the courtroom as a tool for incentives or sanctions is a natural extension of the notion of the drug court session as theater where the judge performs to influence the client in front of him (Nolan, 2001). In this theater, the judge displays his judicial orientation through his interactions with the client. A judge can use the traditional courtroom setting to emphasize the punitive, repressive side of the court, or he or she can transform it to present a more restitutive setting for drug court clients. This transformation is representative of the transformation of the judge from a repressive authority figure to a therapeutic agent as well as of the transformations the court is expecting the client to undergo – that of seeing the judge not as a punisher but as an instrument of therapeutic intervention helping the drug addict change into an abstinent member of society.

Steen (2002) opined that the placement of the defendant close to the judge and between the judge and both attorneys (the more typical drug court configuration) is a way to bring the judge into a relationship with the client while minimizing the notion that the defense attorney is there to protect the client from the judge. In this way the physical layout of the courtroom can be used to support the goals of therapeutic intervention in a courtroom setting. Both observation and judicial interviews supported the notion that the physical layout of the courtroom could be used either to support a progressive process or reinforce the authoritative power of a traditional judge (see appendix courtroom diagrams).

The decision by a judge to physically alter the traditional workspace is a specific aspect of his judicial orientation. It is a physical manifestation of his or her desire to move from a courtroom that is viewed by defendants as a punitive system to a totally different configuration in the hopes that the defendant will abandon that traditional view and replace it with a more therapeutic view. This alteration of the environment was found to be an extension of a judge's progressively-oriented model in order to emphasize treatment and positive reinforcement.

The most noticeable physical alteration of the courtroom is used by Court D where the judge presides, *sans* robe, at what is normally the defense table (with the drug court coordinator at his side), sitting across from the drug court client (with his treatment provider at his or her side). When the client approaches the table to sit down, the judge rises and shakes his hand.

Non-traditional courtroom setup:

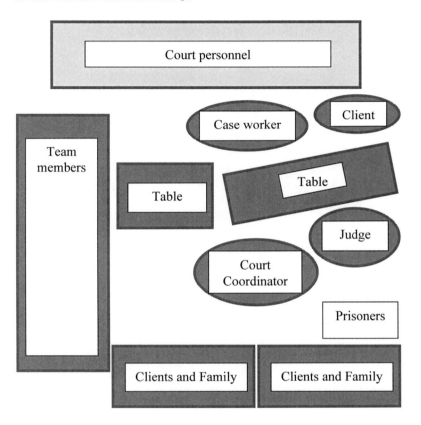

When asked about this procedure, the judge indicated that he (along with his team) instituted this change after attending the National Drug Court Institute sponsored by the National Association of Drug Court Professionals (NDCI/NADCP) conference "Incentives and Sanctions Workshop" with Judge William Meyer (ret.) held in Coral Gables, Florida in 2006.

Judge Meyers (2007) outlined the different ways a drug court team can influence client behavior through rewards and sanctions. Judge Meyer stressed the need for rewards, as long-lasting behavior change can only be achieved through positive reinforcement coupled with motivational negative reinforcement (Meyer, 2007). Meyer detailed ten specific principals to help guide drug court teams in developing appropriate responses to influence behavior change (e.g., responses should be delivered swiftly and reliably and for every targeted behavior, but should not be painful, humiliating, or injurious).

While not specifically recommended by the workshop, the judge of Court D interpreted the message from that conference as informing him about the physical layout of his courtroom. As the judge saw it, the courtroom configuration was a "means to help build trust in the participants...The level physical position hopefully shows unbiased neutrality that doesn't scream 'I'm over you. Listen to me. Do what I say.'" In addition, the judge related that the list of sanctions and rewards he gleaned from the conference article included handshakes, hugs, verbal praise, cookies, and so on.

During observations, the judge in this court would shake the client's hand before and after talking to the client and often brought in homemade cookies for the clients. It was in these ways the drug court judge and team could put into practice the information presented on incentives. In the courts where clients were physically next to their defense attorneys for issues related to non-compliance, judges often focused more on rewards and problem-driven treatment plans during the drug court session. For example, one judge discussed pushing his treatment team to look for and propose creative solutions for clients who struggle the most with their addiction. In another court, the judge rarely pointed out that the client was being sanctioned. For clients who were to receive a punishment such as jail, the judge merely set bail and a return date. For repeated non-compliance, clients were asked to relate how things "would be different this time" and to list the ways in which they were going to act in order to ensure compliance in the future. In this way, judicial condemnation was taken out of the drug court sanction for many of the reward-oriented drug courts.

It was in this particular court where another novel change to the courtroom occurred – the creation of the Penalty Box. As previously discussed, the Penalty Box was used by this court to quickly identify those clients who were non-compliant so that they could be isolated and called last for whatever sanctioning seemed appropriate.

<u>Penalty Box setup:</u>

COURT E

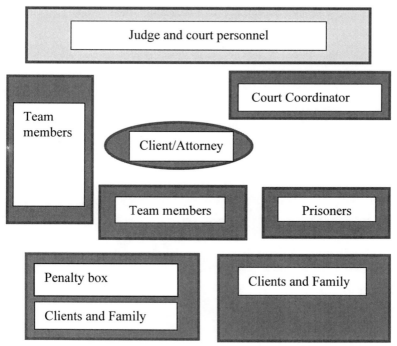

Non-compliant clients would enter the courtroom and seat themselves in the penalty box and wait until they were called, thereby declaring themselves to everyone in the courtroom "who" and "what" they were. This use of the courtroom is a form of reintegrative shaming. The use of the Penalty Box is based on the idea that an individual can be stigmatized by placing himself in the Penalty Box and then serve his sanction (whatever it is) solely for the purposes of returning to the community. Thus, when finished with the sanction, the client can return to drug court and be treated like everyone else in the community and ultimately become successful.

In contrast to the physical layout of the courtroom as a tool to administer rewards and encouragement, the physical layout of the courtroom can also be used to promote compliance in drug court by simply not transforming it at all (or by removing the most important protection of all – the defense attorney). Most of the drug courts in this study placed the client between the judge and the defense attorney. The placement of the client, as presented by Steen (2002), leaves the client on his own to face the judge over his or her failure to comply with the drug court treatment plan. Observations verified that non-compliance could be dealt with quite harshly by the judge with very little furniture or space standing between the judge and the non-compliant client (e.g., with stern judicial admonishment or significant time in jail).

A few courts placed the drug court coordinator between the judge and the client. Interestingly, only one court, Court J, physically placed the client, drug court coordinator, prosecutor, and defense attorney at the same level (see site descriptions). Court E was unique in that the drug court coordinator was constantly on the move, going from client to judge to client (often with his or her defense attorney) and frequently to the gallery to speak to family members or interested parties.

Those courts where the clients were closest in physical proximity to the judge were found to focus more on treatment compliance and sanctions. Clients were often left on their own to face the judge and account for their failure to comply with the drug court rules (i.e., drugs found in urine sample, were not home for a curfew check, missed treatment appointment, or failure to come to court). Clients would provide an amazing array of reasons why their toxicology exam was positive (poppy seed bagel and close physical proximity to someone else doing drugs) or why they did not answer the door for a curfew check (slept through the doorbell or can't hear it from inside the apartment).

Non-compliance often led to one or more weeks in jail. Clients whose attorneys were allowed to advocate for them often presented better arguments for non-compliance and were often successful if they contested the sanction. For example, one client argued strongly that his positive urine toxicology test was due to a poppy seed bagel (a common reason for testing positive on a toxicology test). The judge of that court allowed the client to repeat the behavior in a controlled setting (the courtroom with a toxicology test before and after the bagel). In this court, the defense attorney did advocate for the client and was ultimately successful in challenging the sanction he faced.

The courtroom, at best, has been used as a tool by the judge to transform his image to the client into a more therapeutic agent by removing the physical constructs that support the image of the judge as a punitive agent. This type of judge would rely on the traditional court setup for some aspects of drug court (e.g., hearing on removal from drug court), but for most of the drug court session the judge remained in the transformed setup to encourage a restitutive outcome regarding drug court clients. On the other hand, the traditional court setup can be used to emphasize the repressive nature of court. By leaving the client on his own before the judge to face the full force of the judge's admonishment and/or sanction is unmitigated. Thus, the repressive nature of the law (in the form of the judge) is not far from the client's consciousness.

This traditional setup can also emphasize the judge's power. Drug court team members., as previously described, collect an incredible amount of information on the client which is relayed to the judge during the case conference. This includes information that is more socially related (e.g., client is seeing a prior partner) than legally related (e.g., actual drug use). Sometimes it can be a treatment provider's hunch or intuition that tells him or her that the client is "dirty" or relapsing. There is really no part of the client's life that is not subject to discussion if there is any possible connection between the information and relapse potential. If the team decides, for whatever reason, that the client is lying or non-compliant with any part of the drug court program, sanctions are entirely possible.

This level of control is simply not present in traditional criminal and civil court systems. Team members were observed to request sanctions on clients based on nothing more than a "belief" that the client was non-compliant or close to actually relapsing. Indeed, one client was observed to be sanctioned to a week in jail for doing nothing more than swearing at a member of the team. While team members may have seen it as a "time out" similar to what we impose on children for being bad, jail is more repressive and invasive than merely being "sent to your room."

As the medical discourse is fully imported into the criminal/civil court systems through therapeutic jurisprudence, the traditional adversarial process is at least partially transformed. Drug courts have changed the perception of justice. In drug courts, the defendant is transformed into client, due process is set aside for treatment, and judges are the enforcers of treatment. This is a natural extension of the medicalization of drug addiction, but with the added problem of drug treatment teams with a vested interest in the success or failure of a drug addict who have the authority to punish clients for failure to succeed. Failure in drug court may have results that are worse than the original criminal sanction may have been. Interview subjects repeatedly spoke of clients who had entered and failed drug court only to be sentenced to more time in jail than they would have received had they gone through the traditional court process without any diversion. Drug courts provide a form of repressive law with a kind face, punctuated and supported by the traditional courtroom setup.

The judge, meanwhile, is the most important person in the room. We speak of drug courts, but the judge is the physical manifestation of the drug court. His or her *persona*, his delivery, and his choices all combine at the front of the courtroom. All eyes are on him during the court session. Given this power, how does the judge construct himself as a therapeutic agent?

THE JUDGE: BACKGROUND AND CONSTRUCTION OF SELF

Looking at judicial orientation begins with how the judges see their role. The judges in this study spoke about their backgrounds and roles in drug court. Most of the judges have spent a considerable amount of their professional lives as judges. The mean years on the bench for the judges in this study came to almost 20 years. Many of the judges in this study came to be drug court judges when the movement was just starting. A few noted how little their legal training had prepared them for the role of therapeutic agent: "These are supposed to be therapy-driven courts for people suffering from a disease. They didn't teach us that in law school. When we went to the one-week training for new judges – here's another shocker – they didn't teach us that there [either]." Another judge spoke about aspiring to be in professional sports as a college student. Most of the judges had long careers as attorneys before they ever became judges.

Often, it was that time as a lawyer that instilled compassion for the clients they would one day preside over in drug court:

And when I talk to people – and I learned this when I was doing criminal defense work.... – and not to condone crime or say these people are not evil or bad or harm you – but in my private conversations with them ... I gained their trust, they'd open up to me, and I would talk to them. Many, and again, I say this with humility – many would just look at me and say to me "No one's ever said that to me before." How many of those people I have reached and made a difference, I'll never know. As I try to do the same thing in the drug court without appearing to be too soft.

Another judge told me that "I was just going to say that another asset has been the fact that, number one, I was a criminal defense lawyer for a lot of years. I was a public defender...which I loved, for several years. I was the prosecutor ... [and] the city attorney for twenty-three years. So all of these diverse backgrounds, really like you're making a cake and this is the ingredients and you put all the ingredients and you wind up with a judge." Other judges spoke of their closeness to the community and family backgrounds giving them the tools to reach people in drug court.

JUDGES AS DADS:

Approximately half of the judges in this study spoke of their role in drug court as being a father figure to the clients. One said, "My role is more so to encourage them, to compliment them and praise them if they're doing positive things in their life...I see my role more or less as father figure. This is the kind of parenting that they probably never got early on in life, and they need to know there are rules. You need to follow these rules. If you follow these rules, everything will go well. If you don't, then you may be sitting in the state prison." Again, "I wholeheartedly believe that it's a like a well-drawn family structure where the judge sits as the father figure." Another said, "[to] many of these people – the percentage is extremely high, and if were to venture a guess... let's just say it's more than a majority – we become a father image. If I was of a different gender, we would become a very strong maternal interest." And, "that's the role that is obvious here to me 17 years later – day one, week one, or year one. I had no idea that I was going to become a father image, and sure enough – it's that and that foremost." Finally, "you do become [invested] because of the family approach that we're trying to take."

Other judges in the study understood their role to be as an agent for transformation and that they were part cheerleader, part authority figure, part manager, and part judge. One judge offered the following description of his notion of his role in the drug court:

> I perceive my role as creating, as best as possible, a therapeutic environment in order to assist individuals to reach stability in their life and sobriety and also to seek to have them redirect their lives with respect to having employment, stable, habitable housing, and for those some are going to school, facilitate that process, so they can go on to school to college. For those that don't have their high school degree, to facilitate the process ...of them getting their high school or GED, the equivalency. And, also, to be mindful of public safety and, in addition, to not have them committing additional offenses and redirecting them out of the criminal justice system.

A different judge said,

> It's what's in the best of our participants and let's try whatever we can try, and if that doesn't work we'll try something else. But...I don't know how best to characterize it. I think compassion is probably the best word for it. What I've come to learn is that most people are good. They may make some bad choices which result in lifestyle situations that wind up in criminal court and wind up in with their having lost family and friends and jobs and all that. So I believe sincerely that people who make an attempt at the program should be given every opportunity to have that light go on. None of us knows when that's going to happen.

Another judge put it this way:

> You know I am certainly there to give encouragement. I am certainly there to assist them and support them in any way I can... and that is really the most satisfying aspect of it. I do, you know, enjoy that aspect of the job. On the other hand, I understand the carrot and the stick and...when I -- when we go to the negative aspect end of the stick aspect you know, I am there to impose whatever punishment may be therapeutic.

JUDGES AS DESPOTS

One judge creatively indicated that he is

> the benevolent despot...sitting up there.... In many cases, I'm
> the first person in the system who's actually taken an interest
> in them in what could be 10, 20, 30 years, so if they want to
> please me in the process of making themselves more whole
> and more able to deal with life...[That] can vary from patient,
> gentle listener to on occasion extraverted and somewhat
> controlled arrogance and I say that because the range of
> emotions depending upon the degree of combativeness or lack
> of integrity or cheating, so to speak of the system,...requires a
> different response from me. My role is to take control of that
> court room. It is my courtroom and I have to function in
> drawing together the different resources that are there.

While only one judge presented his role as a despot, a few
presented their role as a managerial role or figure of public authority.
How each judge would implement that role reflected a personal belief
about how that role should work. In the same way that there are
worker-friendly bosses and worker-unfriendly bosses, they both believe
they are bosses. For drug court judges, how they constructed the role
of drug court judge and how they acted as drug court judge meant they
presented those behaviors they believed to best motivate clients to
achieve sobriety and maintain abstinence.

There are different ways to approach the determination of whether a
judge is viewed as progressively or traditionally oriented. While it is
possible to identify judges who are polar opposites regarding orientation,
there is still an element of the traditional in a progressive judge and a
slice of progressive in a traditionally oriented judge. However, it may be
possible to see which way the judges in this study lean.

PROGRESSIVE VERSUS TRADITIONAL ORIENTATIONS: WHERE DO THE JUDGES FIT?

One way of understanding judicial orientation is to analyze specific
interactions with the client. The observation instruments used in this
study coded judicial interactions for each client on the basis of whether
the judge's interactions fit within the progressive measures of ethic of

care and due process, or fit within traditional measures of ethic of right and crime control.

In Figure 17, the total number of progressive statements made for each court was divided by the number of clients for that court, and a score was created for progressive orientation. A high progressive orientation would be above 1 (meaning more than one such statement, on average, was spoken to the clients). A judge who fell in the middle of the scale would be 1, and a low progressively oriented judge would score below 1, meaning that on average the judge made less than one progressive statement to the clients in his courtroom.

Figure 17: Judges score on Progressive Measures

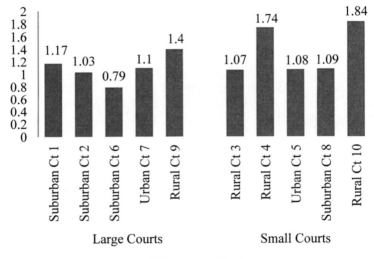

■ Score per client

The results of these scores suggest that Rural Ct 10, Rural Ct 4, Rural Ct 9, and Suburban Ct 1 were the top progressively oriented judges in that they had multiple progressive interactions with clients during the drug court session. However, these scores also demonstrate that virtually all the judges in this study used at least one progressive interaction per client. Thus, the judges relied heavily on positive reinforcement to motivate clients. This was supported by the judicial interviews in which the judges related their training in the drug court model and the emphasis on rewards in drug court (one judge in this study was recently elected to the position and took over the drug court and he was not, as yet, trained in the drug court model). While there were courts observed during the recruitment phase which demonstrated a much more traditional, compliance oriented perspective in their interaction with clients, those courts did not participate in this study.

Like the scores for progressive measures, a score was computed for the total traditional interactions for each court divided by the total number of clients. Figure 18 presents the score of the traditional measures for each court.

Figure 18: Judges score on Traditional Measures

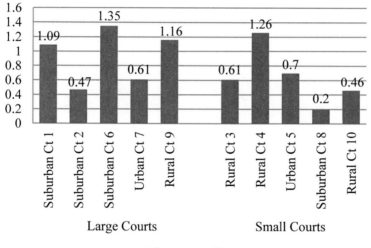

Looking at Figure 18, the results suggest that Suburban Ct 6, Rural Ct 4, Rural Ct 9 and Suburban Ct 1 score high on the traditional measures. Computing the scores this way indicates that it is possible to score highly on each measure, demonstrating that judges can act in both progressively and traditionally oriented ways. However, looking at individual courts cannot demonstrate how the courts would do once grouped in small and large court categories.

Thus, a collapsed mean percentages analysis was calculated for the traditional and progressive orientations for large and small courts in order to see if there were differences across courts within their respective categories. Figure 19 presents those mean percentages.

Figure 19: Score Comparison – Large vs. Small Courts

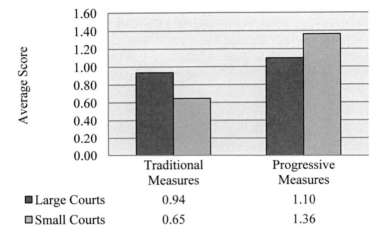

	Traditional Measures	Progressive Measures
■ Large Courts	0.94	1.10
□ Small Courts	0.65	1.36

The results displayed in Figure 19 demonstrate that once the courts are grouped into large and small categories and the percentages collapsed into a mean percentage for each category, clear differences between small and large courts appear in terms of the traditional and progressive measures. Large courts demonstrate that they score higher on traditional measures than small courts, and small courts score higher on progressive measures than large courts.

In the alternative, judicial orientation can be analyzed according to the judge's observed practices in regards to choice or addiction models. During the drug court session, the judge must implement rewards, sanctions, and procedures through the lens of his construction of addiction. Each tool created by the judge and his team is implemented in the drug court session depending on how he views the client in terms of the addiction. Is an addiction a choice or a disease? It is one of the most important constructions each drug court must come to grips with is the nature of addiction. Is drug addiction a disease or a choice? How each drug court answers this question plays a major role in how their drug court is constructed and how it operates.

Chapter 5

Social Construction of Addiction

Drug court incorporates the disease and choice models (Tiger, 2011, 2013). Drug court professionals share the belief that drug addiction is, in part, chosen by the individual and can be impacted by the rational practices of punishment and education.

ARE THE DISEASE AND CHOICE MODELS SOMEHOW INTER-RELATED AND BECOME SOMETHING ELSE?

That disease and choice model terms are used interchangeably and in concert argues for the hybrid notion. Are there any beliefs, terms, or practices that support the notion that drug use and abuse are neither wholly disease-related nor choice-related, thus giving additional credible evidence of a hybrid concept used in drug courts?

Drug courts team members. incorporate language into their daily practice that demonstrates a commitment to the choice model – clients are believed to make choices in relation to where they live, what they do, and how they spend their free time. Drug courts also employ practices related to a choice model for substance abuse through graduated sanctions and rewards to manage client behavior. Sanctions come in different forms, from essays to jail time while rewards for compliant behavior can include ovations from the team, gift cards, or journals for clients to write their thoughts in (Shannon Carey et al., 2008). In reality, drug courts prefer sanctions over rewards (Harrell, 1998; Shannon Carey et al., 2008). Should a client fail to follow the drug court team's recommendations, considered non-compliant with his or her treatment providers, or come up dirty on a drug test, punishment must come swiftly and harshly to satisfy the requirements of specific deterrence. Swift, certain and harsh punishment would also have an impact upon clients who witness the sanction by teaching them a lesson in regards to their own behavior to satisfy the concept of general deterrence (Harrell, 1998).

Another choice construction relates to the idea of people, places, and things. This concept, arising out of Alcoholics Anonymous, refers to the role people, places, and things have in a drug addict's relapse. Incorporated in this concept is the acceptance that addiction is related to habit, and changing addiction means changing habits that lead to use or abuse. Related to the concept of habit is the belief in individual responsibility for acts committed before and after drug use (Burns & Peyrot, 2003). While relapse is accepted as inevitable, the decision to engage in behaviors related to the habit of substance abuse is a rational decision, thus the use of sanctions for the acts committed before the actual use is perfectly appropriate (Meyer, 2007). In addition, any decision to lie about the substance abuse is also a rational decision (unless the client is actually high at the time of his or her court appearance). Sanctions, even jail time, for lying are also accepted as appropriate by drug court professionals. Finally, drug court professionals discuss educating the clients and providing them with tools for their toolbox. This is a belief related to resource capital, and the more resource capital a client has to avoid the people, places, and things that lead to relapse, the less likely relapse will occur (Granfield & Cloud, 1999). The longer you can delay relapse, the less likely relapse will occur (more clean time dictates recovery).

Drug court professionals are taught that drug addiction is a disease that can be treated and cured. Traditional courts care little about whether the defendant is "cured" through the court system, only that there is some measure of justice provided to a victim or society. However, in the case of drug court, the offender becomes the victim and rehabilitation is the focus of all the criminal justice professionals in the room (Burns & Peyrot, 2003). Within drug court, the language used to talk about addiction is very important and demonstrates a commitment to the disease model. In drug court, the defendants become clients, clients are assessed and treated, what is best for the client is discussed in case status meetings, and ideally if the client successfully graduates the client is considered to be in remission (always living with the disease, but never cured of the addiction).

Finally, like any terminal disease, relapse is inevitable and not the client's responsibility.

Drug courts also employ certain practices that demonstrate a commitment to a disease model of addiction. Drug addiction is identified through assessment instruments that assist in the diagnosis of those who are addicted and those who are not addicted. Admission of dependency is essential to the client's recovery. If the assessment indicates that the client is not addicted or the client fails to admit his or her disease, he or she is considered unsuitable for drug court and is excluded from the diversionary court (Burns & Peyrot, 2003). In addition, drug court professionals are committed to a course of treatment that will help cure those individuals who are addicted to controlled substances. Either Alcoholics Anonymous or Narcotics Anonymous, termed self-help by drug court professionals, is a critical part of the treatment process. Clients are discussed in case status meetings, where their case is thoroughly reviewed. The client's progress towards abstinence is addressed and treatment options are evaluated. Finally, it is the team that decides what, if anything, will keep the client from future relapses (Burns & Peyrot, 2003; Nolan, 2001).

Drug court professionals believe that something more than treatment and punishment will help an addict abstain from drug use and abuse. This belief is the essential reason why drug court looks and behaves so differently than any other institution related to the care of drug addicts does. The ideals of storytelling, drama, and consistent team encouragement are believed to provide a missing piece to the rehabilitative aspects of drug court and give the client a different kind of nudge than punishment alone does. The whole idea of storytelling is unique to drug courts (Nolan, 2001). Traditional courts do not typically encourage defendants to tell their side of the story. Moreover, judges are not encouraged to share personal stories or show compassion in traditional court. Storytelling is intended to show empathy and support for the client as well as to illustrate the many pitfalls that lie ahead for them. The narrative found in drug court provides guidance for the client to help him or her negotiate the trials and tribulations that come from abstinence (Nolan, 2001).

Another aspect related to the narrative and drama expected in drug courts is the role of the judge. The judge and his or her role in the drama is arguably the most important aspect of drug court (Bean, 2002;

Hanson, 2002; Marlowe et al., 2004). During drug court trainings, judges are encouraged to create their own style for their drug courts. No one model of how the judge is to act when handling clients is given, but all agree that the role of the judge and the coercive nature of the position as "judge" is the key to ensuring client compliance with treatment. How each judge coerces compliance is a matter left up to the judge and/or team members during their team building (through the trainings). The more compliant with treatment the client is and the longer the client is compliant, then the more likely the client will succeed in drug court and, ultimately, learn to abstain from drug use. The reliance on the judge to coax, scare, or encourage the client into compliance week after week and month after month is the central theme of the drama of every court appearance (Trainers, 2005).

Not quite punitive, drug courts accept the tremendous hold controlled substances have on some individuals who seem unable to live a life outside of the criminal justice system. They return again and again, harming themselves or others. Not quite treatment, drug courts accept the inevitable conclusion that some part of addiction is rational, a decision to use, regardless of the immediate consequences. The hybrid notion of addiction is supported by the treatment model for drug addiction employed in most of America. This treatment model consists of "advocating a 12-step philosophy, typically augmented with group psychotherapy, education lectures and films, AA meetings and relatively unspecified general alcoholism counseling" (W. R. Miller, Wilbourne, & Hettema, 2003, p. 41). It is this model that is most commonly found in drug courts. Then, after treatment is completed, the "once an addict, always an addict" philosophy demands continued participation in AA/NA meetings which also promotes the idea that recovered addicts completely abstain from any future substance use in order to avoid falling back into the drug addict's criminal/quasi criminal lifestyle.

Examining drug court practices implemented daily in America provides insights into how addiction is constructed by those professionals responsible for treatment interventions. Is addiction a disease or a choice? Or is addiction, as treatment professionals and criminal justice agencies intervene with substance abusing individuals, more of a hybrid notion incorporating aspects of both models in the daily practice?

DISEASE MODEL OF ADDICTION IN PRACTICE: REHABILITATION

Treatment, or the idea of rehabilitation for drug offenders, is not a new concept. It is adopted from Prohibition with its disease concept of addiction and the medical model with its focus on treatment (Levine, 1978, 1985; Mays & Ruddell, 2008; Reinarman & Levine, 1997; Valverde, 1998). The criminal justice system, as well as the treatment community, has struggled with the best way to stop substance abuse since prohibition was selected as the primary method for enforcing drug policy. Treatment is simple in concept - it consists of activities intended to assists individuals or families in changing their behavior (Maisto, Galizio, & Connors, 2004). Debate over the specifics of treatments is quite lively however. Typically, drug court judges rely on treatment providers to provide recommendations and services for drug court clients.

Official forms of treatment include in-patient and out-patient care. Substance abusers often have to go through a phase of detoxification before they can even start in a treatment program as the physical ramifications of abruptly ending substance use can be severe. Thus, detoxification includes medical assistance to wean the individual's body from the chemical substance safely (Day, 2007; Lyman, 2011). Once the body is rid of the chemical substance, treatment programs can assist the individual in altering the habit of drug abuse. Long-term or short-term residential treatment are in-patient programs aimed at removing the individual from the environment in which they are using controlled substances (Lyman, 2011; Maisto et al., 2004). These treatment programs can provide different treatment modalities such as the therapeutic community or cognitive behavior therapy, but the essential idea of these programs is to provide intensive supervision with therapeutic support to induce behavior change (Lyman, 2011). Once the individual successfully completes the intensive treatment found in a residential facility, out-patient treatment is available. Out-patient treatment programs can include intensive day treatment, group therapy, and educational programs (Lyman, 2011). These programs often last longer than residential treatment and can help the individual connect with other programs they need to move into a drug-free life.

Narcotics Anonymous, an organization which works with drug addicts to help them stop using drugs, is considered an established self-help program (Lyman, 2011; Maisto et al., 2004). Based upon the model of Alcoholics Anonymous, it is a 12-step program in which individuals work through a specified progression in their journey to become and remain drug-free (Day, 2007; Irvine, 1999). Narcotics Anonymous provides a kind of group therapy where former addicts meet and support each other in their efforts to stay clean (Maisto et al., 2004). After some clean time has passed, former addicts must find a "sponsor" who will be a buddy for that person in order to provide more support and help to the individual. Research has been mixed regarding the efficacy of Narcotics Anonymous and Alcoholics Anonymous (Kaskutas, 2009; W. R. Miller et al., 2003; Straussner & Byrne, 2009; Trice & Roman, 1970). Research into NA and AA has suffered from the same kinds of issues that plagues drug court itself. There is ample anecdotal evidence to suggest that NA and AA work, but rigorous scientific studies would be difficult to carry out. Critics argue that the research presents data showing that NA and AA have little or no impact on client outcomes (Kaskutas, 2009; W. R. Miller et al., 2003). Some recent research has suggested that NA and AA both have a positive impact on addicted clients, but it does not demonstrate clear efficacy (Kaskutas, 2009; Straussner & Byrne, 2009; Trice & Roman, 1970)

Out-patient and in-patient residential treatment and self-help are seamlessly integrated in drug court to treat, monitor, and prevent client relapse. These are the primary tools employed to move clients forward in their recovery from drug addiction, and sanctions as well as rewards are centered on these primary tools. When a client relapses while attending an out-patient program, judges will consider coerced in-patient treatment as a "next step" for that client, but they will often rely upon treatment providers to give their recommendation regarding the necessity and usefulness of in-patient treatment for that client's particular situation. The choice model of addiction, or the idea that addicts choose to engage in substance abuse, plays out differently in practice.

CHOICE MODEL OF ADDICTIONS IN PRACTICE: MEDICATION ASSISTED TREATMENT

Harm reduction is an alternative to abstinence in the drug treatment philosophy (Rothschild, 2010). Harm reduction, or the idea that the negative consequences of addiction can be mitigated while the addiction behavior continues, was implemented for heroin treatment but now includes the use of suboxone and the like for opiate addiction (Vocci, 2008; Witkiewitz, 2005). Heroin addiction is typically treated with methadone maintenance; the drug user is given a steady supply of a chemical similar to heroin which does not have the negative effects, thus allowing the addict to work and live a relatively productive life in the community (Karoll, 2010). Harm reduction accepts the possibility that the individual may remain dependent on the chemical substance for the rest of his or her life and is "maintained" on methadone in order to increase safety and reduce risks to the individual who is addicted (Jarvinen, 2008; Rothschild, 2010). Unlike the situation of most drug addicts, heroin users' continued drug use through methadone maintenance is tolerated through harm reduction strategies.

Harm reduction policies have only recently been encouraged in drug courts which have generally promoted an abstinence-only policy in the past (Vocci, 2008). A drug court can choose to incorporate or discontinue disease model practices and choice model practices during the planning stage, and also after it has been in existence for some time. An important aspect of drug court is its ability to be reflexive and responsive to the needs of its clients and to discard practices that don't work, unlike traditional court which is based upon precedent and legislative control.

MEDICATION-ASSISTED TREATMENT: IS ADDICTION A CHOICE OR A DISEASE?

Indeed, understanding judicial orientation in drug court can be viewed from the perspective of medication-assisted treatment or whether the judge constructs drug addiction as a choice or disease. In the alternative, do drug court judges see drug addiction as some kind of hybrid between the two? Leslie Paik (2011) argues that judgments on client non-compliance boil down to the social constructions created by members of the drug court team (Paik, 2011). Paik relies on the fact that many clients are found to be non-compliant for relatively low level, minor behaviors that are not criminal.

Drug courts' focus on proximal behaviors was also observed in this study. Indeed, what is proximal is the judge and team's assessment (construction) as to what will likely lead the client to relapse. Clients were sanctioned to jail for the act of swearing in court and arguing with staff. Clients were judicially admonished for chewing gum and dressing provocatively for treatment appointments. Finally, some clients were warned that certain relationships could get them removed from drug court and returned to the criminal court calendar. Clients who used drugs would be spared a jail sanction as long as they self-reported the use (they could, of course, lose their cumulative clean time). It was the clients who lied who received jail, which could also be imposed for clients who were not compliant with the treatment provider (failure to actively participate, missing appointments, and smoking on the property of an inpatient facility). Non-compliance could be whatever the staff want to believe is non-compliance (Paik, 2011).

One brewing controversy in the drug court model is whether or not to allow clients to enter into drug court and graduate while using prescribed drugs like methadone, suboxone, or pain killers. All the judges in this study expressed the understanding that drug addiction is a disease. However, if drug addiction is truly a disease, then drugs that help a person combat that disease would be acceptable. People are not jailed for the appropriate use of chemotherapy after they have been diagnosed for cancer. People are not arrested for the appropriate use of anti-anxiety pills or anti-depressants as long as there is a proper diagnosis and prescription.

All of the drug courts in this study had potential clients assessed for a dependency diagnosis. Only one court allowed clients into their program if they were charged with a drug-related criminal offense but did not have a dependency diagnosis, and those clients were referred to the judge's compliance court. This court was specifically for those defendants who did not have a dependency issue. Thus, the clients in the observed drug courts were diagnosed with the disease of drug addiction.

Conventional treatment wisdom is that former substance abusers must completely abstain from drugs from the point of recovery: "Once an addict, always an addict;" thus, a former addict must forever live a drug-free life. This view comes directly from the disease model of addiction. However, harm reduction policies exist within the drug court model in the form of medication-assisted treatment. Individual drug courts daily grapple with whether or not to allow clients to enter their drug court programs while continuing to use suboxone or methadone. If drug addiction is a disease, then it is a natural extension to use medication to help combat the illness. To the extent that is true, drug addicts are prosecuted in court for being sick. Some viewpoints, however, frame drug addiction as a choice; thus, drug addiction must be viewed as something more than a disease – some combination of disease and choice.

Where a judge falls regarding the use of medication-assisted treatment can offer an important clue as to whether a judge believes that drug addiction is a choice (rational choice and abstinence-only policies) with some component of a disease modality (gradual referral to higher levels of treatment care), or whether drug addiction is a disease (medication-assisted treatment and rehabilitation), which includes some element of choice (encouragement of reflection in order to gain insight into the disease model). If a judge believes that drug addiction is primarily a choice (with a disease component), then the client, ruled by rational choice decisions, will be swayed to abstain from substance use by swift, certain, and harsh punishments. The client will be constantly evaluating the costs of engaging in substance use and deciding one way or the other, depending on the likelihood of getting caught and sanctioned. If, however, the judge believes that drug addiction is a disease (with some component of choice), then the client is not struggling with costs and benefits of some action, but struggling with a sickness. The client fights sickness with an appropriate diagnosis and multilayered treatment. The client should stay away from people, places, and things because of the danger of relapse.

Judges in this study were mixed in terms of where they stood on the issue of medication-assisted treatment. Their responses reflected each end of the continuum: "I run a methadone-free court, and if people want to be in this court they have to be in a tight track off the methadone, I think people looked at soboxone as a possible solution but have since become very disillusioned by its problematic nature." Another judge opined as follows:

I've read and heard pros and cons about both. I've had good experiences with both. I've had bad experiences with both. So I'm not qualified to totally answer that. Suboxone, that's such a medical issue, of course, and I'm just sometimes surprised the treatment will have one philosophy about that with other medications, and yet doctors have another one. And I think that the treatment and doctors better get together and talk about that. But I've had cases where doctors prescribed suboxone and valium, and to no success by the way.

Finally, another judge observed:

We have never bought into the idea that methadone is exclusion to treatment court, never. We have accepted people, we have referred people we continue to refer people on methadone and suboxone with the understanding that they will try to get off and try to live a lifestyle without those kinds of supports. But we do use them as a treatment mode. So my opinion is on the side that some people need that, you can call it a crutch, you can call it a tool, you can call it a resource. Whatever you call it, I believe that's important. And we use it.

Based on the interviews, Suburban Ct 2, Rural Ct 3, Rural Ct 4, Urban Ct 5, and Suburban Ct 8 allow medication-assisted treatment in some form (i.e. suboxone but not methadone). The judge in Suburban Ct 6 agrees with medication-assisted treatment (but the policy of the drug court was unclear), and the judges in Suburban Ct 1, Rural Ct 9, and Rural Ct 10 do not allow medication-assisted treatment. This suggests that the judges in Suburban Ct 2, Rural Ct 3, Rural Ct 4, Urban Ct 5, Suburban Ct 8 fall on the side that drug addiction is a choice (with some disease component) and the judges in Suburban Ct 1, Rural Ct 9, and Rural Ct 10 believe that drug addiction is a disease (with some component of choice).

Table 9 presents the courts and where they fall in terms of their calendar and position on medication-assisted treatment.

An examination of the judges' scores from the last analysis in terms of a two-by-two analysis using court calendar and medication-assisted treatment for both progressive and traditional measures is found in Tables 10 and 11. Table 10 shows the mean score for judges on the progressive measures. As Table 10 demonstrates, being a judge from a small community/court calendar (regardless whether the judge allows medication-assisted treatment) means that the judge scores higher on the progressive measures of ethic of care and due process.

Table 9: Court Calendars and Medication-assisted treatment

			Medication-assisted treatment	
Courts	Small	Large	Yes	No
Suburban Ct 1		x		x
Suburban Ct 2		x	x	
Rural Ct 3	x		x	
Rural Ct 4	x		x	
Urban Ct 5	x		x	
Suburban Ct 6		x	x	
Urban Ct 7		x	x	
Suburban Ct 8	x		x	
Rural Ct 9		x		x
Rural Ct 10	x			x

Table 10: Mean scores on the progressive measures by small courts and medication-assisted treatment.

Average progressive scores		
	Medication-assisted treatment	
	Yes	No
Small town or Small calendar	1.25	1.84
	N=4	N=1
Large court or large court calendar	1.29	0.97
	N=3	N=2

The results in Table 11 indicate that if the judge presides over a large court and denies medication-assisted treatment, he scores much higher for the traditional measures of ethic of right and crime control.

The above analysis tends to support the proposition that small courts are better able to implement the therapeutic court model. In addition, a large court that does not allow medication-assisted treatment encourages a judge to employ a judicial orientation low on progressive oriented practices and high on traditional oriented practices. Moreover, there is evidence to suggest that a large court with a small court calendar can score high on progressive, reward oriented measures. This means that if larger court calendars were split up into smaller sections throughout the week the judge could implement more progressive interactions in the same manner as a court with a smaller calendar in a rural/mid-sized community can. Another layer of the social construction of addictions relates to the faith judges have in the efficacy of treatment and self-help.

Table 11: Mean scores on the Traditional measures by court size and medication-assisted treatment.

Average progressive scores		
	Medication-assisted treatment	
	Yes	No
Small town or Small calendar	0.69	0.46
	N=4	N=1
Large court or large court calendar	0.81	1.13
	N=3	N=2

DRUG COURT JUDGES AND TREATMENT

Weinberg (2000) used social constructionism to discuss the ecology of the addict's lifestyle in relation to homeless drug addicts – in treatment or "out there" (Weinberg, 2000). According to Weinberg, these homeless drug addicts construct recovery as getting "clean," while relapse is being "dirty" (Weinberg, 2000). Indeed, "out there" refers to the life of a drug addict on the streets, which is degrading, dirty, solitary, and savage and serves to tempt the individual back into drug addiction (Weinberg, 2000). Weinberg proposes that these constructions are in response to the treatment community which proposes that addiction is due to a "loss of control," and control can only come from long-term active involvement in a therapeutic community (Weinberg, 2000). Thus, drug addicts come to understand that their addiction comes from "out there" as being in treatment gives them the ability to control their drug addiction (Weinberg, 2002): "It is precisely the therapeutic community – the ecology of the program – that is held to possess medicinal force, simple logic dictates that whatever forces are held to possess the potential for rekindling addiction (and that, alone, warrant ongoing participation in the program) must be located, as it were, ecologically elsewhere" (Weinberg, 2000, p. 618).

Social construction of the drug addict as "out there" is well documented by Bourgois and Schonberg (2009) in their work *Righteous Dopefiend* which describes the complicated lives of the heroin and crack addicts living on the streets of San Francisco (Bourgois & Schonberg, 2009). Bourgois and Schonberg present compelling evidence that addicts are difficult to place into nice, neat definitions and an addict's life is full of contradictions (Bourgois & Schonberg, 2009). Those involved in drug addiction, like those in Bourgois and Schonberg's ethnographic study, often choose to maintain a life in which they drift between legal and illegal activities, home-based and homeless days, as well as safe and unsafe decisions even when methadone maintenance is readily available (Bourgois & Schonberg, 2009). More importantly though, the drug addicts living "out there" in San Francisco struggled to live the "American Dream," entering into marriage, having dinner parties, and socializing with each other through strong and weak ties. While they drifted between legal and illegal activities, their intention was to maintain control over their lives within their community and live a more "normal" life -- just like everyone else.

However, the conventional wisdom does not account for the fact that some addicts just stop abusing drugs. These spontaneous remitters completely abstain from drug use *without therapeutic intervention* while other drug addicts recover and casually use drugs. (Blomqvist, 2002). Glenn Walters (2000) suggests that when a flexible definition of remission is used rates of remission increase (Walters, 2000). For example, if a harm reduction definition is used to define remitters (e.g., substance abuse is reduced as well as negative consequences related to substance abuse), a mean rate increase of 26.2% for remitters is reported -- as compared to the rate of remitters if total abstinence is required in the definition of remission (Walters, 2000, p. 454).

This contradiction between those self-remitters who walk away from their drug addiction without therapeutic intervention and the disease model which promotes the idea that addiction can only be controlled through "ongoing participation in a therapeutic community" means that drug addiction is more complicated than most addiction professionals would care to admit (Weinberg, 2000). Judges in this study reflected this schism in their interviews.

The medical model is alive and well in drug court and drug court judges are defined by how well they implement the drug court model.

Assessment and treatment are required elements of drug court, and most drug courts are limited to the resources existing within their own community to provide that assessment and treatment. The assessment in drug court is intended to determine whether a client is a mere user (abuse diagnosis) or an addict (dependency diagnosis). This assessment was observed during this study of drug court. One court in this study, as previously mentioned, would send those with an abuse diagnosis to the compliance court while clients with a dependency diagnosis would be placed in drug court. Each judge in this study was observed to rely upon the drug court coordinator to inform him about the appropriateness of the defendant for referral to drug court, and to rely upon treatment providers to inform him on what specific course the client's treatment should take.

In this study, drug court judges relied upon 12-step programs like Narcotics Anonymous and Alcoholics Anonymous to supplement formal treatment programs regardless of any efficacy issues surrounding those programs. This is the model in which the National Drug Court Institute trained drug courts in and nine out of ten of the judges in this study were trained extensively in that model. During those trainings, field observation included drug courts that all used 12-step programs in their drug court. Thus, to find this model in existing drug courts is not unusual. Figure 24 presents the number of observation sessions in which judges emphasized treatment and rewards with the clients during the court session across ten observations. Treatment includes residential, out-patient, and self-help elements. Some courts emphasized self-help more than others, but treatment is the main focus of drug court. Figure 24 demonstrates that each of the judges tended to emphasize treatment during the drug court session even more than rewards. Figure 25 presents each judge's focus during their drug court team meetings. Figure 25 demonstrates how much treatment is emphasized in the team meeting as opposed to in the court appearance in front of clients, thus demonstrating the idea of the "show" that is discussed by judges and team members .as well as related in the drug court literature. Judges act and interact with clients in ways that are predetermined in the status appearances in order to influence client behavior. Asking about and supporting the tenets of treatment is very important to judges and reinforces the concepts the clients are learning in treatment. One judge put it this way when asked about discussing client lives:

Figure 24: Did the judge emphasize treatment and/or rewards?: Judicial Style in Court

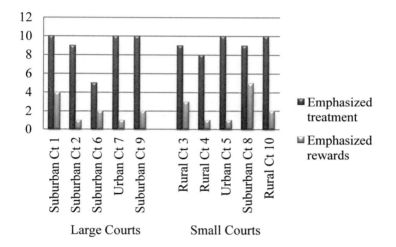

Figure 25: Did the judge emphasize treatment and/or rewards?: Team meeting

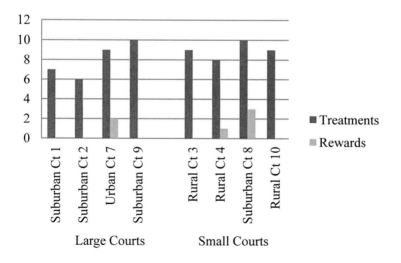

[I]t's very important to the building of relationships that they [clients] feel comfortable discussing things. They also feel the ability to bring things to the court's attention without being criticized for that or embarrassed by that or punished for that...but I think it's extremely important that I know everything about their case, that I know what's going on in their treatment, I know what's going on here and there so that if there is something that needs to be discussed... So I don't get surprised by it when they come up, but also if things are going really well and they don't have things to talk about or things to be praised for currently. It becomes important to let them know that I understand them a little bit, I know what's going on in their life, I know that their kid is going on a basketball tournament, or those type of things that just build that connection...again that family issue of they need to respect you enough to want to please you in what they do and therefore help themselves....

The judge also discussed treatment:

Absolutely, through a lot of training and a lot of classes with respect to treatment they were part of starting the drug court and then learning, and then I learned so much just from staffings and things and other courts may not do it as much as I do it but I think it's important I try not to pitch one type of recovery or one type of philosophy when it comes towards that, but I think being in charge of something like this for so long [I] begin to understand what works for the most part and what doesn't work. And my job I think is to give them the best chance at success so we don't push a particular theory, but I like to advocate if I see them in what I think is either heading in the wrong direction or not addressing what they need to address.

Indeed, each of the judges in this study discussed treatment and the possibility that clients could come clean without the assistance of treatment. Each of the judges in this study was well versed in the drug court model and revealed his opinions on treatment and recovery without treatment. While a few judges in this study believed it was possible to spontaneously remit from drug addiction, they believed it was a relatively rare occurrence. For example, a judge indicated that one way to recover without therapeutic intervention was through self-control, reiterating the treatment philosophy that drug addiction is a loss of control:

> [T]here are some people that can do that, I think that it is a rare commodity, considering temptation and normal human reaction, I look at it with some degree of skepticism, I think that that happens about as much as winning the Lotto.

Another judge put it this way:

> few and far between. I don't know stats, but I can only guess from my experiences that natural recovery is few and far between. It's just a very heavy burden for somebody to do it all by himself or herself. Could it be done? Sure. A spouse gives an ultimatum, okay? Whatever, you know, your children, they won't talk to you, 'If you're going to drink don't come around my grandchildren, Dad.' I mean that can be - it is so difficult.

Another judge was clear about his belief that drug abuse is about self-control:

> I think for those people they probably are not in a situation where they let it get so far out of their control that they have made it a drug court. There are probably individuals that are out there that are alcoholic that caught themselves at some point and just chose not to do that anymore. I hate to use choice because that implies something, but they just don't use anymore. They were never arrested DWI or put in jail. They hit rock bottom somewhere where -- you know. ..Yes, I think people can control addiction on their own. hose people are in our drug court. These people need the extra incentive. Are they doing it on their own? Absolutely, I am not out there making decisions for them. I am not out there absorbing it for them. Even if they graduate our program after us pounding on them for 3 years to do what they need, they did it on their

own. We just put them in what I believe to be a structure that
gives them the most likelihood of success. So they do it all.
We just have to enforce punishment.

Another judge presented the possibility of spontaneous remission this
way:

> God love them if they can, you know…I think probably the
> best avenue for some person to stop using is probably to be
> treated. You know, period. Other people you know swear that
> they can do this "by myself," "with my family." " I can do it
> through god's assistance." "I can go to Alcoholics
> Anonymous or NA and they will assist me." If they can do it,
> more power to them. I guess I don't discourage any of that. In
> our program obviously we are looking toward treatment.

That most of the judges suggested that treatment is a required
component of recovery is not surprising given the drug court trainings
these judges have had on the drug court model, which itself does not
allow for recovery without treatment, or at least not for those
individuals who are diagnosed with a dependency to drugs. Judges in
this study reflected that model; one judge put it thusly:

> Yes. But it depends on the level of the addiction. I know
> people that have. I know people that have corrected their
> lifestyle. They've stopped drinking or they stopped using
> drugs for a variety of reason. They got married. They had
> kids. You, too, probably know people that were probably
> heavy drinkers or drug users that have changed their life on
> their own without any intervention or without any treatment.
> But every person is different. I still believe that in some
> people – and some medical journals say that there's a
> predisposition toward addiction, that possibly we're all
> predisposed to be a different level of an addict. For instance,
> one person can drink and stop, and another person can drink
> and not be able to stop. We don't know which ones they are
> until we get them into the criminal justice system, and it's that
> revolving door that keeps on bringing them back because of
> their addiction. So yes, to your question – it is possible; but

that all depends on the level of the addiction and the type of personality the person has that has the addiction – whether they're able to correct that on their own without intervention or treatment.

A few judges discussed the treatment model in more detail. One judge used the treatment model despite mixed efficacy results for treatment in general (not just for AA/NA):

I mean and I think that is the best way to get somebody sober and stay sober. But the question it's kind of -- people who have you know have gotten to a point in their life, sunk down so deep you know they want to climb that ladder do and is it going to be easier for them later on to slip back down if they don't have treatment. Probably it will be a lot easier for them to slip back down and get into the depths of it again. Does treatment...guarantee that they are not going to? Obviously no. I mean the stats on treatments aren't very good you know. Eight out of ten or nine out of ten people will get back into it. I don't mean to you know knock treatment because I think it is the best way. You know we have professional people who can assist you through times.

Another judge was very supportive of AA:

Yes, we have a support group that meets Monday morning that's pretty strong. So that's been very helpful.

Many of the judges were trained in the neurological model found within the treatment literature and spoke about that in terms of addiction (Weinberg, 2002):

You've got to look at how insidious the disease is. The addiction is so powerful that - and I think that part of the problem is that people think that they can naturally recover if I put my mind to it. What they don't know is how much damage they have already done to their mind... It comes out a little more and more as the time goes on, because you start to realize that there an involuntariness here as to why there's subsequent use.

One judge said in this regard:

> I have to be honest with you… [considering] true addiction cycles, I don't know of anyone without some sort of outside intervention, and it could be treatment alone, it doesn't have to be a judge, I don't think it's an easy task to, to be on your own, I really don't…I would venture to say that ninety-nine percent or higher need some sort of intervention and, and again, I'm, I'm not saying it needs to be an organized problem solving court team, but it needs to be something. And the reason I say that now is when I first saw what happens in the brain to somebody…

Another judge elaborated on the physical changes that come from addiction:

> [i]t's a craving. It's a strong, strong craving to feel well…with insecurities and problems. People get hooked on Lortabs. Sometimes they'll take a Lortab or two for an injured back or leg. Then they find out that not only is it taking care of your lower back, they don't wake up so paranoid and scared about everything in life from not having money, from having a dysfunctional family. That is the nerve endings. You function better. You just function better because you're so scattered and nervous and insecure in this scary world we live in…The brain will ask for the drug immediately. Start taking four Excedrin every morning. You need those Excedrin after the third day, or you're going to have a bad headache if you don't take it.

One of the judges spoke of treatment in terms of whether the client has an abuse diagnosis (as opposed to a dependency diagnosis) and the neurological model:

> I guess anything is possible if it is an abuse diagnosis. I think that a person is more likely to be able to make some changes

in their lifestyles. To be successful I think in many instances again if it isn't an abuse diagnosis, time results in a maturity and growing up adjustment -- "I can't do this anymore" type of surrender and that is successful. If it's a full-blown addiction [dependency diagnosis], they cannot do it themselves as far as I'm concerned. They need the support, they need the direction, they need the tools and they need that clean time to help their brains rewire themselves and reestablish those synopses so that they can function somewhat normally, and that takes years. And without that they are always in danger of reusing and relapsing returning down that road.

One judge put it bluntly that if they are able to spontaneously remit then, they don't hit rock bottom by getting to criminal court:

I wouldn't say that it's impossible, but we don't see those because the people come in...this isn't a first legal involvement or the first repercussion of their youth. So, if there are people out there who do it, we're not seeing them because they wouldn't be here. That they would have done it already. My inclination from the people we deal with is only when they're tremendously forced to do it. You used to say when they hit bottom, but you don't hit bottom. You can be hitting bottom several months or years into the program, so...

A different judge was clear about the ongoing nature of addiction as he referred to successful completion of drug court not as a graduation, but rather as "A Day of Recognition:

[We]... also like to call it "A Day of Recognition." Recognizing where a person stands today in their recovery and their sobriety or stability in their life and at the same time, it affords us an opportunity to further emphasize that it does not end today, but it's a continuation in the things that they need to do in order to keep the disease of addiction in remission.

The observation data and judicial interviews show the extent to which judges rely upon treatment and treatment providers to work with clients. Most of the judges discussed the importance of treatment and the opinions of treatment providers in assisting clients to become abstinent from drugs. The opinions found among drug court judges in this study reflect the considerable disagreement in the research on treatment and the hybrid notion of drug court. Drug addiction is part choice and part disease. The judges in this study spoke about the necessity of treatment to overcome drug addiction, supported the notion of "once an addict, always an addict," and had full support for coercive methods to motivate clients to abstain from substance use of any kind. Virtually all the judges in this study believed that it was unlikely that addicts could recover on their own without the assistance of treatment professionals and continuing self-help.

The drug court judges in this study viewed drug addiction as some combination of a failure of self-control (choice), influenced by the social aspect of the drug lifestyle (people, places and things) which, if left unchecked over time, leads to a change in the chemical composition of the brain or body (disease or conditioning), thus supporting the notion that drug court uses a hybrid model of addiction. Moreover, these judges discussed constructions as to how to intervene in a drug court client's life, reflecting the treatment communities' dialog about the disease model which promotes that addiction can only be controlled by being in drug court. As Weinberg opined, abstinence comes with "ongoing participation in a therapeutic community" so as to not return to "out there" (Weinberg, 2000, 2002).

Of course, it is only through analyzing drug court outcomes in relation to progressive or traditional judicial orientations that we can pull all of this together and understand whether having a more progressive, reward-oriented drug court is a desirable policy.

Drug Court Outcomes

In terms of the drug court outcomes of graduation and retention rates., Figures 19 and 20 display graduation rates and one-year retention rates from August 2011 to August 2012. The courts with the highest graduation rates appear to come mainly, although not exclusively, from the smaller communities. One large court with a high graduation rate (Court Suburban Ct 2) has a judge who is closely tied to the community as is generally found in smaller, more rural communities.

Figure 20: Graduation Rates by Court

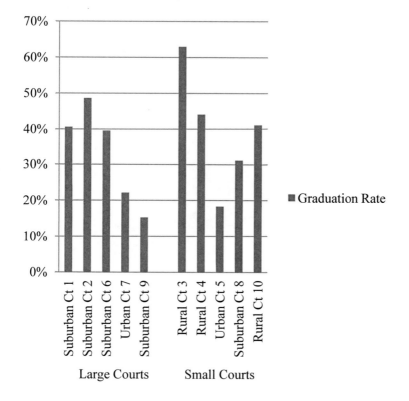

However, collapsing mean percentages of small and large courts (shown in Figure 21) demonstrates that clear differences can be observed in terms of graduation rates. Small courts produce higher graduation rates, which is the ultimate goal of drug court.

Finally, Figure 22 lists the courts in terms of the average number of clients on any one status date who have hit a one-year retention rate (this is how New York State categorizes retention rate. in its drug courts). It should be noted that all of the courts in this study have a high retention rate, attesting to each court's ability to keep clients in its drug court and maximizing the opportunity to graduate clients from drug court.

Figure 21: Graduation Rates – Large versus Small Courts

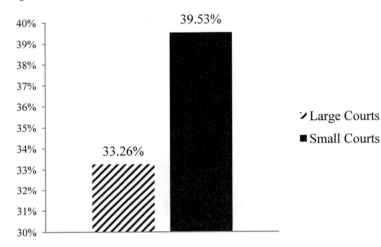

Figure 22: Retention Rates by Court.

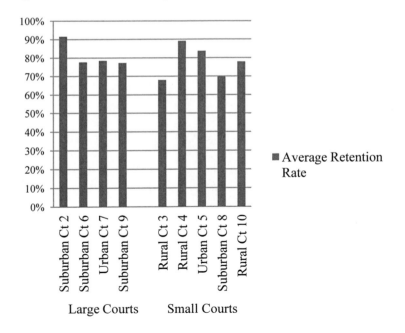

Figure 23 portrays the drug courts in this study in terms of small and large courts, and retention rates .in terms of their collapsed mean percentages in order to determine if any differences could be documented between those two categories. This analysis provides insight into whether there is any difference between small and large courts.

Figure 23 Average Retention Rates – Large versus Small Courts

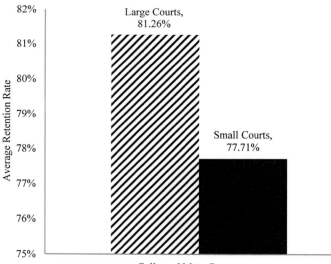

Collapsed Mean Percentages

Here, contrary to other evidence presented herein, it seems as if the larger courts have a slight advantage in terms of one-year retention rates.. Further analysis would be needed to understand why large courts have a better retention rate. However, the data presented in Figure 20 suggests that, notwithstanding their advantage in retention rates, large courts tend to lose more of their clients before they can successfully graduate.

As this analysis demonstrates, all the courts in this study seem to be doing relatively well in terms of client outcomes. Whether judges act as more progressive or traditional in their approach to drug court may depend on the size of the community from which they come, the size of their calendar, their ability or capacity to alter the look and feel of the court in which they preside, the nature, extent and quantity of rewards, sanctions, and unique procedures they use, and, finally, how the judge constructs his or her role in drug court and how the judge constructs the very clients who come before the court.

The results of this study suggest that a progressive orientation has a beneficial impact on graduation rates. Equally important is the suggestion that small courts (and/or courts with small calendars in large urban communities) produce better graduation rates, but the question remains whether this is because of the court's greater capacity to spend more time on individual clients or because those small calendars promote a more progressive orientation by allowing judges to create a stronger relationship with individual clients. Small court efficacy is supported by some of the drug court literature as well. Given these results, further analysis is needed to explore the link between small and large drug courts and a judge's construction of self in order to better understand the respective role of each of these factors in client outcomes.

Chapter 6

Critical Issues and Concluding Thoughts

While drug courts struggle to create a sense of organizational presence, drug court continues to evolve with every new revelation, from its earliest beginnings to the more solidified, contemporary version that will shape future drug courts. In the meantime, an in-depth analysis of drug court's black box is critical to having a more complete understanding of drug courts and their impact on today's system of justice. Through this deeper understanding of the black box, trainings can be developed for judges to help them understand their role in drug court from this more sociological perspective, as well as the benefits of a more progressive orientation. This awareness should encourage policy makers to begin to limit drug court judges' court calendars to more manageable numbers to increase the possibility of creating a relationship link between judge and client, thus increasing the potential for successful therapeutic intervention. Drug court professionals should also keep in mind the dangers inherent to drug court.

CRITICAL ISSUES IN DRUG COURT .– CONFLICTS OF INTEREST AND CONFLICTS OF VALUE

When consensus regarding the laws that govern does not exist and the "rightness" of the rules of society are questioned, there is dissention, use of power to control and coercion overpowers collaboration. It is in the world of conflict and coercion that we find the insights of Karl Marx and Michel Foucault most helpful. Like Durkheim, Vilhelm Aubert was a major theorist who reflected upon the evolution of law.

Aubert categorized conflicts into two specific categories according to the role they fulfilled in society: conflicts of interest, and conflicts of value. Conflicts of interest are based on disputes arising over commercial interests and can be resolved through bargaining or mediation, while conflicts of value are disputes based upon ideas or principles which must be resolved through the use of authority and/or coercion (Friedman, 1983). Thus, if a society does not have a consensus over core values and beliefs as Durkheim suggested, then conflicts of value are inevitable.

As human societies became larger in scope and more complex, formal law and coercion became more prevalent (Friedman, 1983). American society, over time, has experienced more conflicts of value in its legal system through the prohibition of morality crimes, including prostitution, gambling, and the use of drugs and alcohol. Termed "victimless crimes," these are behaviors that do not result in direct harm to another individual but the behavior may result in harm to the actor or someone else from related acts. Morality crimes, in essence, are disputes over values (e.g., is a particular behavior – gambling, paying for sex, drinking alcohol, taking drugs – deemed to be counter to the right way to act according to God).

Consensus on particular penal code statutes are relatively easy to draft and codify for crimes when an identifiable victim results from the proscribed behavior, in contrast victimless crimes can be difficult to codify and enforce. In codifying laws to address conflicts of value, a series of questions must be answered. Who wins? What are the consequences of losing? How are the laws enforced and against whom are the laws enforced? Who and what purpose do the laws serve? Finally, if and when prohibition of a particular behavior is decided upon, how will society deal with individual members who attempt to circumvent the law? When conflicts of value exist, they often benefit from a Marxian analysis.

Conflicts of values fall within the realm of Karl Marx. Essentially, Karl Marx focused on the evolution of society (synthesis) through the clash of thesis and antithesis (Deflem, 2008). Marx proposed that history can be conceived of as a series of struggles between social classes (based upon the modes of production) that culminates in the evolution of society from feudalism to capitalism to communism. Each stage changes the social classes, their modes of production, and the corresponding political and legal systems. Marx (1848) proposed that the communist state was the ultimate evolutionary stage of man and that evolution was based on man's material circumstances (Collins, 1982; Marx & Engels, 1992). To Marx, class consciousness was the key to the next evolutionary stage. Marx saw the rise of working class solidarity (i.e., trade unions) as the beginning of class consciousness and, ultimately, the revolution which would move society toward communism (Collins, 1982). Along the way, the evolution of law would be the mechanism that those in power used to legitimatize and maintain their power through all facets of civil and criminal law (Deflem, 2008).

Marx's crude materialism of law (law is a "reflection of the economic base") was a simple approach with no analysis of the need for law or the relationship between the law and the social system within which it existed (Collins 1982). The problem with this theory of law is in determining which came first, the chicken (the oppressive laws) or the egg (the ruling class consciously enacting laws that oppressed). The consensus view of class consciousness (class instrumentalist theory) proposes that the ruling class as a whole knows what is in its best interests and enacts laws to promote its best interests (the egg), and thus the subordinate class is oppressed. Marxism seeks a theory of legal development that explains how the laws develop over time: "Ordinary social practices and experiences are the breeding-ground for ideologies, which in turn determine the content of the laws" (Hay, 1975, p. 41). These social practices are created and related to the modes of production for that society's developmental stage (Hay, 1975). Marxism accounts for the evolution of law through changes in the mode of production. The evolution of Marxism would embrace the loosening of the philosophical framework regarding the relative autonomy of the law (Spitzer, 1983). Laws evolve from functional to dysfunctional as the revolution moves society from one stage to another. Law becomes a part of the basis of society through the modes of production, a "bottom up" process, and the law serves societal interests.

Marx, however, did not write extensively on law, the role of law, or his theory of law. Marxism and the creation of a theory of law ends with the problem of "legal fetishism," which involves certain assumptions: 1) legal order is necessary; 2) law is a unique phenomenon in and of itself, requiring its own focus of study; and, 3) the rule of law, that law is known and knowable. Marxists have rejected these principles and are thus disinclined to develop a general theory of law (Deflem, 2008).

The historical progression of the English vagrancy laws supports the idea that the ruling class can co-opt remnants from a prior societal stage, arguably that dysfunctional time period between stages, and use these remnants to further its own interests. Vagrancy laws, a remnant from feudalism, were transformed as laws attempting to control individuals who were not gainfully employed (and who might have enough free time to steal or cause trouble). These laws first utilized relatively minor punishments to control individuals and culminated in felony convictions and death for multiple convictions. In this light, the laws appear to be the first "Three Strikes Laws." The evolution of vagrancy laws coincided with the need for cheap labor, the industrial revolution, and a reduction in the labor force due to famine, poverty, and war. Thus, enforcing work through the criminal law upheld the interests of the ruling class (Chambliss, 1964).

Conflict and fear have been at the very heart of drug prohibition. Throughout history, every prohibited drug has gone through a public relations phase of demonization where it is portrayed as the root of all evil to scare the general public. Marijuana allegedly caused "madness and horror" (Inciardi, 2008, p. 31). Opium use led to prostitution, gambling, and moral decline (Levinthal, 2006). Cocaine was the cause of criminal activity and prostitution in the South (Provine, 2007). It is this conflict and fear that have moved American drug policy ever onward.

Some have argued that drug prohibition provides a dialog in addition to the idea that the policy keeps society safe from the evils of drugs; that is the dialog of institutional racism (Provine, 2007). Provine (2007) argues that drug laws were enacted in response to racism and have endured because they serve a racist agenda. Provine points to the history of drug legislation enacted through the demonization of the drug as it was linked to a specific minority. Those drugs co-opted for demonization often connected to the ethnic group mainstream Americans feared. Marijuana legislation, for example, was enacted after marijuana use was linked to Mexican immigrants (Provine, 2007). Crack cocaine, arguably cheaper and more potent than powder cocaine, was more harshly penalized in the law than powder, thereby disproportionately affecting poor African American communities (Walker, 2011). Thus, drugs framed as evil are prohibited and this policy reflected back on a particular ethnic group. Moreover, drug legislation offered society a way to control those they perceived as the "dangerous classes" among them.

After analyzing Marx on law, some questions remain: Does the law preserve the current state of affairs between the ruling class and the subordinate class in order to serve the social order? Does the law serve the interests of the ruling class in order to label some people criminal so as to keep those individuals in a subordinate position to perform some of the worst roles in society (i.e., as prostitutes and drug addicts)? In other words, the ruling class must have people to exploit, thus, the law serves to force individuals to remain in the position to be exploited systematically. Aubert, Marx, and conflicts of value are directly related to the social movements that led to the regulation of chemical substances.

Historically, different societies have used chemical substances for celebrations, rituals, coping, and pain relief. In the United States, alcohol has always been a popular choice for coping and common products sold for medicinal purposes during the 1700's and 1800's contained chemical substances (Inciardi 2008). Drug use and abuse has played an integral role in society since before recorded time (Inciardi 2008). In fact, it would be difficult to find a person who has not used drugs at some time to relieve pain, recover from an illness, or relax after a bad day. However, U.S. society chooses to label drugs with the concepts "good" and "bad" and drug use as either "healthy" or "sick." A glass of wine drunk with your meal, Vicodin pills taken after surgery, or morphine prescribed for back pain are all considered healthy applications of drugs, while, the use of marijuana, cocaine, and methamphetamine, regardless of the reason is viewed as an unhealthy use of illicit drugs. However, there is significant disagreement on decriminalization and/or legalization of drugs across the United States. To date, twenty-three states and Washington D.C. allow for the medical use of marijuana while the federal government remains staunchly on the side of prohibition of this type of use of cannabis (ProCon.org, 2012). While there is little or no discussion about legalizing other forms of drugs, the use of medication-assisted treatment is also an area where professionals disagree. It is clear that the government remains prohibition-minded, but the daily use and misuse of drugs across the nation is a reminder that there is little or no consensus on the issues of drug use.

Drugs, in fact, are inanimate objects that have no inherent "badness" or "goodness" in any absolute sense; they are created by man and are merely tools to be used one way or another. Thus, the way society controls drugs is a choice and the perception society has of drugs is a social construct (Conrad and Schneider 1992; Jenness 2004). Like Marx, Michel Foucault focused on the exercise of power in society but at a different level. While Foucault did not discuss drug use or drug prohibition directly, he detailed the medicalization of mental illness in terms of power (Foucault 1984a). This understanding of power, as well as the creation of a profession, can be applied to drug prohibition and drug court.

Foucault (1984) describes the process of scientism, or the application of medical methods, rules, and procedures to the mentally ill, a process which resulted in the creation of the asylum for the mentally ill (Foucault, 1984; Turkel, 1990). Foucault proposed that in order to achieve that end a transformation of the ways in which the mentally ill were discussed, labeled, examined, and finally treated had occurred (Foucault 1984a). This method of discussing, labeling, examining and treating the mentally ill, from a Foucauldian perspective, is more properly termed as a "discourse" involving the exercise of power (Allan, 2006). Foucault theorized that knowledge about the mentally ill was changed forever as knowledge was transformed into new technologies and understandings about the human condition developments, which in turn affected health care practices and legal regulations in society itself (Allan 2006; Foucault 1994).

In addition, Foucault wrote about the gaze of science which he proposed was the transformation of society during the Enlightenment era (Allan 2006). It is through scientism, or the application of a scientist's methods, rules, and procedures, that man is objectified and controlled through discipline. Gaze includes the idea of the Panopticon, (most often understood in the form of a prison where a single guard is able to observe the entire prison from a central location), or the "all seeing" eye that comes from scientism and the use of power which allows society to discipline man, not through punishment but through surveillance (Allan 2006; Foucault 1984b.)

Finally, discourse for Foucault plays a fundamental role in society as it had such a powerful impact on how society worked (Foucault 1984c). Discourse is more than the "rules and practices" beneath the words and concepts of a particular area of society. Discourse creates the world in which people, within that sphere of knowledge, function and negotiate (Allan, 2006). There are the practices of inclusion and exclusion for an area of society (Turkel, 1990). Moreover, the discourse is self-legitimizing; the more the discourse is insinuated into the society, the more the society conforms itself to the discourse through regulations and social institutions, and the more firmly rooted the discourse becomes within a society (Turkel, 1990). Where a person exists within the discourse is pre-defined (i.e. the role a person plays in the world within that sphere of knowledge) (Allan, 2006). The place a person occupies within the discourse determines how he or she will think, talk, act, and feel within that world (Allan, 2006). Within the discourse is the power in naming, the naming of yourself, and the naming of others (Felstiner et al., 1980).

Marx and Foucault shared a similar understanding that social construction penetrates deeply within the individual, shaping ideas and conforming conduct. Moreover, the use of power and coercion creates the individual, social groups, and social phenomenon from both the inside out and the outside in to completely transform the human condition. The necessity of power rises in need and ferocity as consensus among community members declines. Applied to the world of the drug court, power and coercion are part of its existence and drug court could not function without them.

Foucault describes five methodological propositions for analyzing and understanding power. (Foucault 1980). The first of these propositions encourages viewing power at its most extreme end, as it is there that you will find the exercise of power to be the least legitimate: "One should try to locate power at the extreme points of its exercise, where it is always less legal in character" (Foucault, 1980: 96). Thus, the practice of torture is harder to justify the more gruesome the acts become.

Drug court, one of the practices employed within the world of "abstinence only" treatment, has its own extreme points where legitimacy is more fully based upon the goal of abstinence than upon jurisdictional authority. Therapeutic jurisprudence is the idea that abstinence from drug use and abuse would be ensured if compliance with treatment were backed by the authority of judicial oversight. Ultimately this is the marriage of the criminal justice concepts of rehabilitation with deterrence (swift, certain and harsh punishment).

Clients, identified through a violation of some criminal or civil penal code, are required to sign a contract whereby they give up certain constitutional rights in exchange for some break on their sentence. Within this contract, the client agrees to abide by any sanction the treatment team decides to impose should there be any non-compliance with drug court rules. For example, relapse does not automatically lead to a short jail sentence; however, denying a relapse can result in a week in jail.

Moreover, a jail sentence sanction in drug court is immediate, often without any legal representation or appeal as drug court is a diversionary court outside of the regular court system. Jail is employed by all of the therapeutic jurisprudence courts and is referred to as judicial coercion, a key feature in all problem-solving courts (Miller & Johnson 2009; Satel 1999). Jail can be used as a sanction for any non-compliance; that can range from failure to achieve a GED to moving in with a drug-using roommate. Non-compliance can be anything that the treatment team agrees would be harmful to the client and lead that client to drug use, thus violating the "abstinence only" concept.

Foucault's second proposition refers to how power is exercised:

"[I]t is a case of studying power at the point where its intention, if it has one, is completely invested in its real and effective practices" (Foucault, 1980: 97).

The practice of abstinence was not a policy that began in Congress or within the Office of the President. It was not created by some sovereign entity and imposed from above, rather abstinence was formulated within the temperance movement in the 1700's and 1800's and was co-opted by religious organizations (McGrew n.d.). While abstinence was not the initial concept proposed to fight the evils of alcohol, it was the concept that the temperance movement settled on and this concept ultimately found its fullest expression in alcohol prohibition through the Volstead Act of 1919 (McGrew n.d.). The temperance movement, in all its entities, exercised power through its imposition of abstinence.

While the Volstead Act was repealed within a few years of its enactment, abstinence continued as the preferred method for recovery from alcohol addiction and, later, drug addiction. Abstinence is entrenched in the language of treatment and is a goal for any person who abused a controlled substance. "Abstinence only" is found in Alcoholics Anonymous and Narcotics Anonymous principles, while "harm reduction," a different treatment policy, is rarely if ever discussed or utilized in treatment programs. Drug court is one practice used to pursue the goal of abstinence and was created long after abstinence was introduced and accepted as an exercise of power. It is within the discourse of abstinence that drug court has found a home.

The third proposition of power refers to domination: "Power is employed and exercised through a net-like organization. And not only do individuals circulate between its threads; they are always in the position of simultaneously undergoing and exercising this power" (Foucault 1980: 98). For Foucault, power is so infused within the society, like perfume that permeates the air after it is sprayed, that our very behavior is produced by it. As the discourse of sexual desire and shame defines much of our experience with sex ("abstinence only" is also applied to sexual desire), ingesting alcohol and drugs is considered evil and must be avoided. Excessive drinking is looked upon as unseemly or dangerous, depending on who is doing the drinking (McGrew n.d.). Thus, power socially constructs the behavior so as to control people in subtle and overt ways alike.

The fourth proposition of power defines the analysis of power related to a social phenomenon: "One must conduct an ascending analysis of power, starting, that is, from its infinitesimal mechanisms, which each have their own history, their own trajectory, their own techniques and tactics, and then see how these mechanisms of power have been – and continue to be – invested, colonized, utilized, involuted, transformed, displaced, extended, etched, by ever more general mechanisms and by forms of global domination" (Foucault, 1980: 99).

In order to analyze "abstinence only" (as it relates to alcohol and drug use) and the practices that support it, from its humble beginnings within the temperance movement to the here-and-now, is a vast undertaking. Initially, different societies used chemical substances for celebrations, rituals, coping with stress, and pain relief (Inciardi 2008:2). At the dawn of time, drugs were co-opted into society to be an asset used by medicine men and women to treat tribal members and provide insight into the natural world. Current policies for drug prohibition and the concept of abstinence both have roots in the temperance movement of the mid-1800s. For the temperance movement, alcohol was an evil substance that must be fought and for this battle total abstinence was required. The temperance movement culminated in the Volstead Act of 1919 which prohibited the manufacture and sale of alcohol in the United States (McGrew n.d.). While "[t]emperance was not always equated with teetotalism…[t]here developed in the mid-19th century, however, the conviction that all brews, be they 'ardent spirits,' beer, ale, or wine, were anathema" (McGrew n.d.). As the "abstinence only" discourse developed, practices supporting it became entrenched within local communities (i.e., in organizations like AA and NA).

Finally, Foucault proposed that power culminates in an entrenched system that is self-serving: "We need to see how these mechanisms of power, at a given moment, in a precise conjuncture, and by means of a certain number of transformations, have begun to become economically advantageous and politically useful" (Foucault, 1980: 101)." In this regard, it is possible to see parallels between the medicalization of the mentally ill and the medicalization of the alcohol and drug addicted. Professionals who deal with the mentally ill must have a certain education, must discuss the patient in terms of the DSM-IV (Diagnostic and Statistical Manual of Mental Disorders), and must have only so many treatment options. Additionally, the world of the mentally ill is framed within a pre-determined language and way of practicing psychiatry. Even the way laymen discuss the mentally ill is regulated by this language. People who are mentally ill suffer from a disease that can only be cured by a doctor of psychiatry (whether a medical doctor, psychiatrist, or a person with a doctoral degree in psychology). Thus, professionals have taken exclusive control over the area of mental illness and the language used to discuss it.

Once a behavior is medicalized, the discourse changes from a discussion of choices to the application of medical science (procedures, examinations, and treatments) to the behavior. Applying medical science to drug use changes the lens through which drug use and abuse is viewed, the language used to discuss drug addiction, and the selection of individuals who are judged competent to work with those labeled addicts. In addition, applying the medical world to drug addiction and naming it a "disease" implies that the individual who uses and abuses drugs is not entirely responsible for his or her behavior and that, somehow, he or she can be cured with proper treatment.

The creation of drug court, within the auspices of therapeutic jurisprudence, is the extension of treating the disease of addiction through a political body. Everyone who works within these select communities gains more money, resources, and power. Drug treatment is ordered through the court to a select group of providers and coerced through weekly compliance appearances. In drug court, monitoring and surveillance comes in different forms and is virtually "all seeing." Drug court professionals collect and maintain quite a bit of information related to the client, all in the name of effective treatment. Information is obtained through criminal records, social service professionals, probation, informants, assessment interviews, medical records, and urinalysis and other forms of drug testing. Moreover, the information collected through these various forms of surveillance is discussed during case conferences and there is a determination about whether the client is in compliance or non-compliance. Ultimately, whether the client is sanctioned or rewarded is based upon this surveillance, and discipline is thus achieved through this control over the client. The client, before even entering drug court, must sign a release for information that allows drug court, as a team, to obtain information from medical and mental health professionals. These releases have no restrictions on the information that can be obtained on the client and cannot be revoked if the client wishes to remain in drug court (Tiger, 2013).

The "abstinence only" discourse is now a fundamental part of society. A discourse is more than merely the words and concepts, it is the world within which individuals function. The abstinence discourse defines inclusion and exclusion for members involved within the discourse. Moreover, the more the discourse is insinuated into the society, the more society conforms itself to the discourse through regulations and social institutions and the more firmly rooted the discourse becomes within the broader society. More than a place of discourse, though, drug courts are a place of substantial power. Drug court team members .collect a considerable amount of information on the client during the course of drug court. This includes information that is criminally related or socially related, whatever might have an impact on the client's ability to remain drug-free. There is no part of the client's life that is not subject to discussion if there is any possible connection between the information and relapse potential. It is this delving into the client's life where power is exercised to the greatest extent. There is no part of the client's life that is beyond the treatment team's gaze. The initial assessment exam, as well as any later medical and toxicology exams, all increase the treatment team's ability to categorize and control a client's life. This level of control is simply not present in traditional courts where attorneys are more fully empowered to protect the interests of their clients.

As the medical discourse is fully imported into the criminal and civil court systems through therapeutic justice, the traditional adversarial process is transformed. Drug courts have changed the perception of justice in some major respects. In drug courts, the defendant is transformed into the client, due process is set aside for rehabilitation, and judges are the enforcers of treatment. This is a natural extension of the medicalization of drug addiction, but the judge is given the authority to punish clients for failure to succeed, a result of drug treatment teams having a vested interest in the client's success or failure and a courtroom having the concept of therapy (therapeutic justice). This transformation changes the courtroom process from adversarial to cooperative, and fact finding to a process for punishment in the pursuit of coercing social control. The entire language of the process has changed as well as the world in which drug offenses and drug users are handled. Drug courts thus provide a form of repression with a therapeutic face.

Once the abstinence discourse was co-opted by the medical and psychiatric community and finally by the government through the drug court, great amounts of money, resources, and power became invested in a select group of individuals. Drug abstinence was the official face of drug court success until 2008 when the National Institute on Drug Abuse presented a webinar on medication-assisted treatment for opiate addiction, arguing that drug-addicted clients had better outcomes when permitted to use suboxone, naltrexone, or methadone while in treatment (Vocci, 2008).

The 2008 webinar was the beginning of the answer to a long brewing controversy in drug courts – namely, can clients in drug court use prescribed drugs (suboxone, naltrexone, or methadone) while in drug court or graduate from drug court when the goal is abstinence? For some judges, medication-assisted treatment was a bitter pill to swallow. The issue culminated in the 2010 National Association of Drug Court Professionals annual conference, held in Boston, where experts from both sides provided arguments for and against medication-assisted drug rehabilitation treatment. It was rather clear that the National Association of Drug Court Professionals promoted the use of medication-assisted treatment under certain circumstances, and it was up to the individual drug courts to make their own determination whether to allow the use of medication in drug court. This has changed the players and the boundaries of discourse involved in drug court.

In the case of drug courts, methodological practices provide a fuller picture of power, as it relates to alcohol and drug use, and the practices of drug court where power is invested. It is within the policy and procedures employed by drug court teams that has considerable impact on individual drug court clients. Drug court teams, for example, whose members determine that medication-assisted treatment is an unacceptable policy in their mental health court, can demand that clients stop using their prescribed medication for anxiety. Drug court team members. will then find that clients taking their prescribed medications are in non-compliance with drug court and drug court judges will sanction those clients. There are a multitude of other policy decisions that can have similar impacts on drug court clients. Drug court teams meet regularly and cooperatively decide the fate of individual drug court clients for any given week. Drug court teams with team members. who fail to put aside their individual agendas or who have unresolved conflicts may have struggles that can affect the productiveness of team meetings, the quality of treatment provided to drug court clients, and, ultimately, the ability of individual drug courts to help promote the drug addict's rehabilitation.

Proponents of drug courts see therapeutic jurisprudence courts as one of the best ways to address drug addiction. Supporters of the drug court model see the marriage of rehabilitation and punishment as a way to reintegrate drug court clients back into the conventional world (McColl, 1996). Some even see the move from an adversarial system of justice towards a more benevolent court focused on the defendant's needs as a progressive and positive step forward in our current system of laws (Tiger, 2011; Wexler, 1999a, 1999b). Reform and rehabilitation is the goal drug court professionals all struggle to provide, in their own way (Tiger, 2013; Wexler, 2005, 2008).

However, a number of critics of the drug court movement have come forth. Morris B. Hoffman, District Judge in Denver, Co, has been a strong critic of drug courts. Comparing drug treatment courts to early juvenile justice courts, Judge Hoffman proposes that in drug treatment court judges become the most dangerous branch of government, as they:

1) function like therapists with the power of judges;
2) act as a member of a team that includes stakeholders, attorneys, and treatment providers;
3) interfere with other criminal justice members; and,
4) make drug policy unilaterally (Hoffman, 2002b, p. 2072).

Judge Hoffman also believes that drug courts have a net-widening effect in that the mere existence of drug court increases the number of drug cases that are pulled into the system in as much as there is a system of treatment within the court itself. Thus, those cases more likely to be kept out of the criminal justice system are brought into the fold so that the defendant can benefit from the benevolence of the court system (Hoffman, 2002a). In addition, Judge Hoffman criticizes drug court itself, holding that its evaluations are incomplete and improperly conducted, drug court does nothing to reduce drug-related criminal recidivism, and drug court is not less expensive than regular court processing (Hoffman, 2000).

There have been others who have been critical of drug court evaluations to date (David DeMatteo et al., 2011; Sevigny, Fuleihan, & Ferdik, 2013; Smith, 2014). The most consistent criticism of drug court evaluation studies is their failure to use random selection in their research methodology, their failure to use an appropriate control group to compare successful drug court defendants, and their failure to evaluate long-term recidivist measures in their study design (Anderson, 2001; David DeMatteo et al., 2011; Hoffman, 2000; Slobogin, 1995). Without sound methodology in drug court evaluations, it is impossible to truly evaluate the effectiveness of drug courts or the reduction of costs that drug offenders placed in drug court have on the criminal justice system.

Additional criticisms revolve around due process violations (Brank & Haby, 2013; Smith, 2014). For example, Sevigny, Fuleihan and Ferdik (2013) found that, on average, drug court does not reduce the amount of time that clients spend incarcerated as any benefit to a reduction in the incarceration rate is lessened by the increase to the length of time clients are sentenced to who fail are sentenced. DeMatteo, Filone and LaDuke (2011) argued that graduated sanctions can lead to due process violations if sanctions lead to a reduction in judicial/client interactions intended to be a positive intervention (David DeMatteo et al., 2011). This criticism of drug courts based upon due process violations also occurred within the historical development of juvenile justice courts (Hoffman, 2002b; Popovic, 2000). This phenomenon is also part of Foucault's analysis of power. Judges in drug court are given tremendous power to control people's lives with few, if any, checks or balances, all in the name of helping the drug addict, but the risks of judges abusing that power is quite high.

In therapeutic jurisprudence courts, traditional courts are transformed into a different world where constitutional protections and the law are nonexistent (Tiger, 2013). Drug court, like juvenile court, has evolved out of some perceived need within society and has incorporated both traditional and non-traditional court processes in order to fulfill a rehabilitative role... Drug courts have evolved along a similar trajectory as characterized juvenile courts. Until recently, drug courts were left to their own devices in terms of balancing their rehabilitative role against protecting clients from arbitrary and capricious decisions. It wasn't until the 2010 NADCP conference in Boston that there was a real focus on defense attorney issues and legal challenges to drug court practices. The conference encouraged drug courts to institute greater due process protections. In addition, the NADCP has begun to promote best practices in order to standardize drug courts to some extent as well as to address criticism that has been leveled against the drug court movement.

Each of the drug courts in this study have incorporated best practices to differing degrees, mirroring the eclectic and evolving nature of drug courts in general. Drug court judges and teams incorporate the elements they desire in their drug court while refusing the rest. The drug courts participating in this study included assessment procedures in order to weed out those individuals who did not have a dependency diagnosis. While few due process abuses were observed, numerous due process issues were discussed in the interviews with team members.

One due process procedure related to the contesting of non-compliant allegations was observed. Some courts in this study allowed clients to dispute toxicology exams either formally or informally. One court allowed clients to contest a test or allegation that would lead to a sanction, but should the test come back positive from a secondary analysis or should an allegation be proven correct the client would receive a sanction double in length. Clients in this court could also dispute curfew home visits records or allegations of missed treatment appointments, actions which would entail the court contacting the source of the information to determine truth or falsity. This allowed clients to contest their charges, but could lead to lengthy jail times.

At least two courts were understood to have developed procedural mechanisms to address due process concerns related to being released from the court without proper protections. Neither of these procedures was observed during the course of the study, but one termination hearing was scheduled. In the end, this hearing did not take place as the client was given another opportunity to remain in the drug court, but this judge did discuss the termination hearing:

> As for the termination, this is our attempt to provide due process. The report outlines what the participant has failed to do. Specific sections of the treatment court contract are cited together with the conduct or behavior alleged to be in violation. The report is usually at least two pages, but has been much lengthier depending on the participant's history. For instance, if there have been three positive urine screens and a missed screen, the dates and results are listed which are then tied to the contract requirement. If there's been a re-arrest, the details are listed. If a participant has absconded from residential placement, their report is included. This serves to alert the defendant as to the reasons for the termination. The participant is told to review the report with counsel. The participant can elect to terminate voluntarily and then be sentenced or can request a hearing. At that time, the defendant and counsel can present witnesses and testimony why the termination should not occur. We've only had one hearing. The treatment provider was called to testify. This seems to meet the due process requirement.

Despite their value in treatment of drug-addicted offenders, not everything is rosy in the drug courts included in this study. Team members., judges as well as key members, discussed possible due process violations that can occur in drug court. One team member observed the following.:

If I have somebody in my court a year and then that person fails out, all right, and that person is in his or her mid-thirties...Let me tell you something, when those people get into their 40s and 50s, they will not forget what they learned and maybe it's their time to shape up...It's got to be their time. For anybody to think that now is your time, that's not correct. The time is when they tell you it's their time. And they know it's their time and they want to do it. And that's the point, "Do I want to do it or just play lip service to it?" Not all are ready at this point. You cannot, in a sense, frown on that. You cannot double punishment on that. You have to understand. Now one thing I don't do that a lot of judges do is if you fail out of drug court and you get whacked hard during sentencing. I think that if a person was going to get 30 days on the crime committed, prior drug court, and they come to drug court and fails out of drug court, I don't believe you can give somebody six months.

Another team member put it this way

It really depends on the judge. There are some judges who are very fair in that regard and do not punish someone for trying. I truly believe, based on my own observations, that they are not punished or treated more harshly –either in the resolution of the case, or the sentencing of the case – for having been involved in drug court. Even if they were not invested at all. But there are other judges who just as clearly punish someone much more severely for having been in the drug court. In those cases, that's an argument that that judge should have to recuse himself.

Increased sentence for failing to complete drug court was but one result of the increased power of drug court judges. Clients in drug court are more likely to be jailed for such things as lying to the court, swearing at a staff member, or missing treatment appointments, things that would never put them in jail if they had not agreed to participate in drug court. By putting themselves in drug court, clients are placing themselves in a precarious position by agreeing to allow very powerful people make significant decisions in their life about their friends, roommates, employment, even whether to attend school, all in the name of benevolence. Should they fail, they risk even more time in jail than they would have received if they had never tried.

In this study, clients were regularly told to move out of a particular place or leave a girlfriend or spouse in order to remain in drug court. Observed behaviors that bordered on due process violations were the imposition of jail time for swearing in the court lobby and the discussion of a jail sanction for a client on a team member's intuition that the client was doing something wrong. More serious, though, is the possibility that there are drug court judges who punish clients more severely for attempting drug court and failing to accomplish abstinence. While drug courts judges balance the needs of the community, treatment of the client, and the general deterrent effect on clients in the courtroom, there is the potential that the goal of benevolence is lost. That is the lesson found in the juvenile court movement. At some point, the tremendous power given to a judge without some protection for the client can lead to harm.

It is here, viewing power at its most extreme end, where you will find the exercise of power to be the least legitimate (Foucault, 1980). Analyzing these critical issues. with a Foucauldian lens provides an insight into the practices of power in drug court. Drug courts, in the benevolent desire to force clients into a lifetime of abstinence, justify significant intrusions into clients' lives, expecting them to give up control over the minutia of their existence, sometimes for years, in the name of the social phenomenon of prohibition. Police officers, probation officers, case workers, court officials, and client advocates, as a collaboration of community stakeholders, share in the surveillance of clients in order to ensure that they remain abstinent. Even in drug courts that allow medication-assisted treatment, the ultimate goal is to wean individuals from any supportive medication before they graduate. If a client fails to live up to the ultimate goal, jail is the end of the line where trying and failing can mean even more time in jail given by a judge intent upon punishing that individual for failure.

In the midst of ambiguity in drug court, judges fill up the space by asking "who is this client?," "what do they need?," how can I help clients?," and "what is the best way to motivate them?" This is the social construction of drug court. In the same way that prosecutors need to determine the best clients to pursue trials for in rape cases (by social constructing who is a sympathetic rape victim), drug court judges socially construct their experience in drug court (Frohmann, 1997). Judges fill the ambiguity with who a drug addicted client is (making a choice versus diseased), what is in the client's best interest (abstinence versus harm reduction), and what is the best way to motivate them (sanctions versus rewards). Judges must also decide who they are in relation to the client (dad versus despot). Finally, judges construct the members of their drug court teams as the means to the ends determined by their social constructions surrounding addictions and law.

Valuable insight can be gleaned from the understanding that some of those social constructions are based upon information that is not entirely accurate or effective. Treatment modalities are not always effective, a higher level is not always the best next step, and sanctions are not necessarily the most appropriate way to motivate clients. Abstinence, rooted in the Prohibition era and the Temperance movement, may not be the best solution for every drug court client. Finally, the connection between trauma and drug addiction has never been fully explored. Some of the most recalcitrant clients are those individuals who are heavily traumatized by childhood sexual abuse or other significant trauma (e.g., war trauma in veterans), and these clients are the clients who are least able to address it. They may spend years drifting between drug addiction and remission and legal and illegal behavior, without ever being able to identify their trauma, thus never being able to address the causes of their drug addiction. Unless a treatment agency is willing to identify the trauma and simultaneously treat the substance abuse and the trauma, the client may have difficulties achieving success in drug court and, ultimately, reintegrating into the community.

In the end, drug courts have huge potential, but if allowed to go unchecked long enough the availability of power may corrupt even the most well-meaning judges. The leeway given to judges to create a unique drug court can also lead to the potential for arbitrary and capricious behavior, an occurrence even drug court professionals fear (Tiger, 2013). What is the future for drug courts? The NADCP hopes that by encouraging individual drug courts to voluntarily incorporate due process protections and best practices they can avoid appellate court decisions that may restrict drug court effectiveness. History shows that legal challenges are inevitable and may well alter drug court practice in the future, whether for good or bad.

FINAL THOUGHTS, LIMITATIONS AND FUTURE IMPLICATIONS

It is possible to see drug court in the views of the major theorists from sociology of law. Drug courts flow from Durkheim's theories of restitutive law and Weber's logical formal rationality of law (if predictability and guaranteed rights are the key to Formal Rationality), as well as from substantive law, Marx's position on the purpose the law serves (which is not always "justice"), organizational theory, and Black's sociological lawyer (and socialism of the law). These sociological theories both predict and make room for drug court within the framework of legal theory, while also providing a lens through which to analyze and understand. While classical theorists were not alive when drug prohibition occurred and drug courts were created, that does not preclude an analysis of drug court with a classical sociological lens. Taking into account all of the major theorists found within sociology of law, there was an acceptance that traditional legal discourse was insufficient to deal with the complexity of what modernity has done to our system of laws.

In the same way that the juvenile justice system has altered the way juveniles have been treated by the criminal justice system over the century it has been in existence, drug courts have changed our perceptions of the drug offender and what, if anything, society should do to an individual who is addicted to drugs. Perhaps drug courts are better limited to small calendars which provide each judge with the opportunity to capitalize on the relationship that the judge can build and sustain with individual clients. Moreover, drug courts should be mindful of their potential for due process violations. Power always comes with the potential for abuse, and being cognizant of the potential problems can help drug courts reform themselves before a higher court steps in to force reform on them.

The discussion herein suggests that substance abuse and recovery reflects some combination of the disease and choice models of addiction, while the lines between where choice ends and disease begins are not very clear. How judges interact with drug court clients appears, according to the analysis presented, to be influenced by court calendar (small versus large), the social construction of addiction, and organizational theory regarding how well teams are able to work together. Thus, any intervention that is intended to impact an addict's ability to recover from drug addiction, as well as to maintain his or her recovery, must be some combination of disease and choice models incorporating a more complex level of understanding about addiction. Durkheim, Weber, and Black make us aware of the role non-legal factors play in drug court, while Foucault provides some understanding that power is not always used to benefit those within the system. All this provides a contextually grounded understanding of a legal system that can be very ambiguous but, ultimately, remains a legal system which should be based upon fundamental fairness.

Drug court is an alternative to the traditional court system that includes a merging of the choice and disease models. By incorporating both treatment and coercion in its implementation of therapeutic jurisprudence, drug court may be able to succeed where other interventions fail. Knowing the potential, but acknowledging the risks, will help guide drug court judges to use drug courts to their fullest.

One of the most concerning issues that came out in the interviews with the judges and team members. is the danger that budget cuts pose to drug courts. There is less and less money for more and more clients (as well as for Art. 216 clients who arguably have a longer history with drug addiction and more significant criminal history). The results of this study suggest that this trend could impact client outcomes negatively as calendars increase. The interviewees expressed this concern and their inability to find or fund the staff and resources needed to work with the clients who come into their courtroom. This study does echo their fears that future budget cuts will seriously hurt drug courts.

Another concern that was clearly related in the interviews is the impending retirement of the judges who paved the way for the drug courts in this area. The majority of the judges in this study will be retired or face retirement in the near future. The training and experience that will be lost is incalculable. The judges and team members. I spoke to expressed concern for the future drug court judges given that elected judges may not have any interest in being drug court judges and the community will lose its drug court. Also, if an elected judge agrees to be active in drug court, the scarcity of trainings, once abundant, will leave that judge without the tools he or she will need to preside according to the drug court model.

It was suggested that drug court judges could be appointed rather than elected (as child support magistrates are now), thus eliminating the uncertainty of elections and increasing access to trainings over the long term. Indeed, appointed magistrates could potentially train with the current drug court judges to help ease the transition. This is not possible with elected judges now as there is no way to predict the winner of an election, and by the time the judge takes office the prior judge is gone. Appointed judges function in all parts of our justice system, and using them for drug court has advantages.

This study would have benefited from including more drug court judges in the observation, not only in terms of diversity of the sample but also in being able to see more procedures. There is no doubt more judges would have produced a richer list of rewards, sanctions, and unique procedures. In addition, adding client interviews would have added to the ability to assess the role judicial orientation has in motivating clients to stay in drug court, graduate, and live a life of sobriety. This would include not only clients who successfully graduate, but also clients who chose to leave drug court before graduation and those who fail to graduate to provide their perspectives. Moreover, including short- and long-term recidivism rates of clients would be important in knowing the long-term impact of drug court on drug-addicted clients.

Future research should include more client information. Client interviews and various lengths of recidivism rates are important indicators of the long-term success of any treatment modality. A more complete understanding of client characteristics and court intake procedures would also be enlightening regarding the nature of the clients who enter each drug court. An understanding of the criminal history of the clients in drug court as well as those deemed ineligible would be important to any future research.

Another area of research that would benefit drug courts includes examining treatment modalities available to drug courts within the community. A greater understanding of the specific treatment providers, as well as the types of treatment they provide, coupled with their efficacy rates with clients would be useful to drug courts. Any drug court professional can attest to the fact that not all treatment services are equal, and some are better with different kinds of clients. Critical to this examination is assessing what, if any, focus treatment providers put on the identification and treatment of trauma-related issues in drug court clients. Only one court in this study was certified in trauma-informed care, enabling that court to identify the nature and extent of trauma in its drug court clients, thus allowing the court to address the issue in its clientele. Examining judicial understanding of different treatment modalities and/or the use of AA/NA can lead to future trainings to assist drug courts in their goal to impact client outcomes.

The results from this study are the beginning of our understanding of the black box of drug court. The study demonstrated how different each court is and how creative the teams are in working within their communities. A progressive or traditional orientation is just one factor. This research, however, suggests that it is an important factor in motivating clients towards the goal of abstinence and reintegration back into the larger community.

Training manual

Examples of judicial behavior sheet:

Encouragement: If the judge says "Keep the focus," or the equivalent, without any praise: this is coded in Individual Responsibility and Focus on Compliance.

If the Judge says "Keep up the good work," or the equivalent: this is coded as praise.

If the judge sanctions a client to jail, the code sheet should be marked for the following three categories:

Individual responsibility

Focused on Compliance

Sentenced client to jail

If the client graduates, there is always praise, graduation cert and reward

FAQ
What do I enter into the Notes section?

Anything you would like. Please add any additional information that seems important or relevant to the court session, team meeting and/or instance. DO NOT enter any identifying information. However, any impressions or context should be included.

How do I enter Notes?

In the notes section, please write the instance number and any related info can be entered there. Or, if you are writing any general impressions, then write that and enter the information that seems important.

Who is an Instance?

Any drug court client should be included on the observation sheet as an instance. Having said that, it may not be easy to figure out who an instance is. There are some clients who are in patient and the judge hears a "Paper report." The judge may also hear arraignments, clients who are just signing a contract, as well as other criminal matters. Those people would not be considered an "instance" and should not be noted on the observation form.

Who are drug court team members?

You may not always be in the team meeting and cannot figure out who is a team member. and what role that team member plays in drug court. If you think you know who is who and what role they play, then fill out that section, however, if you are not sure then don't fill out that section. Each judge should be interviewed and we shall be able to obtain that information at the end of data collection.

What if nothing that can be noted on the observation form happens for a client?

Please write "nothing happened" in the column for that instance.

Please define "sought middle ground" for the team meeting and observation form. What exactly do you mean by that?

Middle ground applies when there is a disagreement between team members or an active controversy that the team must deal with in regards to rules/procedures or what to do with a particular client. A judge seeks middle ground when he tries to find a compromise between team member's positions or one that the whole team is happy with.

Please define "quick processing based upon rules."

Quick processing means that the judge does not take anything into consideration other than non-compliance, then sanction, non-compliance, then sanction, non-compliance, then sanction. Thus, very speedy due to routine handling of clients.

What is quick in regards to disposal of cases?

This means that the judge does not spend much time on each client. Clients then receive very little interaction with the judge.

What does "relied upon" mean in filling out the observation form?
A judge relies upon the drug court coordinator when he asks the drug court coordinator (or any other team member for that matter) for any information he uses in making a decision in regards to a particular client.

What is an example of the judge sanctioning a client based upon a team's member's assertions?
Basically, if the judge sanctions a client solely on a team members. assertion that something unrelated to drug use occurred (i.e. client was disrespectful to the team member).

What do you mean by "considered violation only?"
This means that the judge sanctioned the client based upon the non-compliant act and did not use any context to mitigate the sanction at all. The judge may ask for context, but if after hearing the context sanctions the client without any leniency, then he considered the violation only.

Information Sheet #1: Drug Court Judges and Judicial Behavior

The purpose of this study is to examine drug court judges during their drug court session/team meetings so that we can better understand judicial orientation and how it plays out in court. The sole subject of the study is the judge and the data collected is what the court watcher can observe during the drug court/team meeting session. While there is a section on each of the forms that allows the observer to note the team members in attendance during the session/team meeting and the sex/race of those team members (if possible to note), there will be no way to link the general information noted on the court watching form to any particular court. No client related data is collected other than number of clients in attendance, as well as sex and race of those clients (if possible to note). Furthermore, no information related to the names of any participants/non participants is collected on the team meeting watching form.

Each form contains a pre-printed number associated with the court, however the list which contains the connection between the pre-printed number and the actual court associated with that number is only accessible to the principle investigator of the study and will be destroyed after data collection is over. Once the code sheet is destroyed there will be no way to associate the actual court to the data in the study. The privacy of the court, team and clients is a primary concern of this study.

Information Sheet #2: Drug Court Judges and Judicial Behavior

Drug Court, a relatively recent innovation within the criminal justice system, exists as a diversionary court (set apart from the traditional court system) to treat drug abuse in order to reduce criminal recidivism. The purpose of this study is to examine drug court judges during their drug court session and team meetings in order to understand judicial orientation (whether treatment orientated or sanction orientated) and the judicial orientation's impact on drug court client retention and graduation. It is through this more contextual understanding of how drug court can impact client success that drug court professionals can come to understand the inner workings of drug court in order to increase effectiveness in regards to client outcomes. This will be an observation based qualitative study utilizing drug court and team meeting observation forms to collect specific information related to the judges behavior in both settings supplemented with semi-structured interviews with key team members..

The sole subject of the study is the judge and the data collected is what the court watcher can observe during the drug court/team meeting session. While there is a section on each of the forms that allows the observer to note the team members in attendance during the session/team meeting and the sex/race of those team members (if possible to note), there will be no way to link the general information noted on the court watching form to any particular court. No client related data is collected other than number of clients in attendance, as well as sex and race of those clients (if possible to note). Furthermore, no information related to the names of any participants/non participants is collected on the team meeting watching form.

Each form contains a pre-printed number associated with the court, however the list which contains the connection between the pre-printed number and the actual court associated with that number is only accessible to the principle investigator of the study and will be destroyed after data collection is over. Once the code sheet is destroyed there will be no way to associate the actual court to the data in the study. The privacy of the court, team and clients is a primary concern of this study.

Information Sheet #3: Drug Court Judges and Judicial Orientation

Who: Drug court judges New York State

What: The black box*
Judicial interactions
Unique practices & procedures and sanctions & rewards

Where: Ideally, team meetings and court sessions

How: Field Observation (2 person research teams-kind of like "flies on the wall")
10 observations per court
Semi-structured interviews - 2 interviews of the judge during the course of the study
Court specific data on client retention and graduation rates

Drug Court Watching Form

Date: _____ Court: _____
Time: _____ Observation # _____ Observer_____

Sanctions
(21) Increased AA/NA meetings
(22) Increase case management contacts
(23) Day reporting
(24) Work Release Program
(25) Work Crew
(26) Electronic Monitoring
(27) Community Service Hours
(28) Jail Time
(9) Other

Rewards:
(30) Speech upon graduation
(31) Small gift
(32) Reduced community service
(33) Reduced drug testing
(34) Reduced treatment requirements
(35) Reduced status appearances
(36) Reduced homework assignments
(37) Applause
(38) Praise
(39) Stage certificates/diplomas.
(9) Other

Team member	Judge	Prosecutor	Defense	Project coordinator	Treatment Providers	Treatment Providers	Treatment Providers
Sex							
Race							

Judicial Instances	1	2	3	4	5	6	7	8	9
	M/F B/C/ O	M/F B/C/ O	M/F B/C/ O	M/F B/C/ O	M/F B/C/ O	M/F B/C/ O	M/F B/C/ O	M/F B/C/ O	M/F B/C/ O
(Treatment, Due Process and Rehabilitation focused)									
Reward given									
Compliant act (reason for reward)									
Client Reaction to reward									
Asked client or team for context or additional information									
Encouraged the client to use community support (family, friends, AA/NA)									
Discussed the client's community service project or sanctioned client to community service									

Judicial Instances	1	2	3	4	5	6	7	8	9
	M/F B/C/ O	M/F B/C/ O	M/F B/C/ O	M/F B/C/ O	M/F B/C/ O	M/F B/C/ O	M/F B/C/ O	M/F B/C/ O	M/F B/C/ O
(Offense & Punishment, Crime Control and Deterrence focused)									
Considered violation only (no context asked for)									
Sanction given									
Considered context of any violation									
Non-compliant act (reason for sanction)									
Client reaction to sanction									
Focused on compliance									
Emphasized Individual responsibility									
Client sentenced to Jail									

NOTES (i.e. unique rewards, unique procedures, impressions)
Use back page if needed   Page

Client, compliant behavior	Client non-compliance behavior
(1) attended treatment appointments	(11) drugs found in urine/admitted use
(2) followed team requests/stage requirements	(12) failed to go to treatment appointments
(3) drug free urines/no admitted use	(13) failed to follow team requests
(4) phase advancement/graduation	(14) associated with drug addicted friends
(5) obtained employment/GED	15) lied about non-compliance
	(16) new criminal charges
(9) other	(9) other

Date:_____ Court_____ Observation#_____ Observer_____

Judicial Style (select yes, no or not applicable based upon overall impression from session)	Yes	No	n/a
Sought middle ground or solution most of the team was happy with *(Consensus)*	o	o	o
Elicited input from treatment team members- beyond the drug court coordinator*(Inclusion)*	o	o	o
Discussed client's employment, family relationships, childhood	o	o	o
Discussed extenuating circumstances	o	o	o
Emphasized treatment/rewards *(please circle which applies)*	o	o	o
Agreed with treatment recommendations *(in court or from Team Meeting-if you can tell)*	o	o	o
Relied on Input from others-beyond just the drug court coordinator	o	o	o
Considered the context of offense *(if any)*	o	o	o
Focused on attitude and demeanor of client in courtroom	o	o	o
Discussed client rights *(those he have in drug court)*	o	o	o
Discussed whether client could be innocent *(related to an incident while drug court client)*	o	o	o
Discussed client need to talk with attorney *(before or after a sanction)*	o	o	o
Relied on the presence of the defense attorney	o	o	o
Relied upon the Drug Court coordinator	o	o	o
Considered each client on a Case by Case basis	o	o	o

Judicial Style (select yes, no or not applicable based upon overall impression from session)	Yes	No	n/a
Allowed for the contesting of evidence *(i.e. a dirty urine or accusation before a sanction)*	o	o	o
Made unilateral decisions *(without consulting others)*	o	o	o
Quick processing of cases based upon rules	o	o	o
Discussed need to be compliant with treatment/law abiding lifestyle *(please circle which applies)*	o	o	o
Discussed past non-compliance with drug court rules	o	o	o
Discussed acts of lying	o	o	o
Discussed offense only: seriousness/prior history *(please circle which applies)*	o	o	o
Emphasized Rules	o	o	o
Emphasized Sanctions	o	o	o
Focused on punishment	o	o	o
Quick to sanction	o	o	o
Assumed guilt	o	o	o
Sanctions based upon team member assertions	o	o	o
Speed in disposal of issue at hand	o	o	o
Uniformity in case disposition	o	o	o
Routine handling of cases	o	o	o

NOTES (i.e. unique rewards, unique procedures, impressions)
V.10/14/11

Drug Court Team Meeting Form

Date:_____ Court _____
Time: _____ Observation #_____ Observer_____

Team member	Judge	Prosecutor	Defense	Project coordinator	Treatment Providers	Treatment Providers	Treatment Providers	Treatment Providers
Sex								
Race								

Judicial Style (select yes, no or not applicable based on the overall impression from the session)	Yes	No	n/a
Sought middle ground or solution most of the team was happy with *(Consensus)*	o	o	o
Elicited input from treatment team members- beyond just the drug court coordinator *(Inclusion)*	o	o	o
Discussed client's employment, family relationships, childhood	o	o	o
Discussed extenuating circumstances	o	o	o
Emphasized treatment/rewards *(please circle which applies)*	o	o	o
Agreed with treatment recommendations *(in court or from Team Meeting-if you can tell)*	o	o	o
Relied on Input from others during team meeting- beyond just the drug court coordinator	o	o	o
Considered the context of offense *(if any)*	o	o	o
Focused on any attitude and demeanor of client in courtroom	o	o	o
Discussed client rights *(those he has in drug court)*	o	o	o
Discussed whether client could be innocent *(related to an incident while drug court client)*	o	o	o
Discussed client need to talk with attorney *(before or after a sanction)*	o	o	o
Relied upon the presence of the defense attorney	o	o	o
Relied upon Court coordinator	o	o	o
Considered each client on a Case by Case basis	o	o	o
Allowed for the contesting of evidence *(i.e. a dirty urine or accusation before a sanction)*	o	o	o
Made unilateral decisions *(without consulting others)*	o	o	o
Quick processing of cases based upon drug court rules	o	o	o

Judicial Style (select yes, no or not applicable based on the overall impression from the session)	Yes	No	n/a
Discussed need to be compliant with treatment/law abiding lifestyle *(please circle which applies)*	o	o	o
Discussed past non-compliance with drug court rules	o	o	o
Discussed acts of lying	o	o	o
Discussed offense only: seriousness/prior history (please circle which applies)	o	o	o
Emphasized Rules	o	o	o
Emphasized sanctions	o	o	o
Focused on punishment	o	o	o
Quick to sanction	o	o	o
Assumed guilt	o	o	o
Sanctions based upon team member assertions	o	o	o
Speed in disposal of issue at hand	o	o	o
Uniformity in case disposition	o	o	o
Routine handling of cases	o	o	o

NOTES (i.e. unique rewards, unique procedures, impressions) v.10/14/2011

Semi-Structured Interview – Judge

Drug Court Judges and Judicial Behavior
Semi Structured Interview - Judge
1) How old are you (please fill in) _____ years?

2) What is your sex? (Please check one answer)
- Male
- Female

3) What is your race? (Please check one answer)
- Caucasian/White
- African American/Black
- Native American
- Asian/Pacific Islander
- Other (please specify) _____

4) What is the highest level of education, or grade in school, that you completed? (Please check one answer)
- Less than high school graduate
- High School Diploma/GED
- Some college/university (1-3 years)
- Trade/technical/vocational training
- College graduate
- Bachelor's degree
- Master's degree
- PhD/JD/Other postgrad degree/training

5) Are you an attorney? (Please check one answer)
  ○Yes
  ○ No
      If yes: How many years have you been an attorney?

6) How long have you been a judge?

7) How do you see your role in Drug Court? (Probes: could you tell me more about that? Can you give me an example?)

8) What is your guiding philosophy for you as a drug court judge? (Probes: could you tell me more about that? Can you give me an example?)

9) What team members are on your team? No names please just the team roles and number of each role that you have recruited to be on your team.

10) Do you attend the team meeting? Why or why not? Have you modified the team meeting in any way?

      a) If you do not attend the team meetings, how do you receive information on the clients?

11 In thinking about how your team performs, can you tell me a little about that? (Probe: can you tell me a story about that? Can you give me a for instance?)

12) What kinds of performance related procedures have your team come up with at is unique to your court? (Probe: can you tell me a story about that? Can you give me a for instance?)

13) What is the most important behaviour, intervention or procedure that you use in your court in your role to impact drug court clients? (Probe: can you tell me a story about that? Can you give me a for instance?)

14) What do you like best about drug court? (Probes: could you tell me more about that? Can you give me an example?)

15) What is your opinion, thoughts, feelings, on your drug court team? (Strengths, weaknesses, what would you do different, what have you learned, what do you do different than the training recommended?)

16) Do you or your team engage in continuing drug court training? (Probes: could you tell me more about that? Can you give me an example?)

17) What is your chief complaint about drug court? (Probes: could you tell me more about that? Can you give me an example?)

18) What client behaviour demonstrates that the client is moving forward? (Probe: can you tell me a story about that? Can you give me a for instance?)

19) What client behaviour demonstrates that the client is moving backward? (Probe: can you tell me a story about that? Can you give me a for instance?)

20) What are your views on client relapse? How do you react to client relapse? (Probe: can you tell me a story about that? Can you give me a for instance?)

21) What is the single defining moment for you as a drug court judge? (Probe: can you tell me a story about that?)

22) The research refers to individuals who are able to kick the addiction habit on their own. This is sometimes referred to natural recovery or spontaneous remission. What thoughts do you have on this? Do you think it is possible to recover from addiction without intervention?

23) What, in your opinion is an impediment to the future of drug courts? (Probes: could you tell me more about that? Can you give me an example?)

24) Do you have an opinion on the current controversy over Methadone or Seboxone?

Semi-Structured Interview – Team Members

<u>Drug Court Judges and Judicial Behavior</u>
Semi Structured Interview - Team Members.
1. How old are you (please fill in) _____ years?

2. What is your sex? (Please check one answer)
   o Male
   o Female

3. What is your race? (Please check one answer)
   o Caucasian/White
   o African American/Black
   o Native American
   o Asian/Pacific Islander
   o Other (please specify) _____

4. What is the highest level of education, or grade in school, that you completed? (Please check one answer)
   o Less than high school graduate
   o High School Diploma/GED
   o Some college/university (1-3 years)
   o Trade/technical/vocational training
   o College graduate
   o Bachelor's degree
   o Master's degree
   o PhD/JD/Other postgrad degree/training

5) What is your role in Drug Court? (Please check one answer)
- ○ Prosecutor
- ○ Defense attorney
- ○ Treatment Provider
- ○ Drug Court coordinator

6) How do you see your role in Drug Court? (Probes: could you tell me more about that? Can you give me an example?)

7) In thinking about how your team performs, can you tell me a little about that? (Probe: can you tell me a story about that? Can you give me a for instance?)

8) Can you tell me a bit about who you regard as your client?
- a. Could you explain what your duty is to your client?
- b. Or, if you don't regard your actions as part of a client relationship, how would you describe what you do? Could you give me an example?

9) What do you like best about drug court? (Probes: could you tell me more about that? Can you give me an example?)

10) What is your opinion, thoughts, feelings, on your drug court team? (Strengths, weaknesses, what would you do different, what have you learned, what do you do different than the training recommended?)

11) Do you have any unique procedures, rewards or sanctions? (List them)
- a) How did _____ develop? (Probes: could you tell me more about that? Can you tell me a story about that?)
- b) What purpose does_____ serve? (Probes: could you tell me more about that? Can you tell me a story about that?)

12) What is the most important behaviour, intervention or procedure used by your court to impact recovery in a drug court client? (Probe: can you tell me a story about that? Can you give me a for instance?)

13) Which sanction used by your court has the greatest impact on clients? (Probe: can you tell me a story about that? Can you give me a for instance?)

14) Are rewards used regularly? Are they effective in motivating clients? (Probe: can you tell me a story about that? Can you give me a for instance?)

15) What are your thoughts about the role of the judge in drug court? (Probe: can you tell me more about that?)

16) What impact does the judge/judges have on clients (that you have been able to observe)? Is there any way that the judge interacts with the clients that has had the greatest impact on them? (Probe: can you tell me a story about that? Can you give me a for instance?)

Judge: Informed Consent – Team Meeting

UNIVERSITY AT BUFFALO, STATE UNIVERSITY OF NEW YORK

Drug Court Judges and Judicial Behavior
Informed Consent Document - Judge

This consent form explains the research study. Please read it carefully. Ask questions about anything you do not understand. If you do not have questions right now, you should ask them later if any come up.

FOR QUESTIONS ABOUT THIS RESEARCH, CONTACT:

This study is being conducted by Kathleen M. Contrino, J.D., PhD. Candidate at the University at Buffalo Sociology Department and Adjunct Professor, Criminal Justice Department at Buffalo State. Any questions, concerns or complaints that you may have about this study can be answered by Ms. Contrino or Dr. Robert Granfield, faculty contact at UB. Ms. Contrino can be reached by telephone at (716) 417-2626. She may also be reached via email at: contrino@buffalo.edu. Dr. Granfield can be reached at (716) 645 – 8462 or by email at: rgranfield@buffalo.edu.

If you have any questions about your rights as a participant in a research project, or questions, concerns or complaints about the research and wish to speak with someone who is not a member of the research team, you should contact (anonymously, if you wish) the

Social and Behavioral Sciences Institutional Review Board, 515 Capen, University at Buffalo, Buffalo, NY 14260, e-mail SBSIRB@research.buffalo.edu, phone 716 / 645-6474.

PURPOSE:

You are invited to participate in a research project that examines judicial behavior of drug court judges during the team meeting setting. The purpose for the research is to observe and collect information on judicial behavior in drug court. Approximately 10 drug court judges, during their team meeting, will be involved in this study.

PROCEDURES:

If you agree to participate in this study, you will be asked to allow a research team of two to watch your drug court team meeting for up to ten (10) drug court sessions.

This is an observation based study, thus being able to observe your normal behavior during the drug court team meeting is essential. You will not be asked to do anything different to accommodate the research team, nor will the research team do anything more than make note of your judicial style during the course of the team meeting. No questions will be asked before or after the team meeting.

Before we leave we will ask your permission to contact you, or your drug court coordinator, in about a week or two in order to schedule another team meeting session for the research team to watch. You can say yes or no at that time. Even if you say yes today, you can still change your mind when we contact you again.

RISKS:

There is a risk of breach of confidentiality regarding your behavior should the master list detailing the pre-coded number of your drug court being linked to your specific court become known.

However, that master list is currently locked up in a file cabinet in 660 Baldy Hall and only accessible to Ms. Contrino. Once the data collection is over, the master list will be destroyed. We worked very carefully to prevent any breach of confidentiality from happening.

BENEFITS:

There is no direct benefit to you from participating in this study.

CONFIDENTIALITY:
Identifying information that we use during the course of the study to contact you will be kept in a separate locked file from the observation forms. This information will be destroyed as soon as we have finished collecting data for the study. This consent form will be the only indication that you participated in this study; it will not be linked to your study data and will be secured in a separate locked file. All forms will only be coded with a code number, not your name.

Only the researchers will have access to master list that links participants with their data. This list will be destroyed as soon as data collection for the study is completed.

COSTS and COMPENSATION:
There is no cost to you to participate in this study. You will not be compensated for participating in this study.

DECEPTION:
There is no deception in this study.

JOINING OF YOUR OWN FREE WILL (VOLUNTEERING FOR THE STUDY):
Your participation is voluntary. Your refusal to participate will involve no penalty or loss of benefits to which you are otherwise entitled. You may withdraw from the study at any time by contacting the investigator and all data that can still be identifiably attributed to you will be withdrawn by the investigator.

SUBJECT STATEMENT:
I have read the explanation provided to me. I have had all my questions answered to my satisfaction, and I voluntarily agree to participate in this study. I HAVE BEEN GIVEN A COPY OF THIS CONSENT FORM.

NAME OF SUBJECT (Please Print)

SIGNATURE OF SUBJECT and DATE

"I certify that I obtained the consent of the participant whose signature is above. I understand that I must give a signed copy of the informed consent form to the participant, and keep the original copy on file in the repository location designated on my IRB application files for 3 years after the completion of the research project.

SIGNATURE OF INVESTIGATOR (or PERSON OBTAINING CONSENT) and DATE

V.10/14/11

Team Members: Informed Consent – Team Meeting

UNIVERSITY AT BUFFALO, STATE UNIVERSITY OF NEW YORK

Drug Court Judges and Judicial Behavior
Informed Consent Document – Team Members.

This consent form explains the research study. Please read it carefully. Ask questions about anything you do not understand. If you do not have questions right now, you should ask them later if any come up.

FOR QUESTIONS ABOUT THIS RESEARCH, CONTACT:

This study is being conducted by Kathleen M. Contrino, J.D., PhD. Candidate at the University at Buffalo Sociology Department and Adjunct Professor, Criminal Justice Department at Buffalo State. Any questions, concerns or complaints that you may have about this study can be answered by Ms. Contrino or Dr. Robert Granfield, faculty contact at UB. Ms. Contrino can be reached by telephone at (716) 417-2626. She may also be reached via email at: contrino@buffalo.edu. Dr. Granfield can be reached at (716) 645 – 8462 or by email at: rgranfield@buffalo.edu.

If you have any questions about your rights as a participant in a research project, or questions, concerns or complaints about the research and wish to speak with someone who is not a member of the research team, you should contact (anonymously, if you wish) the Social and Behavioral Sciences Institutional Review Board, 515 Capen, University at Buffalo, Buffalo, NY 14260, e-mail SBSIRB@research.buffalo.edu, phone 716 / 645-6474.

PURPOSE:

You are invited, as a team, to participate in a research project that examines judicial behavior of drug court judges. The purpose of the research is to observe and catalog judicial behavior in drug court team. The Judge is the actual subject of this study and this study hopes to include in its analysis judicial behavior during team meetings in addition to the drug court proceedings. Approximately 10 drug court judges, during their team meetings, will be involved in this study.

PROCEDURES:

If you agree to participate in this study, you will be asked to allow a research team of two to watch your team meetings for up to ten (10) drug court team meeting sessions.

This is an observation based study, thus being able to observe your normal behavior during the drug court team meeting is essential. You will not be asked to do anything different to accommodate the research team, nor will the research team do anything more than make note of your attendance during the course of the team meeting and the sex and apparent race of each team member in attendance. No questions will be asked before or after the team meeting.

Before we leave we will ask your permission to contact you, or your drug court coordinator, in about a week or two in order to schedule another team meeting session for the research team to watch. You can say yes or no at that time. Even if you say yes today, you can still change your mind when we contact you again.

RISKS:

There is a risk of breach of confidentiality regarding your behavior should the master list detailing the pre-coded number of your drug court being linked to your specific court become known.

However, that master list is currently locked up in a file cabinet in 660 Baldy Hall and only accessible to Ms. Contrino. Once the data collection is over, the master list will be destroyed. We worked very carefully to prevent any breach of confidentiality from happening.

BENEFITS:
There is no direct benefit to you from participating in this study.

CONFIDENTIALITY:
Identifying information that we use during the course of the study to contact you will be kept in a separate locked file from the observation forms. This information will be destroyed as soon as we have finished collecting data for the study. This consent form will be the only indication that you participated in this study; it will not be linked to your study data and will be secured in a separate locked file. All forms will only be coded with a code number, not your name.
Only the researchers will have access to master list that links participants with their data. This list will be destroyed as soon as data collection for the study is completed.

COSTS and COMPENSATION:
There is no cost to you to participate in this study. You will not be compensated for participating in this study.

DECEPTION:
There is no deception in this study.

JOINING OF YOUR OWN FREE WILL (VOLUNTEERING FOR THE STUDY):
Your participation is voluntary. Your refusal to participate will involve no penalty or loss of benefits to which you are otherwise entitled. You may withdraw from the study at any time by contacting the investigator and all data that can still be identifiably attributed to you will be withdrawn by the investigator.

SUBJECT STATEMENT:
I have read the explanation provided to me. I have had all my questions answered to my satisfaction, and I voluntarily agree to participate in this study. I HAVE BEEN GIVEN A COPY OF THIS CONSENT FORM.

NAME OF SUBJECT (Please Print)

SIGNATURE OF SUBJECT and DATE

"I certify that I obtained the consent of the participant whose signature is above. I understand that I must give a signed copy of the informed consent form to the participant, and keep the original copy on file in the repository location designated on my IRB application files for 3 years after the completion of the research project.

SIGNATURE OF INVESTIGATOR (or PERSON OBTAINING CONSENT) and DATE

V.10/14/11

Judge: Informed Consent – Semi-Structured Interview

UNIVERSITY AT BUFFALO, STATE UNIVERSITY OF NEW YORK

Drug Court Judges and Judicial Behavior
Semi-Structured interview
Informed Consent Document - Judge

This consent form explains the research study. Please read it carefully. Ask questions about anything you do not understand. If you do not have questions right now, you should ask them later if any come up.

FOR QUESTIONS ABOUT THIS RESEARCH, CONTACT:
This study is being conducted by Kathleen M. Contrino, J.D., PhD. Candidate at the University at Buffalo Sociology Department and Adjunct Professor, Criminal Justice Department at Buffalo State. Any questions, concerns or complaints that you may have about this study can be answered by Ms. Contrino or Dr. Robert Granfield, faculty contact at UB. Ms. Contrino can be reached by telephone at (716) 417-2626. She may also be reached via email at: contrino@buffalo.edu. Dr. Granfield can be reached at (716) 645 – 8462 or by email at: rgranfield@buffalo.edu.

If you have any questions about your rights as a participant in a research project, or questions, concerns or complaints about the research and wish to speak with someone who is not a member of the research team, you should contact (anonymously, if you wish) the

Social and Behavioral Sciences Institutional Review Board, 515 Capen, University at Buffalo, Buffalo, NY 14260, e-mail SBSIRB@research.buffalo.edu, phone 716 / 645-6474.

PURPOSE:
This study is an observation based study that examines judicial behavior of drug court judges during the drug court and team meeting setting. The purpose for the research is to observe and collect information on judicial behavior in drug court. Approximately 10 drug court judges, during their team meeting, will be involved in this study. This specific potion of the study is interested in your role as a drug court judge.

PROCEDURES:
If you agree to participate in this study, you will be asked a series of questions about how your behavior in the drug court session and team meeting. In addition, you will be asked to relate your opinion on a variety of matters related to drug court, drug court effectiveness and the treatment of drug court clients. We would like to tape record the interview to allow us to make sure we capture your thoughts accurately. Tapes will be transcribed as soon as possible following the interview. We will use code numbers on the transcripts and .wav files. Once the interviews have been transcribed, we will destroy the .wav files and any information containing the link between the transcript and your court (and name as well).

RISKS:
The questions are not asking for personal information so discomfort in answering should be minimal.

There is a risk of breach of confidentiality regarding your behavior should the master list detailing the pre-coded number of your drug court being linked to your specific court become known.

However, that master list is currently locked up in a file cabinet in 660 Baldy Hall and only accessible to Ms. Contrino. Once the data collection is over, the master list will be destroyed. We worked very carefully to prevent any breach of confidentiality from happening.

BENEFITS:
There is no direct benefit to you from participating in this study.

CONFIDENTIALITY:

All information that you provide during the interview will be strictly confidential. Only a code number will appear on the .wav file and transcript.

Identifying information (the pre-coded number for your court) that we use during the course of the study to contact you will be kept in a separate locked file from .wav file and transcript. This information will be destroyed as soon as we have finished collecting data for the study. This consent form will be the only indication that you participated in this study; it will not be linked to your study data and will be secured in a separate locked file. All forms will only be coded with a code number, not your name.

Only the researchers will have access to master list that links participants with their data. This list will be destroyed as soon as data collection for the study is completed.

Your identity will not be revealed in any description or publication of this research.

COSTS and COMPENSATION:

There is no cost to you to participate in this study. You will not be compensated for participating in this study.

JOINING OF YOUR OWN FREE WILL (VOLUNTEERING FOR THE STUDY):

Your participation is voluntary. You may refuse to participate or withdraw from the research project after it has begun. You have the right to refuse to answer particular questions during the interview. You may withdraw from the study at any time by contacting the investigator and all data that can still be identifiably attributed to you will be withdrawn by the investigator.

DECEPTION:

There is no deception in this study.

SUBJECT STATEMENT:

I have read the explanation provided to me. I have had all my questions answered to my satisfaction, and I voluntarily agree to participate in this study. I HAVE BEEN GIVEN A COPY OF THIS CONSENT FORM.

NAME OF SUBJECT (Please Print)

SIGNATURE OF SUBJECT and DATE

"I certify that I obtained the consent of the participant whose signature is above. I understand that I must give a signed copy of the informed consent form to the participant, and keep the original copy on file in the repository location designated on my IRB application files for 3 years after the completion of the research project.
SIGNATURE OF INVESTIGATOR (or PERSON OBTAINING CONSENT) and DATE

V.10/14/11

Team Members: Informed Consent - Semi-Structured Interview

UNIVERSITY AT BUFFALO, STATE UNIVERSITY OF NEW YORK

Drug Court Judges and Judicial Behavior
Semi-Structured interview
Informed Consent Document – Team members.

This consent form explains the research study. Please read it carefully. Ask questions about anything you do not understand. If you do not have questions right now, you should ask them later if any come up.

FOR QUESTIONS ABOUT THIS RESEARCH, CONTACT:
This study is being conducted by Kathleen M. Contrino, J.D., PhD. Candidate at the University at Buffalo Sociology Department and Adjunct Professor, Criminal Justice Department at Buffalo State. Any questions, concerns or complaints that you may have about this study can be answered by Ms. Contrino or Dr. Robert Granfield, faculty contact at UB. Ms. Contrino can be reached by telephone at (716) 417-2626. She may also be reached via email at: contrino@buffalo.edu. Dr. Granfield can be reached at (716) 645 – 8462 or by email at: rgranfield@buffalo.edu.

If you have any questions about your rights as a participant in a research project, or questions, concerns or complaints about the research and wish to speak with someone who is not a member of the research team, you should contact (anonymously, if you wish) the

Social and Behavioral Sciences Institutional Review Board, 515 Capen, University at Buffalo, Buffalo, NY 14260, e-mail SBSIRB@research.buffalo.edu, phone 716 / 645-6474.

PURPOSE:

This study is an observation based study that examines judicial behavior of drug court judges during the drug court and team meeting setting. The purpose for the research is to observe and collect information on judicial behavior in drug court. Approximately 10 drug court judges, during their team meeting, will be involved in this study. This specific potion of the study is interested in your role as a drug court team member.

PROCEDURES:

If you agree to participate in this study, you will be asked a series of questions about your role in drug court and the impact, if any, of your judge's behavior in the drug court session and team meeting. In addition, you will be asked to relate your opinion on a variety of matters related to the drug court judge, drug court effectiveness and the treatment of drug court clients. We would like to tape record the interview to allow us to make sure we capture your thoughts accurately. Tapes will be transcribed as soon as possible following the interview. We will use code numbers on the transcripts and .wav files. Once the interviews have been transcribed, we will destroy the .wav files and any information containing the link between the transcript and your court (and name as well).

RISKS:

The questions are not asking for personal information so discomfort in answering should be minimal.

There is a risk of breach of confidentiality regarding your behavior should the master list detailing the pre-coded number of your drug court being linked to your specific court become known.

However, that master list is currently locked up in a file cabinet in 660 Baldy Hall and only accessible to Ms. Contrino. Once the data collection is over, the master list will be destroyed. We worked very carefully to prevent any breach of confidentiality from happening.

BENEFITS:
There is no direct benefit to you from participating in this study.

CONFIDENTIALITY:
All information that you provide during the interview will be strictly confidential. Only a code number will appear on the .wav file and transcript.

Identifying information (the pre-coded number for your court) that we use during the course of the study to contact you will be kept in a separate locked file from .wav file and transcript. This information will be destroyed as soon as we have finished collecting data for the study. This consent form will be the only indication that you participated in this study; it will not be linked to your study data and will be secured in a separate locked file. All forms will only be coded with a code number, not your name.

Only the researchers will have access to master list that links participants with their data. This list will be destroyed as soon as data collection for the study is completed. Your identity will not be revealed in any description or publication of this research.

COSTS and COMPENSATION:
There is no cost to you to participate in this study. You will not be compensated for participating in this study.

JOINING OF YOUR OWN FREE WILL (VOLUNTEERING FOR THE STUDY):
Your participation is voluntary. You may refuse to participate or withdraw from the research project after it has begun. You have the right to refuse to answer particular questions during the interview. You may withdraw from the study at any time by contacting the investigator and all data that can still be identifiably attributed to you will be withdrawn by the investigator.

DECEPTION:
There is no deception in this study.

SUBJECT STATEMENT:
I have read the explanation provided to me. I have had all my questions answered to my satisfaction, and I voluntarily agree to participate in

this study. I HAVE BEEN GIVEN A COPY OF THIS CONSENT FORM.

NAME OF SUBJECT (Please Print)

SIGNATURE OF SUBJECT and DATE

"I certify that I obtained the consent of the participant whose signature is above. I understand that I must give a signed copy of the informed consent form to the participant, and keep the original copy on file in the repository location designated on my IRB application files for 3 years after the completion of the research project.

SIGNATURE OF INVESTIGATOR (or PERSON OBTAINING CONSENT) and DATE

V.10/14/11

Appendix L

Sanctions, Rewards, & Policies in each Court

There are additional components to a drug court's black box: individual sanctions, rewards and procedures. Listed above with each site description are the observed sanctions, rewards and unique procedures which are described below.

Rewards, sanctions and unique procedures, though selected during the team meeting when the case is discussed, are issued by the judge during the court session. While these policies are intended to motivate clients to remain abstinent while in drug court, they are also intended to provide the client with the tools to continue to live an abstinent lifestyle and encourage the client to become productive community members.

Each of the observed policies is described in Tables 12, 13 and 14.

Table 12: Observed Sanctions

Observed Sanction	Description
Verbal Warning	Client is told that any future non-compliance will lead to a serious sanction. This is typically issued to a client who is newly admitted to drug court, has committed a low level non-compliant act, and/or may have had a long period of time of compliance and then committed a minor slip-up.

Judicial admonishment	This can be used in combination with the verbal warning or alone to indicate to the client that his/her behavior is unsafe or non-compliant. It is during this kind of discussion with the client that the Judge will mention treatment related terms, reinforcing what they may have learned with the Treatment Provider (i.e. "People, Places, Things" or contacting sober supports during times of trouble).
Penalty Box	A section of the client seating area is sectioned off and designated as the "Penalty Box." This section of seating is for clients who know they are somehow non-compliant or informed that they are non-compliant (i.e. positive toxicology screen). A non-compliant client enters the courtroom, seats himself/herself in the penalty box, and waits until the end of the court session to be seen by the Judge
Essay/Letter	Essays or letters on a particular topic are homework assignment given by the judge in order to invoke thoughtful insight in the client. Sometimes the client has to write an apology for inappropriate or non-compliant behavior or an essay discussing substance use triggers. Other times the client must write a letter to the court explaining why they should be retained in drug court or what will be different if the client is retained in drug court.
Small Gift (i.e. Calendar)	A small gift given to the client as a sanction is intended to increase client compliance. A pocket calendar, for example, can be given to a client after missing an appointment (of any kind) with instructions to keep it with him/her at all times. Future sanctions or rewards can be issued around client compliance or non-compliance for utilizing the calendar.

Plan for Compliance	Instructing the client to develop a plan for compliance is typically issued after a period of non-compliance or a prior, unsuccessful, attempt to complete drug court. The Judge will look at the client and ask "What is going to be different this time?"
Attendance Contract	The client is instructed that he/she must attend every appointment with their treatment provider or a harsh sanction will be imposed. Attendance contracts can happen when there are a series of late and/or missed appointments with the Treatment Provider but no positive toxicology screen
100% Compliance	The client is instructed he/she must complete each and every task assigned to him/her in between drug court status appearances. A client receive this sanction after repeated low level and/or high level non-compliant behaviors and is close to termination from the program.
Increased Case Management Contacts	A client who is in danger of relapse due to stressors in his/her life may benefit from increased case management contacts in order to work with the drug court coordinator on problem solving discussions or activities. Clients, for example, may lose their job or apartment and have little or no skills to recover from such a loss. The drug court coordinator can assist the client in pursuing options the client may never have considered or the additional contact can help give the client the confidence to come up with a solution.
Day Reporting	For day reporting, a client is instructed to report to the courthouse or drug court coordinator every morning. The client may receive instructions or a task to perform or may just have to relate his/her plan for the day (in order to make sure the client will not do anything that will lead to non-compliant behavior).

Random Toxicology screens	If a client is suspected of manipulating his/her urine, using another's urine or managing his/her drug use so as to not test positive on regularly scheduled toxicology screens, the judge may order random toxicology screens in order to discover client drug use.
Loss of Clean Time	A client who tests positive on a toxicology screen can lose all of the cumulative clean time he/she has earned during drug court. Drug courts require a certain amount of cumulative clean time (6 or 12 months) before the client can graduate. Thus, if a client relapses in his/her 11th month in the drug court program he can lose cumulative clean time and be back at day one having to demonstrate an additional 12 months of clean time before successful graduation (with or without regular court status appearances).
Community Service	Community service as a sanction is intended to have the client restore back to the community some of the harm that inevitably comes from individual substance abuse.
Increased AA/NA meetings, 90/90, 60/60 or 30/30	Increased self-help meetings can amount to a one, two, or three more meetings between status appearances or ninety self-help meetings in ninety days, sixty self-help meetings in sixty days, or thirty self-help meetings in thirty days. Any amount of additional self- help meetings are utilized for major or minor non-compliant behaviors and may help re-focus the client on maintaining abstinence. Other intended or unintended side benefits include keeping the client occupied during the day and evening hours and increasing the client's investment in abstinent activities (abstinent "people, places, things")
Higher Level of Care ("Door to Door" or "Bed to Bed")	The drug court team will resort to a higher level of care when out-patient treatment and sober supports fail to keep a client from relapsing. In-patient can be recommended when a client is clearly not moving forward in their recovery. If in-patient is

required after a relapse that results in a jail sanction and the drug court team does not believe the client can remain in the community and stay safe, "Door to Door" or "Bed to Bed" will be ordered. If a client is entering in-patient treatment "Door to Door," the client is going from jail to in-patient treatment (court to jail to in-patient with police officer escort) with no opportunity to go home or see anyone thereby reducing the client's opportunity to engage in any form of substance abuse or buy drugs before going to the treatment facility

Sanction pending

Sanction pending is typically a sanction of jail time that is suspended for the client as long as the client remains compliant with the drug court program. Should the client engage in non-compliant behavior of any kind, the client will be required to serve the length of time in jail ordered by the drug court Judge.

Jail: Short term or long term stay

A jail sanction can be imposed for any behavior (from swearing at a drug court employee to a long term relapse or failure to show up to court for any scheduled status appearance). A short term jail sanction (2-3 days) is used by some courts to punish the client for non-compliant behavior but often allowing the client to serve his/her sanction on the weekends or time off from a job so that he/she can remain employed. Long term jail sanctions (one week to one month or more) happen when there are multiple non-compliant behaviors that are addressed at the same court appearance.

Removal from the Program

Removal from the program is not truly a sanction as the client is returned to criminal court in order to be processed in accordance to his/her particular court matter. While not a sanction, the threat of removal from the program (i.e. 100% compliance) can be used by drug courts to motivate a particularly recalcitrant client. Of course, removal from the drug court is punishment in that the client will remain drug addicted and may never recover from their addiction.

Table 13: Observed Rewards

Observed Reward	Description
Applause (from general handclapping to standing ovation)	Drug courts generally give a client applause in order to recognize a client's positive accomplishments. Drug courts differ greatly on the length and frequency of their applause. Court D, for example, provides that recognition to every client who appears in drug court in order to recognize their appearance in drug court and whatever the client may have accomplished between status appearances while other drug courts rarely applauded clients for positive accomplished outside of graduation.
Handshakes	Handshakes in drug court can be a reward for positive accomplishments (i.e. graduation) or a sign of respect and dignity.
Verbal Praise	Verbal praise is the most commonly used reward. Praise can be used as a "pat on the back" for a job well done (i.e. length of clean time or abstinence during a stressful time). In addition, verbal praise can be used in combination with or alone as words of encouragement to bolster a client in their efforts.
Head of the Class	Head of the class is a reward for a client's extra effort and can be used to allow a client to be called ahead of all the other clients scheduled for that day (and leave immediately after being seen by the Judge. A head of the class reward was observed to be given to clients for attending a court alumni group self-help session as well as writing letters to over sea injured soldiers. This was observed in a court that requires clients to be in court from the beginning to the end of the drug court session.
Small Gift	Small gifts were given to clients for graduation or during the court session. Small gifts during graduation were used as a metaphor and opportunity for the Judge to discuss the client's

struggle and success in their recovery. Small gifts were also given as a reward to a particular client for a job well done (lottery for a coffee shop gift card for those clients who brought their pocket calendars to the court session or for doing a particularly good job struggling with their addiction).

Food (i.e. cookies)	Food was used as a reward for clients, not necessarily for individual accomplishments, but for special occasions. Food was also used by one court in order to represent and encourage clients in the idea of drug court as a family (in that families "break bread" and together).
Leave early (i.e. Green Card)	Allowing clients to leave the drug court session could occur before or after the status appearance with the Judge (i.e. Head of the Class) or before seeing the Judge for those clients who are fully compliant with their drug court program.
Group activity	Some courts would plan a summer activity as a treat for the drug court clients. More than one court was observed planning a summer picnic or had summer picnics in the past. Other courts engaged in group bowling or other appropriate group activities.
Phase advancement	Not all courts in this study adhered to the idea of phase advancement. However, even for those courts which did not have "phase advancement," all the courts rewarded clients who completed specific treatment related activities (i.e. in or out patient treatment) with reduced treatment requirements (i.e. one on one individual counseling or fewer self-help meetings a week), and/or reduced status appearance (i.e. clients could go from weekly status appearances to bi-weekly to monthly). Many courts would also provide stage certificates which would mark the move from one phase to the next as a perk to the client for moving forward in their recovery).

Graduation and/or Graduations ceremonies	Graduations (or in one case "Day of Recognition") could range from simple to elaborate. Most graduations would combine applause, praise, handshake from the judge, and a small gift (i.e. whistle, book brunch) while offering the client an opportunity to the client to speak to other drug court clients in order to give words or wisdom or thanks to the team for supporting him/her.

Table 14: Observed Procedures

Observed Procedure	Description
On time court attendance (i.e. Roll Call)	Court attendance at the beginning of the court session could be required for each client through a procedure such as a roll call (where sanctions could result from a late appearance) or for most client's where individual absences at the beginning of the court calendar could be excused for good reason (i.e. job or class).
Clients stay to end of court/leave after case was heard	Some courts required clients attend the court session from beginning to end while other courts allowed clients to leave after they were seen by the judge. Of course, notable differences were courts that used exceptions such as the Green Card or Head of the Class.
Client Confidentialit y (i.e. microphone is turned off for discussions)	Drug courts all struggle with the tension between the public nature of courts and client confidentiality. Some courts "close" their courtroom to everyone but clients and/or important people in the client's life, some courts require non-court personnel to sign confidentiality forms in order to sit on a drug court session, while other courts retain their public nature. One court allows the client to converse with the drug court coordinator or his/her attorney but have the microphone turned off during the conversation thereby protecting the client's communication (from both the judge and the audience) about various issues.

Weekly Order   In order to encourage compliance with the Drug Treatment program, the Judge and drug court coordinator write a list of the client's required tasks for the week on a form that is given to the client at the end of the status appearance. This "weekly order" will detail the number of self-helps, if any, treatment meetings, required toxicology drug screens and/or job, community service, school requirements in addition to any sanctions such as day reporting or additional self-help meetings. One copy of the "weekly order" was given to the client to remind him/her of what must be accomplished during the week and one copy was retained by the court for record keeping.

Self-helps verified in court   Many, but not all, courts would verify self-help attendance during the court session. Self-helps sheets marking which meetings that the client attended could be verified by the staff before the court session (outside of the client audience). Some courts, however, would verify that self-helps during the court session in front of the rest of the clients in attendance so that failure to do self-helps could be result in the client being sanctioned while other courts would verify self-helps during the court session and then discuss the number assigned for the next week. Thus, clients could be rewarded (or sanctioned) for self-help attendance as well as be encouraged to go to self-helps in the future. One court was observed to ask the drug court coordinator for the number of self-helps and then reward clients with praise for doing additional self-helps. Many clients were observed to have more self-helps than required. In addition, that court would mention the number of self-helps that would be required for the next week or until the next status appearance.

GED
Employment
School
Enrollment   Courts were often observed to require clients to obtain their GED (lots of clients drop out of high school), employment or enroll in a vocational program or college. Those courts try to focus on the whole individual providing the client with the tools they will need to become successful after the client graduates from drug court. These courts recognize that abstaining from substance abuse is one piece of a client's life and looking ahead to the client's future.

Community Service required during phase	Some courts were observed to require a certain number of Community Service hours when a client was unemployed or not in enrolled in some kind of school program. The requirement of Community Service for phase advancement is intended to encourage the client to re-engage with the community, establish sober activities and become a part of the productive member of society.
Essay required for phase advancement	One of the courts in the study was observed to require an essay from every client before they were allowed to advance to the second phase of their drug court program. This essay gave the client and opportunity to engage in a thoughtful look at their struggle with addiction, their family and friends who have been impacted by their addiction and any hopes and dreams they might have. The Judge would ask the client if they wanted to share the essay with the other clients or allow the judge to read it to the audience. If the client requested privacy in regards to the essay, the judge would read it privately and praise the client for any insights or positive things that the essay might contain. This essay provided clients with an opportunity to obtain some insight into their addiction.
Community Improvement Project	Along the same vein of phase required Community Service is the Community Improvement Project. One of the courts was observed to require each client to propose and complete a Community Improvement Project before the client could successfully graduate from drug court. This Community Improvement Project would require the client to give back to the community he/she lived in and encourage the client to think about how he/she could become a more productive, positive, member of the community.
In court intake procedure	A few courts would engage in an intake procedure for new clients which would cover the client's drug history. This entailed the Judge going over a pre-set selection of questions with the client in order to elicit some history (whether drug, medical or social history). One of the courts in this study was observed engaging the

client in an extensive criminal, social, medical, and drug history which was intended to ensure client honesty in regards to his/her addiction. Some clients were observed to tell the Judge one thing and the Treatment provider something else while telling the probation officer another history. The Judge could then address any client dishonesty in court and encourage the client to be more honest in the future.

In Court GED program	An in court GED program allows the client to attend GED classes in the courthouse (often a central location along public transportation routes) and attendance in the GED program is court monitored. Thus, clients will be rewarded or sanctioned according to their compliance with the program. In addition, one of the GED staff would also be a member of the drug court Team as a treatment provider.
In-Court Self-help group	The in-court self-help/alumni group held in the courthouse (often located in a central location in the community along public transportation lines) makes it easier for clients to attend meetings.
Alumni Groups	Alumni groups are made up of drug court graduates of a particular drug court who meet regularly and hold self-help meetings. The groups can also function as community mentors for clients.
Helpful tips upon first appearance	One court was observed to provide an in court information session were the Judge provided the newly admitted client with some helpful advice on how to be compliant with the drug court program.
Time limit to complete drug court	Drug courts can set a specific time period that they will be able to provide services and client monitoring. Clients must complete all the treatment requirements within this period of time or be returned to criminal court for court processing in accordance with their criminal matter.

Cumulative Clean Time before Graduation	Cumulative clean time is that period of time, set by individual drug courts, for which the client must demonstrate abstinence from substance use. Whether a single use or longer relapse will reset the cumulative clean time clock is a decision each drug court makes. Some drug courts may decide the clock reset on a case-by-case basis while other drug courts may set a bright line rule that any use will reset that time clock to zero. Common cumulative clean times were six months or a year.
6 month goal sheet	One drug court was observed to assign newly admitted clients a 6 Month Goal Sheet as homework. Clients were instructed to go home and write out on a sheet of paper specific goals they would like to meet six months from that date, fold the goal sheet and place it into an envelope. The Judge would tell the clients to bring this goal sheet with them to court the next status appearance and give it to him. Six months from that date, the Judge would return the goal sheet to the client, unread, for the client to review by him/herself to see what, if any, progress was made and/or what the client was thinking when they started drug court.
Compliance Court	Compliance court was designated for clients who were screened for drug court but did not show a dependency diagnosis. Clients in Compliance Court report for random/regular drug toxicology screens but would not be required to report to the Judge unless the client was arrested on new charges or had a positive toxicology screen.
Monitoring status	For some drug courts, the time period between when a client has completed all of his/her treatment requirements and has demonstrated the required amount of cumulative clean time is referred to as Monitoring status. This Monitoring status is a time period with dramatically reduced court appearances but random/regular drug toxicology screens to ensure the client is remaining drug free. Once this time period is completed the client can be scheduled for graduation

Transfer	Transfers could occur to other appropriate courts if it was discovered that clients would be able to be more compliant in the other court (due to travel restrictions or availability of treatment or public transportation or a client needed to move). Both courts would need to be in agreement with the transfer. Also, courts would transfer drug court clients to a different specialty court should the client needs warrant it. Many clients, for example, have trauma related issues and the drug addiction is a form of self-medication. Some trauma may not exhibit itself until the drug addiction is addressed and the trauma will interfere with the client's ability to be complaint. Once the trauma surfaces, drug courts can transfer the client to Mental Health Court or Veteran's Court where specific issues of trauma can be addressed in addition to the substance abuse.
Client self-sanction	Judges were observed asking the client to think about and propose their own sanction. This self-sanction was used to give the client an opportunity to consider their actions and come up with an appropriate sanction (a punishment that would fit the crime). One Judge would assign a team member to work on that sanction with the client to help him/her problem solve some sanction. This same judge was also observed giving the client less than he/she came up with on their own.
Client mentor	Newly admitted clients would be assigned a mentor to help them through the drug court. This mentor (a drug court client who has demonstrated long term sobriety and compliance with the drug court program) would help them with the requirements of drug court and provide a sober support in the community.
Curfew	Clients would be told how early they needed to be in their residence so they would be home for bed checks. Police departments or probation were responsible for doing home visits and clients would be sanctioned for any failure to respond to the doorbell.
Permission	A few of the drug courts were very close to the state border. In

required to leave the County	order for the drug court to verify Self-Helps and/or keep track of the clients in the community, the drug court required the clients to fill out a form to request permission to leave the county and receive judicial permission.
Potential partners/room mates investigated	Clients who change addresses, move in with other people or become involved with a significant other must inform the drug court of their new circumstances. Judges were observed questioning Team Members (Probation or treatment providers) and client's on their choices. This gave the Judge the opportunity to discuss "people, places and things" with clients in an effort to keep them compliant with the drug court program.
Termination Due Process Hearing	Termination or due process hearings are intended to allow the client an opportunity to hear the facts against them and provide information in his/her defense before being terminated from drug court. The client has attorney representation for the hearing.

Each reward, sanction and policy is unique and can be used by each court to motivate clients in different ways. Table 15, 16, 17, 18 and 19 are complete lists of rewards, sanctions, procedures as well as compliant and non-compliant behaviors observed during the course of the this study.

Table 15: Complete list of observed compliant behaviors by court

Compliant behavior	Courts										Total	% used
	A	B	C	D	E	F	G	H	I	J		
Attended treatment sessions	3	44	23	12	20	6	206	12	5	190	521	19.95%
followed team requests	8	79	37	24	40	17	196	41	31	208	681	26.07%
drug free urines	4	18	21	11	13	5	165	37	1	58	333	12.75%
phase advancement	41	12	7	8	8	22	7	3	7	23	138	5.28%
obtained employment/ged/graduated hs	1	2	2	8	8	0	2	8	2	12	45	1.72%
new to program	1	0	0	2	0	0	0	0	0	0	3	0.11%
positive attitude	0	1	0	0	1	0	0	1	0	0	3	0.11%
doing well/good reports/doing better	1	4	2	0	1	0	0	4	4	2	18	0.69%
rescheduled appt	0	0	0	1	0	0	0	1	0	0	2	0.08%
extra self-helps	0	0	0	0	0	0	0	0	6	15	21	0.80%
6 month goal sheet	0	0	0	0	0	0	0	0	2	0	2	0.08%
paid bills	0	0	0	2	0	0	0	0	1	9	12	0.46%
started school	0	0	0	1	3	0	2	0	2	5	13	0.50%
taking care of business (surgery/quitting smoking/making dr appts)	0	0	0	1	3	1	0	1	7	5	18	0.69%
extra community service	0	0	0	1	1	0	0	0	0	0	2	0.08%
self-report	0	0	0	2	1	1	3	1	2	1	11	0.42%
unkown/other	1	2	0	0	4	0	0	2	2	7	18	0.69%
Total	60	162	92	73	103	52	581	111	72	535	1841	70.48%
Total Judicial interactions	294	291	95	168	225	192	447	133	401	366	2612	
% of total for court	20.4%	55.7%	96.8%	43.5%	45.8%	27.1%	130.0%	83.5%	18.0%	146.2%		

Table 16: Complete list of observed rewards by court

Rewards	A	B	C	D	E	F	G	H	I	J	Total	% used
Speech upon graduation	27	1	1	0	0	10	7	1	0	5	52	1.99%
small gift	46	1	3	1	1	7	7	0	1	2	69	2.64%
reduced community service hours	0	0	0	0	0	0	0	0	0	1	1	0.04%
reduced drug testing	0	0	0	0	0	0	0	0	0	0	0	0.00%
reduced treatment requirements	0	0	1	2	1	1	1	0	3	6	15	0.57%
reduced status appearances	0	16	4	2	0	4	0	3	6	6	41	1.57%
reduced homework assignments	0	0	0	0	0	1	0	0	0	0	1	0.04%
applause	35	14	83	8	9	20	7	32	2	21	231	8.84%
praise	19	61	67	18	32	31	18	81	52	159	538	20.60%
stage certificates	21	7	4	0	4	8	7	2	8	10	71	2.72%
head of class	0	0	0	0	0	0	0	0	7	0	7	0.27%
approved travel	2	0	0	0	0	0	0	0	0	0	2	0.08%
released (ror)	0	0	0	0	0	0	6	0	0	0	6	0.23%
retained in drug court	0	0	0	0	0	0	1	0	0	0	1	0.04%
handshake	20	2	1	168	2	0	0	0	0	0	193	7.39%
ACD	0	1	0	0	0	0	1	2	0	0	4	0.15%
encouragement	0	0	3	1	1	2	0	0	10	0	17	0.65%
Favorable resolution of criminal charges	1	0	1	0	0	0	0	0	0	0	2	0.08%
transfer to a different court	1	0	0	0	0	0	0	0	0	0	1	0.04%
Unknown/Other	0	0	0	0	7	0	1	0	0	0	8	0.31%
Total	172	103	168	200	57	84	56	121	89	210	1260	48.24%
Total Judicial interactions	294	291	95	168	225	192	447	133	401	366	2612	
% of total for court	58.5%	35.4%	177%	119%	25.3%	43.8%	12.5%	91.0%	22.2%	57.4%		

Table 17: Complete list of observed non-compliant behaviors by court

Noncompliant behavior	A	B	C	D	E	F	G	H	I	J	Total	% used
drugs found in urine	54	22	5	9	14	32	36	5	30	19	226	8.65%
failed to go to treatment appts	26	20	8	13	16	34	34	7	15	21	194	7.43%
failed to follow team requests	13	3	2	6	0	9	31	1	12	7	84	3.22%
associated with drug addicted friends	0	1	0	0	0	0	1	0	5	11	18	0.69%
lied about non-compliance	10	1	1	3	0	2	14	2	17	1	49	1.88%
New Charges	7	5	0	4	13	9	10	2	5	9	64	2.45%
denied something	1	0	0	0	0	0	0	0	0	0	1	0.04%
failed to go to court	5	2	0	0	5	11	4	1	4	2	34	1.30%
no tox provided or diluted sample	6	1	1	0	2	7	4	0	3	2	26	1.00%
interlock failed	1	1	0	0	0	0	0	0	0	0	2	0.08%
found with extra urine	1	0	0	1	0	0	0	0	0	0	2	0.08%
failed to pay fines/treatment	1	1	2	0	0	0	5	0	1	2	12	0.46%
self-report use	10	0	0	0	1	2	1	1	2	0	17	0.65%
Ran, violated rules, kicked out of program	4	0	0	1	1	6	3	0	6	2	23	0.88%
curfew violation, failed to call in	6	1	0	3	0	0	0	0	9	6	25	0.96%
suspected drug use or inappropriate behavior	7	0	1	0	0	1	0	0	2	1	12	0.46%
late for court, treatment appointments	5	4	0	3	0	0	2	0	1	0	15	0.57%
bad attitude	1	1	0	1	0	1	3	1	0	0	8	0.31%
Violation of probation	0	2	0	0	0	0	3	0	0	0	5	0.19%
dress code violation, chewing gum	0	1	0	1	1	0	0	0	0	0	3	0.11%
traffic violation	0	0	0	3	0	0	0	0	0	3	6	0.23%
fired from job	1	0	0	2	0	0	0	1	0	0	4	0.15%
police contact	0	0	0	0	0	0	0	0	7	1	9	0.34%
unkown/other	11	6	1	2	1	8	3	1	6	12	51	1.95%
Total	170	72	21	52	54	122	154	21	125	99	890	34.07%
Total Judicial interactions	294	291	95	168	225	192	447	133	401	366	2612	
% of total for court	57.8%	24.7%	22.1%	31.0%	24.0%	63.5%	34.5%	15.8%	31.2%	27.0%		

Table 18: Complete list of sanctions by court

Sanctions	A	B	C	D	E	F	G	H	I	J	Total	% used
increased self-helps	1	1	0	1	3	4	0	0	7	0	17	0.65%
increased case management contacts	2	0	1	0	9	6	2	0	1	13	34	1.30%
day reporting	0	0	0	1	0	0	1	1	0	1	3	0.11%
work release program	0	0	0	0	2	0	0	0	0	1	3	0.11%
work crew	0	0	0	0	0	0	0	0	0	0	0	0.00%
electronic monitoring	0	0	0	0	0	0	0	0	0	0	0	0.00%
community service hours	2	0	0	0	6	5	0	0	4	2	19	0.73%
jail	45	17	1	13	4	31	55	0	47	18	231	8.84%
100% compliance	2	0	0	0	0	6	0	0	0	0	8	0.31%
returned to criminal court	12	3	0	1	1	0	0	0	0	2	19	0.73%
modified sanction	2	0	0	0	0	0	0	0	0	0	2	0.08%
additional requirement (get doctors note/make a plan/Doctors visit)	4	1	2	3	1	6	2	0	0	1	20	0.77%
denied something (trip)	1	0	0	0	0	0	0	0	0	0	1	0.04%
higher level care/detoxification program	4	4	0	5	4	3	5	2	2	2	31	1.19%
no sanction	9	10	5	5	3	8	23	8	25	14	110	4.21%
curfew	1	0	0	0	0	0	0	0	0	0	1	0.04%
Sanction pending	2	1	2	0	0	16	0	0	0	1	22	0.84%
warning	2	5	0	5	0	6	1	1	3	6	29	1.11%
Judicial admonishment	0	2	1	0	0	0	0	0	0	1	4	0.15%

Table 18: Complete list of sanctions by court (Cond't)

Sanctions	A	B	C	D	E	F	G	H	I	J	Total	% used
increased supervision	0	1	0	0	0	1	1	1	0	0	4	0.15%
penalty box	0	0	0	0	4	0	0	0	0	0	4	0.15%
essay/letter	0	0	0	0	0	3	3	0	6	0	12	0.46%
loss of clean time	0	0	0	0	5	0	0	1	0	0	6	0.23%
back to previous phase	0	0	0	1	0	0	0	0	0	0	1	0.04%
transfer to different court	0	0	0	0	1	0	0	0	0	0	1	0.04%
serve sanction pending	0	1	0	1	0	0	0	0	0	0	2	0.08%
unkown/other	3	1	1	2	7	2	1	0	0	3	20	0.77%
Total	92	47	13	38	50	97	94	14	95	64	604	23.12%
Total Judicial interactions	294	291	95	168	225	192	447	133	401	366	2612	
% of total for court	31.3%	16.2%	13.7%	22.6%	22.2%	50.5%	21.0%	10.5%	23.7%	17.5%		

Table 19: Unique policies observed during the drug court session by court

Unique Policies and Procedures	A	B	C	D	E	F	G	H	I	J
On time court attendance (i.e. Roll Call)	x		x		x	x	x		x	
Exceptions to on time attendance for good reason		x	x					x		x
Clients stay to end of court				x					x	
Clients leave after case is heard	x	x	x			x	x	x		x
Client Confidentiality		x			x					
Weekly Order		x		x						
Self-helps verified in court				x					x	x
GED/Employment/School enrollment	x			x			x		x	x
Community Service required during phase			x	x						
Essay required for phase advancement			x							
Community improvement project			x						x	
In court intake procedure									x	
In Court GED program	x	x			x	x	x	x	x	
In Court Self-help group							x	x		
Alumni group									x	
Helpful tips upon first appearance					x					
Time limit to complete drug court				x						

Table 19: Unique policies observed during the drug court session by Court (Cond't)

					Courts					
Unique Policies and Procedures	A	B	C	D	E	F	G	H	I	J
Cumulative Clean Time before Graduation	x	x	x	x	x	x	x	x	x	x
6 month goal sheet									x	
Compliance Court	x									
Monitoring status	x						x			
Transfer	x						x		x	
Client self-sanction		x								
Client mentor				x						
Curfew	x									x
Permission required to leave the county				x						
Potential partners/roommates investigated							x		x	
Termination/Due Process Hearing				x						

References

Abel, Richard L. (Ed.). (1982). *The Politics of Informal Justice* (Vol. 1). London: Academic Press, Inc.

Allan, Kenneth. (2006). Defining the Possible and Impossible. *Contemporary Social and Sociological Theory Visualizing Social Worlds* (pp. 287-309). Thousand Oaks, CA: Pine Forge Press.

Anderson, John F. (2001). What to do about "much ado" about drug courts? *International Journal of Drug Policy, 12*, 469-475.

Bavon, A. (2001). The effect of the Tarrant County Drug Court Project on recidivism. *Evaluation and Prgram Planning, 24*, 13-22.

Bean, Philip. (2002). Drug Courts, the Judge, and the Rehabilitative Model. In J. James L. Nolan (Ed.), *Drug Courts in Theory and in Practice* (pp. 235-253). Hawthorne, NY: Aldine De Gruyter.

Belenko, Stephen. (1999). Research on Drug Courts: A Critical Review, 1999 Update. *II*(2), 1-58.

Belenko, Stephen. (2001). *Research on Drug Courts: A Critical Review 2001 Update* (Vol. 1). New York: Columbia University.

Black, Donald. (1989). *Sociological Justice*. Oxford: Oxford University Press.

Blomqvist, Jan. (2002). Recovery with and without treatment: A comparison of resolutions of Alcohol and Drug Problems. *Addiction Research and Theory, 10*(2), 119-158.

Blumberg, Abraham S. (1967). The Practice of Law as Confidence Game. *Law & Society Review, 1*(2), 15-39.

Bouffard, Jeff, & Taxman, Faye. (2004). Looking inside the "Black Box" of Drug Court Treatment Services Using Direct Observations. *Journal of Drug Issues, 34*, 195-218.

Bourgois, Philippe, & Schonberg, Jeff. (2009). *Righteous Dopefiend*. Berkeley: Univeristy of California Press.

Boyum, Keith O., & Mather, Lynn (Eds.). (1983). *Empirical Theories About Courts*. New York: Longman.

Brank, Eve M., & Haby, Joshua A. (2013). The Intended and Unintended Consequences of Problem-Solving Courts. In R. L. Weiner & E. M. Brank (Eds.), *Problem Solving Courts: Social Science and Legal Perspectives*. New York: Springer Publishing.

Burns, Stacy Lee, & Peyrot, Mark. (2003). Tough Love: Nurturing and Coercing Responsibility and Recovery in California Drug Courts. *Social Problems, 50*(3), 416-438.

C. West Huddleston, III, Douglas B. Marlowe, J.D., Ph.D., & Casebolt, Rachel. (2008). *Painting the Current Picture: A National Report Card on Drug Courts and Other Problem-Solving Court Programs in the United States*. Alexandria.

Castellano, Ursula. (2009). Beyond the Courtroom Workgroup: Caseworkers as the New Satellite of Social Control. *Law & Policy, 31*(4), 429-462.

Chambliss, William. (1964). A Sociological Analysis of the Law of Vagrancy. *Social Problems, 12*(1), 67-77.

Cissner, Amanda B., & Rempel, Michael. (2005). *The State of Drug Court Research*. Washington D.C.: National Drug Court Institute.

Collins, Hugh. (1982). *Marxism and the Law*. Oxford: Clarendon Press.

Cullen, Francis T., & Gendreau, Paul. (2000). Assessing Correctional Rehabilitation: Policy, Practice, and Prospects. In U. D. o. Justice (Ed.), *Criminal Justice 2000* (Vol. 3: Policies, Processes, and Decisions in the Criminal Justice System, pp. 109-175). Washington D.C.: National Institute of Justice.

David DeMatteo, J.D., Ph.D., Sarah Filone, M.A., & Casey LaDuke, M.S. (2011). Methodological, Ethical, and Legal Considerations in Drug Court Research. *Behavioral Sciences and the Law, 29*, 806-820.

Day, Ed (Ed.). (2007). *Clinical Topics in Addiction*. London: RCPsych Publications.

Deflem, Mathieu. (2008). *Sociology of Law Visions of a Scholarly Tradition*. Cambridge, NY: Cambridge University Press.

Eisenstein, James, & Jacob, Herbert. (1977). *Felony Justice: An Organizational Analysis of Criminal Courts*. Boston: Little Brown.

Felstiner, William L. F., Abel, Richard L., & Sarat, Austin. (1980). The Emergence and Transformation of Disputes: Naming, Blaming and Claiming. *Law & Society Review, 15*(3-4), 631-655.

Fora, Peggy Fulton, & Stalcup, Theodore. (2008). Drug Treatment Courts in the Twenty-first Century: The Evolution of the Revolution in Problem-solving Courts. *Georgia Law Review, 42*(3), 717-811.

Foucault, Michel. (1984). The Birth of the Asylum. In P. Rabinow (Ed.), *The Foucault Reader*. New York, NY: Pantheon Books.

Foucault, Michel (Ed.). (1980). *Power/Knowledge: Selected Interviews & Other Writings 1972-1977*. New York: Pantheon Books.

Fox, Richard, & Sickel, Robert Van. (2000). Gender Dynamics and Judicial Behavior in Criminal Trial Courts: An Exploratory Study. *The Justice System Journal, 21*(3), 261-280.

Friedman, Lawrence. (1983). Courts Over Time: A Survey of Theories and Research. In K. O. Boyum & L. Mather (Eds.), *Empirical Theories About Courts* (pp. 9-49). New York: Longman Publishing.

Frohmann, Lisa. (1997). Convictability and Discordant Locales: Reproducing Race, Class, and Gender Ideologies in Prosecutorial Decision Making. *Law & Society, 31*(3), 531-556.

GAO. (2005). *Adult Drug Courts Evidence Indicates Recidivism Reductions and Mixed Results for Other Outcomes*. Washington D.C.: United States Government Accountability Office.

Gifford, Elizabeth J., Eldred, Lindsey M., McCutchan, Sabrina A., & Sloan, Frank A. (2014). The Effects of Participation Level on Recidivism: A Study of Drug Treatment Courts Using Propensity Score Matching. *Substance Abuse Treatment, Prevention and Policy, 9*, 40.

Gilligan, Carol. (1982). *In a Different Voice*. Cambridge: Harvard Universtiy Press.

Goldkamp, J. S., White, M. D., & Robinson, J. B. (2001). Do Drug Courts Work? Getting Inside the Drug Court Black Box. *Journal of Drug Issues, 31*(1), 27-72.

Granfield, Robert, & Cloud, Willam. (1999). *Coming Clean Overcoming Addiction without Treatment*. New York New York University Press.

Granfield, Robert, Eby, Cynthia, & Brewster, Thomas. (1998). An Examination of the Denver Drug Court: The Impact of a Treatment-oriented Drug Offender System. *Law & Policy, 20*(2), 183-202.

Green, Mia, & Rempel, Michael. (2010). *Do Adult Drug Courts Work? National Results from the Multi-Site Adult Drug Court Evaluation (MADCE)*. Paper presented at the NIJ Conference 2010 Arlington, VA.

Gusfield, Joseph. (1986). *Symbolic Crusade: Status Politics and the American Temperance Movement* (2nd ed.). Chicago: University of Illinois Press.

Guydish, Joseph, Tajima, Barbara, Wolfe, Ellen, & Woods, William J. (2006). Drug Court Effectiveness: A Review of California Evaluation Reports, 1995-1999. *Journal of Psychoactive Drugs, 33*(4), 369-378.

Hanson, Roger. (2002). The Changing Role of a Judge and Its Implications. *Court Review*, 10-16.

Harrell, Adele. (1998). Drug Courts and the Role of Graduated Sanctions. *National Institute of Justice Research Preview*. http://www.ncjrs.gov/pdffiles/fs000219.pdf.

Hay, Douglas (Ed.). (1975). *Property, Authority and the Criminal Law*. New York: : Pantheon Publishing.

Heck, Cary. (2006). *Local Drug Court Research: Navigating Performance Measures and Process Evaluations*. Washington DC: National Drug Court Institute.

Heinz, John P., & Manikas, Peter M. (1992). Networks among Elites in a Local Criminal Justice System. *Law & Society, 26*(4), 831-861.

Hemmens, Craig, Brody, David C., & Spohn, Cassia C. (2010). *Criminal Courts A Contemporary Perspective*. Thousand Oaks: Sage Publishing.

Hoffman, Morris B. (2000). The Drug Court Scandal. *North Carolina Law Review, 78*, 1437.

Hoffman, Morris B. (2002a). The Rehabilitative Ideal and the Drug Court Reality. *Federal Sentencing Reporter, 14*, 172-178.

Hoffman, Morris B. (2002b). Therapeutic Jurisprudence, Neo-Rehabilitationism, and Judicial Collectivism: The Least Dangerous Branch becomes Most Dangerous *Fordham Urban Law Journal, 29*, 2063-2098.

Hull, Kathleen E. (2003). The Culture Power of Law and the Cultural Enactment of Legality: The Case of Same-Sex Marriage. *Law and Social Inquiry, 28*, 629-657.

Inciardi, James A. (2008). *The War on Drugs* (4th ed.). Boston, MA: Pearson Education, Inc.

Inciardi, James A., McBride, Duane C., & Rivers, James E. (1996). *Drug Control and the Courts*. Thousand Oaks: Sage Publications.

Irvine, Leslie. (1999). *Codependent Forevermore*. Chicago: University of Chicago Press.

Irwin, Darrell D. (2002). Identifying the Process of Drug Court Treatment in Small Towns and Mid-sized Cities. *Journal of Crime and Justice, 22*, 63-77.

Ismaili, Karim (Ed.). (2011). *U.S. Criminal Justice Policy A Contemporary Reader*. Sudbury: Jones & Bartlett.

Jacob, Herbert, Blankenburg, Erhard, Kritzer, Herbert M., Provine, Doris Marie, & Sanders, Joseph. (1996). *Courts, Law & Politics in Comparative Perspective*. New Haven: Yale University Press.

Jarvinen, Margaretha. (2008). Approaches to Methadone Treatment: Harm Reduction in Theory and Practice. *Sociology of Health and Illness, 30*(7), 975-991.

Jellinek, E. M. (1952). Phases of Alcohol Addiction. *Quarterly Journal of Alcohol Studies, 13*(4), 673-684.

Johnson, Charles Michael, & Wallace, Shana. (2004). Critical Elements to Consider for Methodologically Sound Impact Evaluations of Drug Court Programs. *Drug Court Review, IV*(2), 35-47.

Joseph Guydish, Phd, Ellen Wolfe, Phd, Tajima, Ed. M., & William J. Woods, Phd (2001). Drug Court effectiveness: A Review of California Evaluation Reports, 1995-1999. *Journal of Psychoactive Drugs, 33*(4), 369-378.

Karoll, Brad R. (2010). Applying Social Work Approaches, Harm Reduction, and Practice Wisdom to Better Serve Those with Alcohol and Drug Use Disorders. *Journal of Social Work, 10*, 263-281.

Kaskutas, Lee Ann. (2009). Alcoholics Anonymous Effectiveness: Faith Meets Science. *Journal of Addictive Diseases, 28*, 145-157.

Kennedy, Duncan. (2004). The Disenchantment of Logically Formal Legal Rationality. *Hastings Law Journal, 55*, 1031-1076.

Knepper, Paul. (2001). *Explaining Criminal Conduct Theories and Systems in Criminology*. Durham: Carolina Academic Press.

Levine, Harry. (1978). The Discovery of Addiction: Changing Conceptions of Habitual Drunkenness in America. *Journal of Studies on Alcohol, 15*, 493-506.

Levine, Harry. (1985). The Birth of American Alcohol Control: Prohibition, the Power Elite and the Problem of Lawlessness. *Contemporary Drug Problems*, 63-118.

Levinthal, Charles F. (2006). *Drugs, Society, and Criminal Justice.* Boston, MA: Pearson Education, Inc.

Lloyd, Margaret H., Johnson, Toni, & Brook, Jody. (2014). Illuminating the Black Box from Within: Stakeholder Perspectives on Family Drug Court Best Practices. *Journal of Social Work Practice in the Addictions, 14*(4), 378-401.

Longshore, Douglas, Turner, Susan, Wenzel, Suzanne, Morral, Andrew, Harrell, Adele, McBride, Duane, Deschenes, Elizabeth, & Iguchi, Martin. (2001). Drug Courts: A Conceptual Framework. *Journal of Drug Issues, 31*(1), 7-26.

Lyman, Michael D. (2011). *Drugs in Society Causes, Concepts and Control* (6th ed.). Boston: Anderson Publishing.

Maisto, Stephen A., Galizio, Mark, & Connors, Gerald J. (2004). *Drug Use and Abuse* (4th ed.). Belmont, CA: Wadsworth.

Marlowe, Douglas B., Festinger, David S., & Lee, Patricia A. (2004). The Judge is a Key Component of Drug Court. *Drug Court Review, IV*(2), 1-34.

Marx, Karl, & Engels, Friedrich. (1992). *The Communist Mafifesto.* Oxford: Oxford University Press.

Maynard, Douglas W. (1984). *Inside Plea Bargaining The Language of Negotiation.* New York: Plenum Press.

Mays, G. Larry, & Ruddell, Rick. (2008). *Making Sense of Criminal Justice.* New York: Oxford University Press.

McColl, Willam. (1996). Baltimore City's Drug Treatment Court: Theory and Practice in an Emerging Field. *Maryland Law Review, 55*, 467-520.

Meyer, Judge William. (2007). *Developing and Delivering Incentives and Sanctions.* Paper presented at the Incentives and Sanctions, Coral Gables, Fla.

Mileski, Maureen. (1971). Courtroom Encounters: An Observational Study of a Lower Court. *Law & Society Revew, 5*, 473-538.

Miller, JoAnn, & Johnson, Donald C. (2009). *Problem Solving Courts: New Approaches to Criminal Justice.* Lanham: Rowman & Littlefield.

Miller, William R., Wilbourne, Paul L., & Hettema, Jennifer E. (2003). What works? A summary of alcohol treatment outcome research.

In R. K. H. a. W. R. Miller (Ed.), *Handbook of Alcoholism Treatment Approaches: Effective Alternatives* (3rd ed.). Boston: Allyn and Bacon.

Mulcahy, Linda. (2007). Architects of Justice: The Politics of Courtroom Design. *Social & Legal Studies, 16*(3), 383-403.

NADCP, National Association of Drug Court Professionals. (1997). *Defining Drug Courts: The Key Components.* Washington DC: Office of Justice Programs.

NADCP, National Association of Drug Court Professionals. (2004). *Drug Court Planning Initiative Family Dependency Treatment Court Introductory Training Program.* Pensacola, FL: Office of Justice Programs.

NADCP, National Association of Drug Court Professionals. (2005). *Use of Jail Sanctions in Family Drug Courts.* Washington, DC: American University Retrieved from http://spa.american.edu/justice/documents/2020.pdf.

NADCP, National Association Of Drug Court Professionals. (2014). http://www.ndci.org/.

Nardulli, Peter F. (1978). *The Courtroom Elite: An Organizational Perspective on Criminal Justice.* Cambridge: Ballinger Publishing Company.

Nardulli, Peter F. (1979). *The Study of Criminal Courts: Political Perspectives.* Cambridge: Ballinger Publishing Company.

Nardulli, Peter F., Flemming, Roy B., & Eisenstein, James. (1985). Criminal Courts and Bureaucratic Justice: Concessions and Consensus in the Guilty Plea Process. *Journal of Criminal Law & Criminology, 76*(4), 1103-1131.

Neubauer, David W. (2008). *American Courts and the Criminal Justice System.* Belmont, CA: Thomson Higher Education.

Nolan, James L. (2001). *Reinventing Justice The American Drug Court Movement.* Princeton, NJ: Princeton University Press.

Paik, Leslie. (2011). *Discretionary Justice Looking Inside a Juvenile Drug Court* New Jersey: Rutgers Unversity Press.

Peters, Roger H., & Murrin, Mary R. (2000). Effectiveness of Treatment-Based Drug Courts in Reducing Criminal Recidivism. *Criminal Justice and Behavior, 27*(1), 72-96.

Platt, Anthony. (1969). *The Child Savers: The Invention of Delinquency 2nd Ed.* Chicago: The Chicago Press.

Popovic, Jelena. (2000). Court Process and Therapeutic Jurisprudence: Have We Thrown The Baby Out With The Bathwater? Retrieved December 7, 2008, from https://elaw.murdoch.edu.au/issues/special/court_process.pdf

ProCon.org. (2012). 18 Legal Medical Marijuana States and DC: Laws, Fees, and Possession Limits. Retrieved December 21, 2012, from http://www.procon.org

Provine, Doris Marie. (2007). *Unequal Under the Law Race in the War on Drugs*. Chicago, IL: University of Chicago Press.

Ray, Bradley, Dollar, Cindy Brooks, & Thames, Kelly M. (2011). Observations of Reintegrative Shaming in a Mental Mealth Court. *Internation Journal of Law and Psychiatry, 34*, 49-55.

Reinarman, Craig, & Levine, Harry. (1997). Punitive Prohibition in America *Crack in America: Demon Drugs and Social Justice* (pp. 321-333). Berkeley: University of California Press.

Rempel, Michael (2006, December 5, 2006). [The State Of Drug Court Research: What do We Know?].

Roper, Glade F. (2007). Introduction to Drug Courts. In J. E. Lessenger & G. F. Roper (Eds.), *Drug Courts A New Approach to Treatment and Rehabilitation*. New York: Spinger Publishing.

Rosenthal, John Terrence A. (2002). Therapeutic Jurisprudence and Drug Treatment Courts: Integrating Law and Science. In J. James L. Nolan (Ed.), *Drug Courts in Theory and in Practice* (pp. 145-172). New York, NY: Walter de Gruyter, Inc.

Rossman, Shelli, Rempel, Michael, Roman, John, Zweig, Janine, Lindquist, Christine, Green, Mia, Downey, P. Mitchell, Yahner, Jennifer, Bhati, Avinash, & Donald Farole, Jr. (2011). *The Multi-Site Adult Drug Court Evaluation: The Impact of Drug Courts*. Washington DC: US Department of Justice.

Rothschild, Debra. (2010). Partners in Treatment: Relational Psychoanalysis and Harm Reduction Therapy. *Journal of Clinical Psychology: In Session, 66*(2), 136-149.

Sarat, Austin, & Felstiner, William L. F. (1988). Law and Social Relations: Vocabularies of Motive in Lawyer/Client Interaction. *Law & Society Review, 22*(4), 737-770.

Sarat, Austin, & Simon, Jonathan. (2001). Beyond Legal Realism?:Cultural Analysis, Cultural Studies and the Situation of Legal Scholarship. *Yale Journal of Law & the Humanities, 13*, 3-34.

Satel, Sally L. (1999). *Drug Treatment: The Case for Coercion.* Washington DC: The American Enterprise Institute Press.

Schmitt, Glenn R. (2006). Drug Courts: The Second Decade.

Schwartz, Richard D., & Miller, James C. (1964). Legal Evolution and Societal Complexity. *American Journal of Sociology, 70*(2), 159-169.

Sevigny, Eric L., Fuleihan, Brian K., & Ferdik, Frank V. (2013). Do Drug Courts Reduce the Use of Incarceration? A Meta-analysis. *Journal of Criminal Justice, 41*, 416-425.

Shaffer, Deborah K. (2011). Looking Inside the Black Box of Drug Courts: A Meta-Analytic Review. *Justice Quarterly, 28*(3), 493-521.

Shaffer, Deborah K., Hartman, Jennifer L., & Listwan, Shelley J. (2009). Drug Abusing Women in the Community: The Impact of Drug Court Involvement on Recidivism. *Journal of Drug Issues, 39*(4), 803-827.

Shannon Carey, Ph.D., Juliette Mackin, Ph.D., & Mike Finigan, Ph.D. (Producer). (2008, December 13, 2008). Drug Courts: Some Answers to Our Burning Questions. [Power Point for Training Event] Retrieved from http://www.npcresearch.com/Files/NEADCP_2008_Burning_Questions_Adult_Drug_Courts.pptt

Siegel, Larry J. (2010). *Criminology Theories, Patterns and Typologies* (10th ed.). Belmont: Wadsworth.

Siegel, Larry J., & Worrall, John. (2013). *Introduction to Criminal Justice 14th edition.* Belmont, CA: Wadsworth Publishing.

Slobogin, Christopher. (1995). Therapeutic Jurisprudence: Five Dilemmas to Ponder. *Psychology, Public Policy and Law, 1*, 193-219.

Smith, Katie. (2014). Fifty-Six Percent Success Is Still A Failing Grade: Reducing Recidivism and Ensuring Due Process Rights in Drug Courts. *University of LaVerne Law Review, 35*, 315-342.

Somers, Julian M., Rezansoff, Stefanie N., & Moniruzzaman, Akm. (2014). Comparative Analysis of Recidivism Outcomes Following Drug Treatment Court in Vancouver, Canada. *International Journal of Offender Therapy and Comparative Criminology, 58*(6), 655-671.

Spitzer, Steven. (1974). Punishment and Social Organization: A Study of Durkheim's Theory of Penal Evolution. *Law & Society, 9*, 613-638.

Spitzer, Steven. (1983). Marxist Perspectives in the Sociology of Law. *Annual Review of Sociology, 9*, 103-124.

Spohn, Cassia, & Hemmens, Craig. (2009). *Courts: A Text/Reader.* Thousand Oaks, CA: Sage Publications, Inc.

Straussner, Shulamith Lala Ashenberg, & Byrne, Helga. (2009). Alcoholics Anonymous: Key Research Findings from 2002-2007. *Alcoholism Treatment Quarterly, 27*, 349-367.

Team, Family Treatment Court. (2006). Drug Court Planning meetings. In K. Contrino (Ed.). New York.

Tiger, Rebecca. (2011). Drug Courts and the Logic of Coerced Treatment. *Sociological Forum, 26*(1), 169-182.

Tiger, Rebecca. (2013). *Judging Addicts Drug Courts and Coercion in the Justice System.* New York: New York University Press.

Trainers, Drug Court (2005, January). [Drug Court Training (Part 1 out of a series of 3)].

Trice, Harrison M., & Roman, Paul Michael. (1970). Delabeling, Relabeling, and Alcoholics Anonymous. *Social Problems, 17*(4), 538-546.

Turkel, Gerald. (1990). Michel Foucault: Law, Power and Knowledge. *Journal of Law and Society, 17*(2), 170-193.

Turner, Susan, Longshore, Doug, Wenzel, Suzanne, Fain, Terry, Morral, Andrew, Deschenes, Elizabeth, Harrell, Adele, Greene, Judith, Iguchi, Martin, McBride, Duane, & Taxman, Fay. (2001). *A National Evaluation of 14 Drug Courts.* (DRU-2637-NIJ). Washington: Rand Corporation.

Valverde, Mariana. (1998). *Diseases of the Will: Alcohol and the Dilemmas of Freedom.* Cambridge: Cambridge University Press.

Vocci, Frank. (2008). Medication Assisted Treatment for Opiate Addiction. Washington: National Institute on Drug Abuse.

W. Clinton Terry, III (Ed.). (1999). *The Early Drug Courts Case Studies in Judicial Innovation.* Thousand Oaks: Sage Publications.

Walker, Samuel. (2011). *Sense and Non-Sense about Crime, Drugs and Communities* (7th ed.). Belmont: Wadsworth.

Walters, Glenn. (2000). Spontaneous Remission from Alcohol, Tabacoo, and Other Drug Abuse: Seeking Quantitative Answers to

Qualitative Questions. *American Journal of Alcohol Abuse, 26*(3), 443-460.

Weinberg, Darin. (2000). "Out There": The Ecology of Addiction in Drug Abuse Treatment Discourse. *Social Problems, 47*(4), 606-621.

Weinberg, Darin. (2002). On the Embodiment of Addiction. *Body & Society, 8*(4), 1-19.

Weisheit, Ralph, & Wells, L. Edward. (1996). Rural Crime and Justice: Implications for Theory and Research. *Crime & Delinquency, 42*(3), 379-397.

Wexler, David B. (1999a). Therapeutic Jurisprudence and the Culture of Critique. *Journal of Contemporary Legal Issues, 10*, 263-277.

Therapeutic Jurisprudence Forum: The Development of Therapeutic Jurisprudence from Theory to Practice, 68 691 (1999b).

Wexler, David B. (2000). Therapeutic Jurisprudence: An Overview. *Thomas M. Cooley Law Review, 17*, 125.

Wexler, David B. (2005). Therapeutic Jurisprudence and the Rehabilitative Role of the Criminal Defense Lawyer. *St. Thomas Law Review, 17*(3), 743-774.

Wexler, David B. (2008). Two Decades of Therapeutic Jurisprudence. *Touro Law Review, 24*(1), 17-30.

Wiener, Richard L., & Georges, Leah. (2013). Social Psychology and Problem-Solving Courts: Judicial Roles and Decision Making *Problem Solving Courts Social Science and Legal Perspectives*. New York: Springer Publishing.

Winick, Bruce J. (2013). Problem Solving Courts: Therapeutic Jurisprudence in Practice. In R. L. Wiener & E. M. Brank (Eds.), *Problem Solving Courts: Social Science and Legal Perspectives*. New York: Springer Publishing.

Witkiewitz, Katie. (2005). Defining Relapse from a Harm Reduction Perspective. *Journal of Evidence-Based Social Work, 2*(1/2), 191-206.

Index